Praise for Shari Rubinstein

M000107108

"Bravo, Shari! This is a thoroughly enjoya
pathos, and transformation. I heartily rec
tale that reflects the grit and the grace of one family against the backdrop of
America on the cusp of the 21st century."

Eitan Shishkoff, Kiryat Chaim, Israel
Author of *What About Us* and *With All Your Heart*

"Your book was so absorbing that I read it from beginning to Epilogue. From
Baptist to hippie to Messianic Rabbi's wife, Shari has lived a life that few of
us can imagine. Her candid memoirs take us on an odyssey of heart and soul,
laughter and tears, that help us better understanding our own pilgrimage and
the times in which we live."

Dana Sudborough, Adjunct Professor at Epic Bible College

"Shari Rubinstein's story will bless and inspire others to continue in their
walk of faith as God has a plan and a purpose for each one of us. Only God
could turn a rebellious hippie into a Messianic Rebbetzin of a growing
Messianic Synagogue, and then with husband Rabbi Rube pass the baton onto
their son, Joshua Rubinstein!"

Don Compton, Director, Shalom Ministries of Santa Fe, NM.

"Knowing Shari for many years, my life has been enriched by her story,
and God's hand in her life. Her warmth and friendship has touched her
congregation, as well as everyone who has known her. Her life is a testimony
of grace and kindness, and knowing her is an encouragement to persevere.
Her story is both inspiring and motivating."

Rabbi Dr. Michael Schiffman, Executive Director, Chevra USA.

"Once again Shari has opened the door to the heart in this, the story of her
life's journey. Through her memoir, we get a glimpse into an era that brought
forth so many leaders of the Messianic movement, presented with her typical
insight, honesty, clarity, and warm sense of humor."

Carol Lerner, Writer and Editor

"Shari, I'm so excited for your new book, I can't wait to read it! Thank you
for your talk with Women Inspired Network about the power of sharing our
stories!"

Sonia Hassey, Founder, Women Inspired Network

"I trust anything Shari writes. "

Heidi Marie Nelson, Adonai Productions

BECOMING RUTH

dropout
to
teacher

hippie
to
straight

spiritualist
to
believer

- a memoir -
by Shari Rubinstein

Restoration Press
Ripples of Restoration
One Tale at a Time

Published in Roseville, California, by Restoration Press. Restoration Press is an independent publishing venture created by author Shari Rubinstein.

Restoration Press
Ripples of Restoration
One Tale at a Time

Shari can be contacted at www.sharirubinstein.com
or rebbetzinshari@mac.com

Layout and Design by Joshua Rubinstein.
Joshua can be reached at www. jdruby.com
or josh@jdruby.com.

Photography of Author by Heidi Lucille. Contact Heidi at: heidi.lucille@outlook.com.
The "Bent's Old Fort" photo on the cover was taken by Rodger Young
on October 1975 in La Junta, CO.

ISBN 978-0-9986315-2-3

Rubinstein, Shari, 1944 –
    Becoming Ruth : Dropout to Teacher - Hippie to Straight - Spiritualist to Believer / Shari Rubinstein, aka Sharon (Mings) Rubinstein
    1. Rubinstein, Shari, 1944 – 2. BIO026000 Biography & Autobiography / Personal Memoirs, 3. BIO019000 Biography & Autobiography / Educators, 4. FAM046000 FAMILY & RELATIONSHIPS / Life Stages / General

RP-0003pb

Printed in the United States of America by Lightning Source.
Lightning Source can be found at:
https://www1.lightningsource.com/

❦ *Table of Contents* ❧

Chapter Four – Hippie Craze - Page 63

Chapter Five – Out of the Haze - Page 81

Chapter Six – HIS Ways - Page 99

Chapter Seven – West Coast Rays - Page 129

Chapter Eight – Tsunami Phase - Page 165

Chapter Nine - "Red Sky at Night..." - Page 177

ACKNOWLEDGMENTS

I cannot say enough good things about my family, friends and community all of whom are a continual source of encouragement, love and support.

Rube's friends Eitan Shishkoff and Russell Resnik were a source for some of Rube's early hippie days. I only know what Rube shared with me about his life before me. His mother Marjorie Boehm told me stories about her own life, as did my mother and dad about theirs.

My mother's sister, Aunt Becky, and my dad's sister Aunt Peggy McCorkle were valuable resources for stories of my parents' lives from before they married and during the early raising of the family. I also gained perspective from their telling of their own upbringing. A strong bond has been forged with my aunties!

My siblings have been a great resource in compiling this historical document. Carol Lester and Anita Norris stayed with me until the end brainstorming titles for sections, chapters and the book itself. Carol and Dwayne Mings were able to fill in so many details of the family events from when I was a bit young to remember. Linda Marr and Michael Mings told me stories of their life at home after I left to be married. My sister Elaine Mings, our family historian, was able to fill in many historical dates and timelines. Thanks, sibs!

It has been eye-opening to pick the brains of my children for how they remembered various times in their lives. Their perspectives were invaluable. Special thanks to Monicqua Busch, Jacob Rubinstein, Joshua Rubinstein and Sarah Whitley. Spouses Aaron Busch, Rosemary Rubinstein and Michael Whitley also provided a wealth of information that helped set the tone for all of their lives as adults and parents.

My 30-year close friend Julia Schley helped me fine tune the section headings and was the one who hit on the title for the book. She knows so much of my story that it was she who could pull together the perspective needed. Way to go, Julia.

My publicist and confidante for this massive undertaking is my son Joshua Rubinstein. If that were not enough, he also has produced the graphic design for this book while being my sensitive and wise Publicist, extremely knowledgeable Technical Advisor and co-Publisher. For this publication he has positioned all the photographs that help this story take on life. A picture is worth a thousand words.

A special THANK YOU to my granddaughter Raina Whitley, Sarah and Michael's oldest girl, who worked tirelessly with me to sort and catalog many of the pictures in this memoir. She has an amazing gift of organization and administration. It was she who kept me motivated to keep moving forward.

My good friend and talented line editor Carol Lerner has worked her magic AGAIN especially trying to keep my remembrances in better chronological order while making me aware when more explanation is necessary. If you find errors, it would be because my text doubled since I had her edit, and chronology gets muddled when pursuing a concept or series of events.

Much of this story of my life has appeared on my blog, Ripples of Restoration. I am grateful to my readers for their faithfulness in following me, which has served to keep me on task.

It takes a village!

PREFACE

I am a storyteller. I aspire to be a wordsmith. I have long felt that I should publish the story of my life. My path has been unusual and has touched on some of the major eras of our times. If for no other reason, there is some historical value to this undertaking. I also do want my progeny to know from whence I came, hence the roots of their own origin stories. I want them to understand the why's for the various turns in my story.

Mostly I want to show my gratitude to a loving God who has spared my life on multiple occasions when my foolishness could have done me in. I want to thank him for never letting go of me, when I have often refused to acknowledge him. I am the perfect example of the poem "Footprints." It is I the Lord is carrying when I have those lying flashes of being alone. I want to share the story of my path with God when I wandered far afield and when He welcomed me Home again. It's a long story with an undeserved happy ending.

I began the serious task of assembling my memories over ten years ago. I have written, rewritten, sorted, thrown out, ad nauseum. The most difficult part of this task has been to be honest, even with myself, about motives for the various choices I made in this life that recently passed the three-quarters of a century mark. It has been illuminating to pin myself down, as it were, and tell the story like it is, or was.

I hope for two things in putting my story out there. I hope my narrative helps you, Dear Reader, understand the choices you have made in your life and perhaps get on with the business of forgiving yourself when you fall short of what you believe to be the mark. Your God only waits for you to ask for His forgiveness. Secondly, I hope you see that there is value in telling our stories to each other. Please be encouraged to get on with putting yours on the page. Your family will be grateful.

I recommend reading this tome in bite-sized portions with a hot cup of coffee and an orange scone. That's how I preferred to write it.

DISCLAIMER

Anytime I have made one of my reflections available to others, invariably, someone remembers the same situation quite differently. I say this so that you, Dear Reader, will know that I acknowledge that there may be recountings of my life and that of my family and friends that do not match your memories. For this, I do apologize if I indeed missed what you believe to be the essential essence of any given situation or event.

All I can say is that perspectives vary a great deal. It was not my purpose to distort, but sometimes I am dealing with details told to me by others who were more directly involved. How I incorporated their thoughts into my narrative was as they seemed to fit the big picture in my head. My interpretation of my life events has been formed by all that went before. Read the story for how it spoke to me.

When I have found that there is a great disparity in either the details of an event or where it fell on the timeline, I tried to make a note for the Reader. It is interesting for us to go through events and come out with such different impressions. My daughter Sarah reminded me that it's okay to point out the dispute as the story progresses. It's like giving a certain credibility to all sides of the story. Thanks, Dear.

And then, there is the aging factor. I have been writing this life story for so long. The most work on pulling it together has been in the last two years. Not only am I much older than when I started this tale—being now 76—but many of those who contributed details are as old or older than I. Just saying.

BECOMING RUTH

I believe when we suspend the indoctrination of our politically correct culture, it becomes apparent that there is a divine design to the creation of man and woman. We are created equal in value, but we are uniquely different. *Vive la difference!*

Just as men are equipped mentally, physically and emotionally to be conquerors, builders and protectors, women are built to nurture, support and love. It is in men to forge a path and in women to believe in that course and commit to partner in the journey. That has been my quest, albeit quite unconsciously.

My first language is love. There is a drive within me to find someone I can love, honor and respect. Much like Ruth of the Bible, once I have committed, my path is set. The only thing that can cause my foot to falter is to lose respect for the man or lose faith in the mission. Even the death of my loved one does not deter my vision.

It is the Ruth Calling. In Ruth 1:16 in the Bible, we find that Ruth has married a Jewish man who subsequently dies. Instead of going back to her people—which would also take her back to a place where the God of Abraham, Isaac and Jacob was not their god—she chooses to follow her mother-in-law Naomi back to her husband's family and faith.

Ruth said to Naomi, "Don't press me to leave you and stop following you; for wherever you go, I will go; and wherever you stay, I will stay. Your people will be my people and your God will be my God." Complete Jewish Bible

The Reader might recognize Ruth's words as they are the foundation of the marriage vows for many cultures.

My journey has been to find that man I can wholeheartedly give not just my heart, but all that I am. I am a strong, gifted woman. My mission has always been to surrender, but not in defeat, but rather in devotion to a higher calling that we might partner to accomplish.

This memoir is that journey.

MEETING MY LOVE

It seems that all my life was pointed toward the time I would meet the man whose journey was also mine. It did not happen until after I had some false starts. I was 29. This is that moment.

Jolting. Tender. His radiant, twinkling blue eyes cut me to the quick. The effect was heightened by his ample "fro" being transformed into a halo by the early morning rays from the screened-in doorway. From my vantage point up in the open loft, I could not perceive any distance separating us. The connection was visceral, unshakable. It was as if we each were receiving the very essence of the other through the portals of our eyes. Cosmic. That was the word we all used.

It was not exactly the "stranger across the crowded room" experience. Of course, he had not been a stranger for a few months since I had landed here in my VW van. There was no crowd at this early hour in our A-frame hub. Most of our fellow inhabitants were of the sleep-in type, especially considering we all were late-night tokers and trippers. At this moment, we could have been surrounded by huddled masses, but we were only aware of each other.

He did not drop his gaze. Rube stood transfixed, framed by the door jamb. It was the look for the launching of ships. I knew in that instant that we would always be together. I knew that somehow we had always been together. It was a reunion unlike any I could have imagined. It was at once ancient and newborn.

We exchanged some kind of greeting that did not reveal the depth of emotion, the electricity. But we both knew. I was sure of that—as sure as anyone could be still buzzing from tripping at a Grateful Dead Concert.

1
chapter

School Days

Early Images

How far back do we actually remember? You hear so many stories about your deeds and your misdeeds, but mostly the misdeeds. Which ones are your own remembrances versus events recounted? There have been a few encounters from my early life that I heard repeated often enough to believe they really happened.

Surely everyone has a memorable moment involving food. Mine was about oatmeal when I was still in a high chair, which was probably about 1945. I apparently made quite a laughable spectacle having turned my half-full bowl on top of my head at the prodding of my mother's oldest brother, Durward. It is this uncle who retold the story, and since he was the instigator, I believe it. I loved my mother's six brothers and her much younger, still present sister, my Aunt Becky.

It must not be a personal recollection of having sat myself down in an ant bed at about 18 months in that same year. I was evidently happily playing in the dirt, oblivious to the little critters crawling all over me. The scream my mother expelled upon discovering me thus, and the subsequent and instantaneous biting of untold ants is vivid, whether a memory or the ghost of a family tale recounted long ago.

Christmas 1946 at Uncle Cecil and Aunt Leona's house with me in front center, clockwise Elaine, Daddy, Mother, baby Anita and Carol.

The German Shepherd incident may indeed be a direct memory. I was about four, in 1948, when I was "attacked" by a dog. I don't recall having been bitten, but the dog's teeth tore my dress off me. I am not sure if anyone ever explained to me why the dog did such a thing, but I have a hazy picture of having just approached a leaky water faucet with buzzy flying things circling about moments before the dog grabbed my dress. Only years later it dawned on me that the dog may have saved me from bee stings, which would have no doubt deepened my insect bite fears. Instead, I came away afraid of German Shepherds.

One dog memory is surely mine. That next year brought

3

the disappearance of our family dog, Spud. Our Cocker Spaniel was a beautiful golden creature, which loved our family unconditionally. I don't remember how we first got him; however, the day he was gone is remarkably sharp.

Mother was distraught that Spud was gone and stymied that it could have happened; our fence was sturdy and the gate was still shut. That was when we lived on Texas Street in Hobbs. This was the first home we were buying. I don't know if she had a suspect in mind, but she was determined that some people intentionally let our dog out, presumably to keep it for themselves.

At 4 years old with sister Anita. Mother had us take formal pictures whenever she could.

Mother took several of us in tow walking about the neighborhood as well as she could with six children ranging in age from ten years to an infant. In reality she more likely left the oldest, 10-year-old Carol, at home with baby Michael and probably two-year-old Linda and four-year-

Mother with six of the children about the age Spud was lost. Top, Clockwise: Carol, Mother, Elaine, me, Linda, Michael, Anita.

old Anita. I remember at least that Elaine and I, being about eight and six respectively, went on this hunting expedition.

I have memories of mother whistling and calling for our missing pooch. Spud was nowhere to be seen. Not having any luck, we went back home and waited for Daddy to return from work with the family car to continue our search. As we whistled and yelled from our slow-moving Chrysler, several times we were sure we heard Spud's bark calling back to us, but he never appeared.

Losing Spud left an ache in me for some reason. Perhaps because there was always a feeling of not enough love to go around in a household of five girls, an older brother, and a newborn baby boy, no matter how hard my parents tried.

Mother needed a hysterectomy after Michael was born, so she was laid up for a couple of months. Even though a woman came in to help during the day, there developed a sense of being detached that still lingers. To me, it has always been about the heart, about relationships, making connection.

There is a way even outsiders were able to make connection with me. I have a physical characteristic that set me apart from the mostly blonde blur of my siblings, as they all were in our younger years. Being different had its advantages, as well as its disadvantages. I was born with an olive complexion and dark hair, in contrast to all my siblings who all started as "towheads" and mostly were fair. My coloring made it easier for relatives to tell me from the others. It also earned me "color" nicknames such as Dago, Blackie and Brownie. Mostly it was my mother's brothers who used these terms of endearment for me.

Me at 8 years old.

Even though the nicknames were lovingly intended, many of my siblings used them to separate me from themselves. It should be noted here that most of my family was prejudiced against African Americans, overtly at least on my father's side. My sisters and my cousins made jokes about my being Black or African American. We all knew of a girl who was Black with almost the same name, Shannie Marie to my Sharon Marie. I was often addressed by her name. I resisted, not so much because I understood racism, but rather because I understood the harm they intended.

First Love

I still see him, standing there, a glint in his eye, his left leg bent slightly forward as he rested his right foot on the running board of his delivery truck. I can't believe he could have always just eaten, but he was never without a toothpick dangling from his relaxed mouth. No matter. To me, he was the most dashing, handsome man I had ever seen. My heart almost burst when he laughed out loud at something I said or did. Without articulating it, or even understanding how it happened, my goal became to make him smile. To see his eyes sparkle for me. This was my love, my daddy.

Little girls are supposed to love their daddies, and I sure did. There are so many vivid memories of those days. Being in the middle of five girls, I remember wondering how my father noticed me. I was fairly typical at making myself known, distinguishable.

When I was about eight, Daddy announced he didn't like his foam pillow and every night there was a race to see which one of us could trade pillows with him. I did everything I could to be first each night. I won so often, that after a while Daddy just gave me the pillow. You would have thought I was satisfied to finally win once and for all. In reality I was enjoying winning my father over and over again, so it was a hollow victory.

I only remember once getting a spanking from Daddy, even though I know that can't be true, given my contrary nature. It was unusual for me to push the limits with my dad because I wanted so desperately to receive his approval. Usually I got in trouble with him when I was called to account for the ill treatment I gave my mother. The spanking I do remember was when I was caught in a lie during my early teenage years. Daddy had no patience for deception.

It's interesting to note that my values are pretty much what he instilled in me. My mother certainly made an effort to impress me with her code for living, and I am sure that much of how I do things came from her, but it was my father who influenced me on my sense of right and wrong.

Daddy was all about hard work and being accountable. I soon discovered that the best way to his heart was to do a job well. Even though Daddy died many years ago, I still catch myself watching for the glint in his eye, the smile curling at his lips, when I complete projects. In actuality, he knew little of my adult accomplishments for many of the preceding years since we lived 1500 miles apart most of my adult life.

Family Business

In about 1942 Mother and Daddy traveled from their home in west Texas to the west coast for jobs as everyone was still coming out of the Great Depression. Dad went first and then Mother joined him with the family which consisted of Dwayne, Carol and Elaine. They took the train to Washington. I heard a story that baby Elaine got sick on the trip and threw up on Dwayne.

When they arrived, Mother first worked in a dress shop in Tacoma. After I was born in 1944 she joined Daddy working in Kaiser's shipyards where ships for the war effort were built and repaired. Daddy worked directly on the ships and in the beginning Mother did too. She worked as an assistant to a pipefitter, "Jean the Pipefitter's Assistant." Evidently having a woman on the shipyard floor was distracting so she was moved upstairs into Payroll. She only went to the floor when she was delivering paychecks.

Daddy's sister Peggy was a young woman at the time. She came to take care of us kids so Mother could work. It must have been a tight fit at first as we lived in a small apartment over a bakery. Later we moved to a house provided by Kaiser. I found the last War Ration Book I was issued showing our address being in that little company housing community of Salishan.

After the war, the family headed back to Texas, but stopped in Hobbs, New Mexico to visit friends and family. We ended up staying there. The last three children were born in Hobbs: Anita in 1946, Linda in 1948 and Michael in 1949.

Daddy's first job in Hobbs was baking bread at Good Eats Bakery for Mr. Randolph. He worked his way up to driving a delivery truck. It was such a thrill to be invited to go with him on his deliveries. We children were often singled out for that honor during summers.

My World War II ration book.

Daddy with one of his wholesale delivery trucks.

It was more than just getting to be with Daddy; there was also the treat of eating donuts fresh from the bakery. I remember meeting the shopkeepers and grocers to whom we delivered. They always made us feel special, more like we were honoring them with our visits. It made me burst with pride.

After the bakery, Daddy worked for a wholesale business when we lived on Texas Street where Michael was born. The company was called Stansell's and was based in another town so Daddy stored at home a large supply of the goods he was to deliver. He filled our detached garage with all kinds of products. He kept a padlock on that garage door or we would have eaten up all the candy. The building emitted the sweet aroma of tobacco and candy. Hard to resist.

Mother was a very busy homemaker during this time. Her giftings and talents included being a seamstress. She made most of our clothes. One time she made dresses out of dotted Swiss that she called our "button and bow" dresses. The expression came from a line in a popular song by Dinah Shore, "Buttons and Bows." Each dress was a different pastel upon which she sewed little bows with a tiny button at the center. She added an attached hem that transformed the dresses into formals if we should ever have the occasion to wear one. If memory serves, my dress was yellow.

Mostly we wore them as formals for the picture she had taken. Then we wore them without the added ruffle as dresses when we went to church. I was reminded by one of our first Sunday School teachers I visited recently, Ruby Mahan, of how well dressed we always were. I can't imagine how Mother found the time to make our clothes.

Button and bow dresses Mother made for us.
L-R: Carol, Linda, me, Anita, Elaine.

In 1950 Mother got the opportunity to work on the 1950 Census. It paid very well. She attended a two-week training in Roswell, New Mexico, during which time Daddy's sister-in-law Bell came and took care of our family. At that time Bell and Dad's half brother Pete were also living in Hobbs. I was six at the time.

A cottonfield in Texas.

It was at the end of summers that Mother made an effort to supplement the family income by taking us all to pick cotton. The cotton was ready just about the time school started up, so we would take two weeks off from school for the picking. Many of our friends were also taken out of school to pick. A major part of our community's livelihood depended on harvesting this crop.

A typical late summer day in 1950, Mother got Daddy off to work in the morning, and then loaded up a lunch, sweet tea, water and all of us kids and headed to the cotton fields. Being the seamstress she was, Mother custom-made our picking bags so we could all work, with the exception of baby Michael who rode on either her long bag or 10-year-old Carol's as they picked. Mostly two-year-old Linda Kay had to also ride instead of pick. Our little bags got emptied into Mother's for the weighing in. Her bag had to have been at least 8 feet long, which is probably the exaggerated view of a child, but I did know they held 60-70 pounds when full. The work was hot, dusty and painful.

When we set out those mornings, at first we were all excited. It was an adventure. There were cotton fields all around the outside perimeter of our town so we didn't have to drive far. At the side of this particular field was what was left of the original farmhouse, but no one was living there at that time. There was a pool in the back yard that had been drained and abandoned. Massive overgrown trees shed their seasonal leaves and broken branches into the pool and the surrounding yard. The area was cool as a cucumber.

We longed for the chance to take our overheated, sweaty bodies to hang out in the shade of the trees. It usually only happened when we got to take a break to eat the lunches Mom made of cold cut sandwiches, PB&J's and cool sweet tea poured from a gallon jug into Mason jars. All of us tried to drag out these little respites from our hard labor.

But first, there was the picking. Mother conversed with the men by the weigh-in area. There was a large scale with a hook where the pickers' full bags were weighed prior to being emptied into the huge screened-in trailer. When a trailer got full, they hitched it up to a truck and took it to the cotton gin. That sometimes happened several times a day depending upon how many pickers showed up.

Our family didn't set any records. Mother and the older girls helped all of us get our bags over our shoulders. Then we put baby Michael on Mother's bag, usually giving him a bottle. There was no relief from the scalding hot sun. They don't grow trees in cotton fields. We all wore scarves or hats covering our heads and eyes.

We wanted to wear gloves because the cotton bolls are so sharp, but it was impossible to get covered fingers into the boll to extract the cotton. I think I can still see the scars I got from the sharp cotton bolls cutting into my fingers all those years ago. It was a slow, painful process, not the least of which was dragging the bags that were increasing in weight while we were decreasing in energy. By the time we got to the end of a row, we hoped we had picked enough cotton to get them emptied so we could start down another row with an empty bag.

Sometimes one of us got to take Michael from his lumpy cotton bed because he was getting cranky. It was such a relief to be the one to go into the shade with the baby. Usually the younger girls, four-year-old Anita and two-year-old Linda, were also ready for a break. The sun got hotter by the minute the closer we got to noon. It was sometimes hard to see because of the sweat dripping into my eyes.

Just when we thought we couldn't go down another row, Mother called us to the weigh-in so we could go to lunch. I have had some favorite meals throughout my life, but I don't think I have ever tasted anything so wonderful as those sandwiches and big gulps of sweet tea after picking cotton. The contrast with the work of the day made it seem that this must surely be Heaven.

We usually did not pick all day. Mostly we went home after the lunch break. Sometimes Mother picked on and she let us play together in the cool of the trees while the younger ones napped. The sun in Southern New Mexico is pretty unforgiving in the summertime. Every time I hear that line from the old song, "Summertime and the livin' is easy," I want to launch a protest. That songwriter knew not of what he wrote. Nobody we knew ever got to relax in the summer heat. When your existence is tied to growing things, the work has to be done in the full heat of the season.

Picking the cotton is only the tail end of this job. Another equally difficult part of this work is referred to as "chopping cotton," which is oddly labeled since the chopper is not cutting down the cotton, but rather chopping the weeds that want to take over the cotton field and threaten the existence of the cotton plants. I don't remember our whole family going out to chop cotton, but I did it one summer when I was visiting an aunt and uncle and cousin.

Uncle Lester Kluting, Aunt Jesse and my cousin Pat grew cotton and we all went out to chop those weeds. For this job, the problem is blisters and always the relentless sun and dry earth. It didn't do much good to cut off the weeds, because they just grew back from their roots. The challenge was to cut them out of the earth. Their gnarly tentacles seemed to have minds of their own as they clutched the soil for dear life. I lost many a battle with them that summer.

Uncle Lester's house was in the middle of cotton fields in eastern New Mexico, an hour or so from where we lived. They were only renting the house while they took care of those cotton fields. The place was dubbed The Rat Camp Ranch for a reason that escaped me then but now seems obvious. Why glorify the presence of these sneaky, snarly creatures? I couldn't think why it was called a ranch, except my aunt and uncle had a horse the landowners allowed us to ride, but the poor thing was at least 30 and pretty much done. Pat and I rode as much as the old mare could take it when we were in between our various chores.

We helped Jesse in the house most of the time. It was she who taught me how to shave my legs. I was amazed at how adept she was at it. Jesse was glamorous from my perspective as a teen-wanna-be. She did the cooking and baking, but on this visit, she was making several cakes to have when my folks came to fetch me. It was great fun and I suspect more of the cake dough went into our bellies than went into the pans. All that survived were put in the freezer that was outside the door of the tiny two-room house. The bathroom was an outhouse, but there was electricity in the house and a bathtub.

At her kitchen sink was not a usual faucet but a pump. When we needed large quantities of water, we just dropped a bucket into the well outside the kitchen door and hauled up a bunch at a time. All of these activities to take care of basic living took up all our time. Sometimes we went out with Uncle Lester to help, but mostly we thankfully stayed in the house. I have described the unforgiving New Mexico summer sun!

Uncle Lester was the biggest of my mother's seven brothers at 6' 4", and I can't even imagine how much he weighed. He was large, but it was all muscle. He had quite an appetite. When he came in from the fields he favored a snack of an entire box of Post Toasties in a bowl big enough for making bread, which was its other use. He didn't have the temperament I would have expected from a giant. Lester was a big teddy bear. He was always laughing and joking with us. He taught me kindness and joy.

My chopping cotton experience was when I was 12, the summer of 1956, and included the incident with the Tarantula. I got one of the biggest scares of my life one day when we were all out in the fields chopping cotton. I was worn to a frazzle from the heat and the exertion. I sat down to take a breather when suddenly I was aware of a dark fuzzy blur in my peripheral vision. By the time I turned to see what it was, my hero Uncle Lester was using his hoe to chop up a large, hairy spider the likes of which I had never seen. My fear of Tarantulas persists.

I look at cotton clothing with more reverence than most. I cannot take for granted what has been created at such personal sacrifice and hard work by so many. When my family went out to pick cotton, we weren't the only family out there. We were fortunate that this was not the only income for our family. We knew that if we didn't pick one day, we still ate and had a roof over our heads. I never knew about the other families. And as for my Uncle Lester's family, growing, chopping and picking cotton provided their living. It did for many in those days in our part of the country.

The Flying Saucer

Some time after our cotton picking days, our family got the opportunity to own a café. Daddy made the acquaintance of a man named Red Crowe when he was still working at Good Eats Bakery. Both men talked of their desire to own a burger place. It had been my dad's dream since before he married my mom. When Red left the bakery, he opened such a café—The Red Crowe—and it became popular very fast. It was at a great location on a major thoroughfare in Hobbs. Red was going to expand his business, so he offered my dad the lease on the building he was leaving. Daddy left his job working at Stansell's Wholesale to become an entrepreneur.

Those were exciting times. During five years of my pre-teen and early teen years, Mother and Daddy leased a small café named The Flying Saucer. Our town was 120 miles from Roswell and the "saucer sighting," the locals took the double meaning. This kind of burger place was cropping up all over the country. The year was 1954 and things were hopping.

The Flying Saucer was pretty much a family business. Daddy did the prepping and cooking and Mother did most of the serving. Carol and Elaine both got to carhop – which is taking orders from customers who stayed in their cars. Carhopping was glamorized by movies depicting the era, but it was very difficult work. I remember my parents also hired a person to wash dishes and there were several women through the years that took over waitressing and helping with food prep so Mother could be with us at home.

Our café was a single small building on a corner lot. Inside there was the one rounded counter with enough room for only ten stools. The single thing visible behind the counter was a small glass case with a couple of shelves to display Mother's pies. Every week our house was the scene of her whipping up a cream base and then adding what was required to make chocolate, lemon, banana cream, coconut and egg custard pies. She also made pecan, cherry and pumpkin in season. I grew up having pies for dessert at home every week, almost every day.

To the right of the diner's entry door was a window to the outside with a ledge where the cook set the food for the carhops to deliver. An outside bench under that window was the only place they could rest between orders, but in

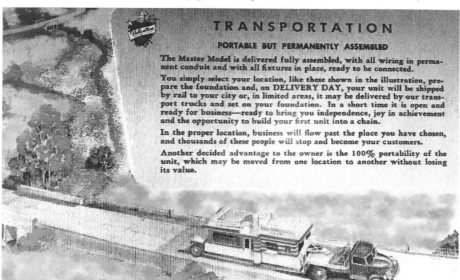

TRANSPORTATION

PORTABLE BUT PERMANENTLY ASSEMBLED

The Master Model is delivered fully assembled, with all wiring in permanent conduit and with all fixtures in place, ready to be connected.

You simply select your location, like these shown in the illustration, prepare the foundation and, on DELIVERY DAY, your unit will be shipped by rail to your city or, in limited areas, it may be delivered by our transport trucks and set on your foundation. In a short time it is open and ready for business—ready to bring you independence, joy in achievement and the opportunity to build your first unit into a chain.

In the proper location, business will flow past the place you have chosen, and thousands of these people will stop and become your customers.

Another decided advantage to the owner is the 100% portability of the unit, which may be moved from one location to another without losing its value.

Valentine Manufacturing Kansas City, Kansas   "The Flying Saucer"

Our Flying Saucer Cafe was one of many trucked all over the country to meet the new demand for "fast" food. Courtesy of my brother, 3M - Michael Monroe Mings.

reality, they rarely got to rest. Cars wanting drive up service parked under the awning Daddy put in at the back for six to eight cars or they could also just park in front of the building. My sisters ran to each of those cars to ask if they were eating in or out. There were so many repeat customers, however, that they usually knew who wanted to go inside and even what they wanted to order.

Since the ground around the cafe was just hard-packed dirt, the carhops couldn't even wear the popular roller skates to lighten their task. I don't think my sisters got paid, but just got customer tips. Boy, but what all they could buy with that money! They began to develop wonderful wardrobes from that job. I envied them, and waited impatiently to be old enough to be allowed to work there, too. In the meantime, I often "sneaked" some of their clothes to wear.

My parents specialized in hamburgers and hot dogs, french fries – typical fast food fare. The only exception was Dad's steaks and Mother's homemade pies. Daddy's steaks, which could only be served to the inside diners, were famous in our town. Since there were only ten stools at the counter, Daddy would say he sold 200 steaks or even 2,000, but always just ten at a time.

Our town of 50 thousand was, and still is, an oil town. The single high school's song is all about the oil derricks. With the oil industry came scouts from a variety of oil companies. They were always looking for new sites to drill. Carol told me that the scouts, who might be in town for just a few days, always topped off their evenings at the Flying Saucer eating one of Daddy's steaks. The quality of his steaks was well-publicized by word of mouth.

Food storage and food preparation took place in the full basement. I remember helping Daddy use the press to cut the french fries in that cool hideaway. That was about all he would let me do since I wasn't old enough to have a job. The potato press was not electric so it took a lot of strength. We used very long potatoes for our French fries. Some customers came in and just ordered fries, they were that good.

Daddy told my sister Carol his two secrets for making them so tasty. He would cut out any bad spots, run the potatoes through the press, then rinse them in cold water. The trick then was to leave them in fresh cold water until time to fry them. Daddy believed it was also frying in lard that made the fries so crispy and full of flavor. He mastered the science of getting the vats of oil to the right temperature.

Daddy took issue, however, with some of our customers who used just about a whole bottle of ketchup with their one plate of fries. This was typically teenage boys. Dad had no qualms about limiting them on the ketchup. The customer was not always right in our establishment! Daddy could lose his meager profit from eaters slurping through what was meant to be merely a condiment.

There were two dishes Daddy made that were his own creation. He developed his own recipes for making his hamburger mix and his chili for the hot dogs. I felt like I was part of some great conspiracy when I was included while he was mixing up his hamburger concoction. I still don't remember all he put in it, but I know there were breadcrumbs and special spices. Everyone raved about his hamburgers.

Even though Daddy specialized in cooking a steak to perfection for the many regular steak customers, my all-time favorite was his hot dog with chili. I watched him make his chili starting with a solid orange block of oily substance for his starter. By the time he was done, there was no rival anywhere of the quality. He poured a generous dollop over a hot dog and added onions and some cheese for the best chili dog ever.

My parents chose not to renew their lease on the café just when I reached the employable age of 15. It seems their profits were cut into more than by the ketchup guzzlers. There may have been a myriad of reasons, but the end result was no more café.

Those years were fun, but also not so fun. We loved to have one of our parents deliver us lunch to our schools. You can imagine the reaction of the other kids when we got chili dogs, fries, milkshakes and sodas while they were eating their dry bagged lunches. This was in the 50's. We felt rich.

The hard part was how demanding the café was on our parents and how much we were left to fend for ourselves. It always fell to the oldest girl, Carol, to watch us and make sure we stayed out of trouble. Her task was impossible.

Carol was only 14 years old in 1954 when she was put in charge of all of us while our parents were at work at the cafe. She was only two years older than Elaine at 12, me 10, Anita 8, Linda 6 and Mike 5. Dwayne was 19 and already in the Marine Corps by then. Carol has her own story to tell of how hard it was on her. It didn't help that taking care of us was like herding cats.

Great Performances

Carol was pretty creative in trying to get compliance from her young charges. One of her more notable performances was when she went through the house with a butcher knife dripping blood (ketchup), pretending she was deranged. We believed her!

Many times she got blamed for what we did. One time, trying to avoid getting into trouble, she told a traveling pony guy to return when our parents were home. I always remembered that it was Carol who gave the photographer permission to take a picture of each of us on his

Family shot at Byers Street in Hobbs on "traveling" horse. Anita and Linda are on the horse. Standing are Carol, Elaine, and me with Michael in front.

I loved horses, real or pretend.

Me at about age ten as a singing diva.

horse, but she told me recently that it was mother who allowed it. Phew! She could have been in a lot of trouble if she decided it on her own. It was a bit expensive to have individual pictures of each of us, plus a group shot in front of the pony. I can't imagine why Mom authorized it.

We were a fairly lively and inventive bunch. Horses figured in more than one mishap. Once when I was about 11—in about 1955—sister Elaine submitted to being my steed. When we turned out of our bedroom into the tiny L-shaped hallway, my "horsie" was insisting that I get off. I wasn't going for it. Let her buck away, I could hold on! Well, she bucked, and I couldn't hold on. I was deposited on my face onto the hardwood floors of that cramped little hall. My gold-rimmed glasses gashed my forehead causing an instantaneous profusion of blood.

Carol came running, while someone ran to the neighbors to use their phone—we didn't have one yet—to call our parents. There was a whole lot of scurrying about. Carol took me into the bathroom and attempted to stop the flow of blood. Everyone was pretty shook up, not the least being me. I confess, however, that I wasn't upset until I saw the blood. It didn't actually hurt right away. My parents took me to the doctor where I received multiple stitches.

Carol insists that she was always getting in trouble for "allowing" us to get in so much trouble. On this occasion, she truly did get in trouble and Elaine received her share of the scolding. All I remember is the pain. I probably escaped the scolding that time.

Whether it was just after school, or in the summertime, Carol usually turned us out into the yard. We possessed a jungle gym where we got pretty good at tricks. We found this so entertaining that we thought others might pay to see us do gymnastics.

A couple of us walked to a little market to buy penny candy while the others went up and down the neighborhood soliciting an audience. We charged a penny to see the show and sold the candy that we purchased at the store at two for a penny, for one penny each. We didn't make much, but it was great fun.

We also ran the typical little kid businesses such as lemonade stands. We thought we were quite the entrepreneurs, not realizing that we were practically giving away the family's treasured supply of sugar.

Once we got on a roll, we began having talent shows for the neighborhood. All of us fancied ourselves great singers and dancers, so we gathered up all the stray kids in the neighborhood and a few parents to provide an audience for our shows. We basically wanted the chance to show off.

My favorite song contribution was "Que Sera, Sera," which I belted out to our little captive audiences week after week. I don't remember being good at any other song. Sometimes we were a sister-singing group, usually harmonizing hymns. All pretty entertaining, at least for us, and big sister Carol liked it because it helped keep us out of trouble.

We played some evening games in our front yard or a neighbor's. Postman and Spin the Bottle were great favorites. There was also Truth or Dare. Most of these games were focused around having to kiss someone, which appealed to us more as we got older. What probably spared us from inappropriate attachments and intimacies was that we were pretty much all friends, practically

Mother and Daddy walking down a street in Tacoma, WA circa 1944.

siblings, in the neighborhood. Who wanted to kiss a sister or brother! No love matches resulted, if memory serves.

Our Parents

Daddy was impatient if he perceived his children being disobedient or lazy. On days when we were home with Mother, she would warn us all day that we were going to get it when Daddy got home. Seems like every day Mother would meet Daddy at the door and give him the run down of who got out of line that day. It was left to Daddy to mete out the punishment.

For whatever reason, it seems that our older brother Dwayne and oldest girl Carol were the most often headed for discipline by Daddy. I can only guess why Mother singled these two kids out, but I think she expected Carol as the oldest girl—which Mother also was in her family of eight siblings—to be a grownup early on. Of course, Carol sometimes just acted like the kid she was. Dwayne was not always around, being five years older than Carol and either staying with his maternal grandparents or going to the Marines right after he finished high school.

Mother was pretty much just a yeller but occasionally got physical. I never responded well to her form of parenting. I was very stubborn and the harder she pushed, the more I pushed back. On at least one occasion our verbal altercation ended up with her grabbing me by my long hair and yanking me around. I think I actually slapped her. I got it from Daddy that time.

Daddy, however, was a little too quick—in my opinion—to whip off his belt when he thought one of us needed it. He would size up what he believed was going on and react without anyone having a chance to explain. I know at least on one occasion one of my little sisters as a young teen went to a park without permission. Daddy drove to that park, took off his belt, and whipped her all the way home. She was black and blue but the embarrassment took a longer time to leave her. They went back later for the car.

I think in Daddy's mind even

Brother Dwayne as a Marine.

when he was what anyone would call physically abusive, he thought he was doing it to protect his children. If someone else hurt any of us, he went to great lengths to let that person know they would not do it again. Once when Elaine was just a newlywed, having married a guy named Ronnie, she ran to Carol's home all beat up. Carol knew Daddy was to be told, which was a big deal to call him while he was at work.

Daddy went to Carol's and teamed up with Carol's husband Kenneth to go over to Ronnie and Elaine's little house to "have a talk" with Ronnie. I don't think they touched Ronnie, but they let him know in no uncertain terms that if he EVER hit her again he would regret it. Elaine's marriage lasted only a few months.

The last time Daddy was out of control with Carol was when she was a senior in high school. She asked Daddy for permission to go somewhere with her friends, which included a boy who was not a love interest for Carol. Daddy rarely let us go somewhere if a boy was also going. Daddy said for Carol to ask her mother. Mother said for her to ask her daddy, so Carol just decided that was permission and went on.

Daddy was full of rage when he learned that she left without proper permission. When Carol returned, he grabbed her as she got out of the car. Carol told her friends to leave. As they sped away, Daddy started hitting her with his fists and kicking her in a fit of anger. Mother was inside the house during this whole scene but did not try to intervene. Carol was traumatized, and having no safety net at home, she ran to a friend's house where she stayed a few days. After this she went to live with Daddy's sister Peggy and Uncle Robert to finish school. It was Carol that I remember suffering the most at Daddy's hands.

In spite of their frequent failings in parenting, they were always good providers of food and shelter. They managed to keep a roof over our heads in hard times. When we first moved to Hobbs from Tacoma, Washington, we lived in a little farm house on the Styles property outside of town. Daddy was able to get the downpayment for us to have our own house in town on Texas Street from working at the

At about 18 months old with sisters Carol and Elaine. Probably outside the Styles Ranch where we lived after returning from Washington after WWII.

bakery. Sadly, Daddy lost the title to that house from gambling.

At that time we moved into the worst part of town into what was referred to as a "shotgun" house. It was all about ten feet wide. The tiny "living room" was about 8 by 10, barely enough room for our loveseat couch and a chair. The couch sported wagon wheels on each side and folded down into a small regular size bed which is where a couple of us always slept. Going back from there was a kitchen with a bathroom tagged on it. Beyond that was a bedroom or two. Very makeshift.

Daddy saved up enough money about halfway through the café lease to put a down payment on a better house for us across town right across the street from the high school. Moving there really opened up our world. The house was small but very well constructed and we were hopeful of enlarging it.

In about 1960, directly after he gave up the café, Daddy went to work for Ponca Wholesale primarily as a bookkeeper. What I remember most is that Daddy drove a panel truck he bought from the company. He delivered goods and also kept their books. This was the job he was in at the time I left home having gotten married in 1961.

I have some fond images of what happened when Daddy received his once-a-year bonuses at Ponca. He lined us all up by age and gave us a proportionate share in his windfall. By the time he got to me, it might be a quarter, but it was great. We felt like we were a big part of his success. And a quarter got me into the movies and paid for a Butterfinger—much larger than the supposedly super-sized ones of today—AND a very large dill pickle. Plus movie goers were allowed to stay in the theater all day for just the entry fee of 15 cents.

It seems that our life during that time settled into a routine surrounding Daddy's work at Ponca and Mother's job of operating the switchboard at The Leawood Motel, a well-respected motel frequented by oilfield executives. Mother worked the night shift, returning home in the early morning before we woke to go to school. She then went through our Yucca Street house at the appointed hour, whistling—short bursts—and calling for us to get up. Actually it sounded exactly like it would if you were calling the dog!

I never quite understood why she whistled. It's not like there was a lot of ground to cover. Our house was only a two-bedroom. All we girls slept in the bigger bedroom, with my parents in the smaller one while our little brother slept on the living room couch—our older brother Dwayne having already gone into the Marines. Nevertheless, whistle she did, every morning.

I was difficult to rouse because I stayed up late every night. For some reason I got scared every night, thinking I was going to die if I fell asleep. I habitually read myself to sleep. Upon Mother's return, she found the light on and my glasses askew on my face. Often she received my phone calls at about midnight when I called to ask her to convince me I wasn't going to die in my sleep. I am not sure where I got that notion, but I was terrible about watching horror movies at our weekly outings to the movie theater. I don't remember ever waking up Daddy for reassurance, even though he was just in the next room.

It was interesting that my mother worked at this job. Their intention after selling the café was for her to be home with us. My memory is it all began when she opened a charge account at a local department store. The story I heard was that Carol needed a dress for a Rainbow's dance. There was not really money for it. Either Carol or Mother put the dress on a charge account. When Daddy found out, he told Mother she was to go to work until she got it paid off. Mother always worked after that.

Early Job – Babysitting

I was always too young for most jobs, but starting at the age of 12, I was old enough to babysit. So, in 1956 I began my career of taking care of kids for money. The going price was 50 cents an hour, regardless of how many kids! Even during the school year I babysat just about every weekend. There is one family that I will never forget. That was the closest I had ever come to death.

This family consisted of about four children. Their five-year-old daughter had leukemia. These parents and the parents of another large family frequently got together to go out for some fun. Consequently, I was left with about nine kids. It wasn't really so hard for someone coming from a large family. I used every bit of creativity I could muster to make up exciting games to play with them before bedtime. I kept them hopping around, literally, until time to put them to bed, which was tough after so much excitement. I just wanted to take that little girl's mind off her illness.

My heart was so broken for this little girl for whom there seemed no hope. I don't remember how long I babysat for them, but I will always remember the phone call informing me that the little girl had died. That was the saddest funeral I have ever attended, and I believe it was my first ever. I still see her in my mind's eye lying in the casket. Her hair was gone by then, but they put what seemed like cotton around her head. It still seems odd to this day.

I couldn't grieve for that loss. I was not really attached to their family in any other way than as a babysitter. These families were

Me at 14 years old in stylish cat eye glasses.

grief-stricken at the loss. I found it difficult to explain how deeply that death affected me because no one else in my family or close connections knew this family. I am surprised my parents didn't understand I needed help coping. I realized much later what an awful thing that was to experience alone.

I don't know if that was the year, but one year after having made what seemed like a large sum of money babysitting, I made Christmas gift-giving the focus of my funds. I don't remember what I bought for Mother and Daddy, but for each of my siblings still at home, I bought an item of clothing—usually pajamas—and some kind of game or toy.

I still had enough money to buy myself a two-piece straight skirt and long-sleeve blouse outfit I had admired at a local department store. It was predominantly turquoise in polished cotton. I felt stunning in it.

Money Matters

From babysitting I went to working the concession in our largest local movie theater. At last I was in a "grown up" job, even though it was definitely just teens running things. The year was 1959 and all the kids of my acquaintance spent their free time watching the latest releases, which were musicals, westerns and some dramas. There I was making popcorn, selling snacks and even taking a turn with the flashlight going up and down the aisles discouraging young lovers. I loved it all.

I cleaned out the popcorn machine at the end of the day, swept, mopped, cleaned bathrooms—your typical teen slavery—but I felt so mature having that job. I also got to see many movies, of which musicals were my favorites.

Money was definitely an issue in our nine-person family. Our house by this time was solid, and in a safe neighborhood; however, it was certainly not big enough for our family. Having only one small bathroom and a house full of girls drove our little brother to go behind our house to an adjoining 5-acre orchard to find a tree when he needed relief.

Most of the trauma and drama of the household revolved around who was taking too long in the bathroom. I was usually the culprit, having very long hair

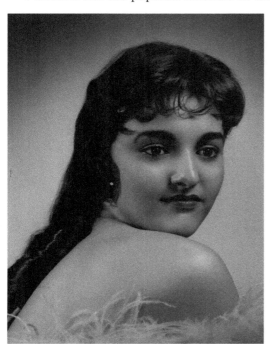
Me with long hair and "Elizabeth Taylor" eyebrows.

styled in a long roll all around the bottom that took so much time to get perfect. And if that wasn't enough, there was my makeup that required equal precision. Not having been born with much in the way of eyebrows, it took great care to recreate the Elizabeth Taylor eyebrows I so admired.

Daddy envisioned closing in the garage of our house to gain another bedroom, which he almost completed. He had the wall built to replace the garage door; however, the room itself never got completely finished. The garage still also housed the washer and dryer all in the same space but it provided a makeshift bedroom. I am sad to say that this became my father's room when he and my mom became more and more at odds with one another.

Things Fall Apart

The 60's brought the breakdown of my family. I remember thinking when I was a sophomore that if I could just help my parents budget their money, their marriage would be fixed. It seemed pretty simple to me. In my young mind, all I observed that was troublesome was their fights about money. There was much more going on—or not going on—that led to their eventual breakup, but money, or the lack of it, was pretty high up on the list by my reckoning.

My parents' system was to divide up the bills and each spend his or her paycheck on separate parts of the budget. I remember that even the grocery buying was divided up. My dad, who was still a great cook, always bought the meats. My mother bought the vegetables and all the trimmings for meals. Mother was the one who bought all our clothes, even Daddy's. It was she who supplied us with milk money to supplement our school lunches and bought all the school supplies. We usually carried a bag lunch to school and it was Mother who bought the fruit, chips, sandwich makings and the occasional dessert.

Mother didn't think Daddy understood all the buying she did for the family and the house. He took care of the car, but that was the extent of his financial involvement in the day-to-day lives of our bunch. Every argument I ever overheard between my parents was focused on their being upset that the other did not carry enough of the financial load with their separate earnings. And they kept their earnings separate, but Mother was not the main breadwinner so she was often in the position of having to ask Daddy to put in money on the things she felt the family needed.

In addition to my father's limited financial commitment to our family, he was also a physically absent dad. My mother was frustrated that he played golf every weekend. Even though he played at a Municipal course that was relatively inexpensive, Mother was not happy about it. It only occurred to me later that she also was upset that he was never around to help her. What must it have been like for her to be the only caregiver for seven kids? I rarely saw her get to go off and do something fun, with or without my dad.

We kids were satisfied—at least when we were younger—if we could go to the movies every weekend. Even now I think about how much we wanted to live vicariously through the lives of those stars on the big screen. Looking forward to films and reading the volumes of books I checked out from the town library were my saving grace.

Mother made a deal with us. If we cleaned our part of the house on Saturday mornings, we got to go to the movies on Saturday afternoon. The other part of the deal was that if we went to church on Sunday mornings, we got to go to the movies again on Sunday afternoon.

In our town the main theater changed movies after Saturday night, so we really got the chance to see every movie that came to town. The biggest and newest movie house was the Frontier. The Reel was a small theater on our main street, but it rarely showed the latest movies. I believe there was also The Scout and The Rig, both named after the main industry of our area – oil rigs.

Since movie watching was such an attraction for me, I was usually pretty motivated to both clean house and go to church. Being decidedly the most stubborn of the kids, however, there were some times I did not get to go to the Saturday movies because I had refused all or part of my cleaning tasks that morning. We girls divided up the big bedroom for cleaning, even down to dividing the closet up. Bickering often ensued.

Then, of course, we cleaned the rest of the house. My mother was imaginative and sometimes we drew tasks written on slips of paper out of a jar, which added some spontaneity to our lives. I still don't know specifically what might have put a burr under my cap about my chores, but, frankly, it did not take much for me to cry injustice. My mother stuck to her guns, and many a time I watched them all drive off to be deposited at the theater, leaving me behind. I showed them.

During those times, I remember Daddy sitting by the front door in his swivel rocker watching television when Mother necessarily walked between him and the TV to leave for work in the evening. She often did not even acknowledge him, much less give him a kiss goodbye. I don't remember his saying anything to her either. It was so unsettling.

Years later this nighttime ritual of my parents came to my mind with a new realization. After my wedding at the grand age of 17—in 1961—my new husband Bob took me back to my parents' house to change for the honeymoon and get my bag. Daddy was sitting in his chair by the front door, television off, watching me leave. I couldn't believe it, but there was a tear in his eye. I gave him a big hug. Later when things got rough for me and Bob I thought if I had known earlier Daddy loved me that much, maybe I wouldn't have been married so young.

My parents managed to keep up appearances only so long. Daddy left the year after I got married. They were married just under 25 years. There were still three kids left at home: Anita at 16, Linda 14 and 13-year-old Michael. I really don't know how my mother made it financially after Daddy left.

Things were especially dicey as my father had just been caught embezzling from his place of work. He told them he would borrow a little here and there to make ends meet, always expecting to pay it back the next payday. It never happened. By the time they found him out, he was in for several thousand dollars. They fired him but thankfully did not press charges. I know we had a 30-year mortgage that wasn't half paid for and her wages were meager. I know it had to have been rough.

Frankly, I was a bit wrapped up in my world at the moment being a wife, a mother of an infant, a secretary and soon-to-be college student. I know those were hard years for my younger siblings, and I hope someday one of them writes that story.

24

chapter

2

Heart
Ablaze

Searching for Daddy

The loves I had in my life all seemed to be my trying to find my dad. It is curious that I still remember several of them and the quality that drew me to each one. In Mrs. Higgins' 1st grade class it was Donald Ainsworth. He was tall and blonde, quiet and the smartest guy in class. I guess he had mastered the ABC's. I am quite certain I never revealed my heart to Donald.

I saw Donald a few years ago at our 50th high school reunion. I finally confessed to him—and his wife whom I never knew—how much I adored him from afar in first grade. I thought it was kind of sweet. They looked mortified.

Who could compare with my dad? Daddy was one of the smartest men I have ever known so I admired men with brains. He had a great sense of humor and would get down on the floor and play with us. I loved it when he chased us on all fours barking like a dog! When I wasn't getting in trouble, I really loved being around my dad.

Daddy graduated from high school just before the Great Depression and didn't get to go to college, going to work instead. He always wanted to be a basketball coach, having been a good player in high school, but he went to work right away to help his family survive.

My next crush was probably in 5th grade—1954—when I fell for Winifred Rains. He was athletic and funny, a definite class favorite. I think he was freckled. My strongest memory of him was how I finagled to go to his house when I was out selling Girl Scout Cookies so he might notice me.

He lived very far from our house. I walked all that distance and then wasn't

Mrs. Higgins first grade class with me (top left) and Donald Ainsworth beside me.

sure which house was his. I trudged dejectedly back home with all my cookies unsold. I don't have any memory of how I got over him, but unrequited love at any age is painful.

The next year it was Bob (last name withheld for reasons that will become obvious). He was classically tall, dark and handsome. When many of us walked home from school, Bob was always among a bunch of boys, laughing and joking and seemingly having a great old time. A few friends or sisters usually accompanied me on my trek home. I couldn't take my eyes off this dreamboat. I fantasized many a time what it would be like WHEN I was his girl. I would have never done anything overt to make my heart known to Bob or any other boy. I don't even know if my friends knew.

One day it all came apart. I thought nothing could shake my love for Bob until that day. There was a Down Syndrome girl in our class who was very openly in love with Bob. She followed him admiringly, not seeming to care that he was not responding.

One day I happened to see Bob give her his books to carry for him. In those days, carrying someone's books—albeit it was usually the boy carrying the girl's—was a sign of true love. What followed next stabbed my heart. He began to joke about the girl to his friends. She walked on oblivious to their taunts, enveloped in her love. What a creep! I was very glad that he never noticed me anyway.

Daddy's basketball team at Peacock High School. He is # 5.

Girl in the Golden Swimsuit

It wasn't until junior high—1959—that my love life picked up. That has to sound scary to many parents, me included! I think I met him at the city swimming pool where I spent almost every day of the summer. Daily I walked to the pool, collecting discarded soda bottles on the way. There was a small store between my house and the pool where I redeemed the bottles for enough money to go swimming. Except for times of bad weather, that was how I spent my summers for a couple of years. It didn't seem so cool a thing to do when I was older.

I was confident at the pool. I usually met friends there. Mary Lou Williams was one of my oldest friends. Often we were at the pool together. Other good friends were Gay Willis (yes, that was her name!) and Gayla Crowe. Cooling off at the municipal pool was pretty much a necessity to beat the triple-digit summers of southern New Mexico.

But, truth be told, we were at the pool primarily to scout and be scouted. Reminds me of the song about looking for love in all the wrong places. *Hmmm.* Regardless of which of my friends came swimming on any day, I was pretty much at the pool every day. We hung out together and encouraged one another in our attempts at diving and boyfriend catching. Both activities were thrilling.

I was a strong swimmer and often dove off the high board. There were many days I stood at the end of the board debating with myself whether it was such a good idea. I don't remember ever exiting back down the ladder, but I was always a bit scared of diving from so high. Usually I made up my mind when either someone was waiting to dive or when one of my friends taunted or encouraged me.

My BFF from junior high and high school, Mary Lou (Williams) Johnston.

I went between swimming and playing in the pool to getting something from the snack bar, then lying on the concrete on my towel usually gossiping about the boys with my girlfriends. Everyone knew you shouldn't go in the pool after having eaten something!

About this time my figure was developed, and I was aware of being ogled. I remember feeling a little embarrassed, but also pleased. My best swimsuit was single-pieced, form-fitting in a golden fish scale kind of material. I was a sleek goldfish.

At a high school reunion some 25 years later, one of the boys of those pool days described that bathing suit to a T. Oops.

It was at the pool that I spent time with Charles Hill and his group of friends. We all goofed off together, playing games of tag in the pool and sometimes just sitting around talking and joking. At some point we all realized that Charles and I were enjoying each other's company and began hanging together, talking, both in and out of the pool.

There is a sensuality of near-naked bodies in the pool together that did not go unnoticed by either of us. There was not much opportunity for anything more than playful pushing in that environment and talking in hushed tones by the sides of the pool. Every so often Charles managed to sneak a kiss in the water when we were close to the side of the water. The pool, being the only public one in town, was always packed, but we managed a few pecks and knowing glances.

Charles asked me to go to the movies with him. We both knew it wasn't about any movie. I tried to pretend I was not aware of the implied consent. Even though I knew I would never go all the way before I was married, I enjoyed the idea of playing around the edges.

My parents did not consider me old enough at 14 to officially date—I wonder why—so Charles and I arranged to secretly meet at the theater. We sought that dark environment for hand holding, his arm being put around my shoulder and the titillating sneaking of a kiss. We were careful to not get caught by the flashlight of the theater worker who was occasionally sent to discourage young lovers.

A couple of years later when I was one of those flashlight-wielding, smooch-thwarters I saw the situation from a different perspective.

When I was one of those girls hoping for a little hand holding or having a guy's arm around me in the theater, it was thrilling. An occasional sneaked peck on the lips felt like true love. It occurred to me later that however much "petting" a guy would do with a girl in a public theater, was only foreplay for what he wanted to do in private. By this age, I rarely watched the movie at all.

Charles Hill in Hobbs High School yearbook 1959-60.

It was all very thrilling to my young heart. Sometimes Charles took me for a ride on his motor scooter afterwards, but I couldn't let him take me home. My parents were even more fearful of their girls riding on motorcycles than their getting involved with boys. Charles' scooter posed no real danger, but I was sure the distinction would have been lost on my parents on both counts if they saw me riding with him on his motorized bike.

Charles was dashing and fun. I think there was as much thrill in the sneaking around as there was in the actual relationship. I began to see problems in his character, however, the longer we dated. He seemed very possessive, but yet I was suspicious on several occasions that he was seeing someone else. He told me I was beautiful, the revelation of which was surprising and soothing at the same time. He gave me a jewelry box and a necklace and earrings set that Christmas. I gave him a wallet.

I am not sure how and why we broke up, but I think that there always seemed to be other girls, or at least the rumor of them. I remember several scenes of explanations being demanded and offered. In the end, I got the word he was going to "break up" with me, which he did. I was not as disappointed as I thought I would be. The more I knew about him, the more I realized that I was dazzled by a few well-placed compliments and his seeming suaveness. He was way less cool than I imagined at the beginning.

My fantasies of having a boyfriend were pretty far afield from the real thing. Isn't that the way it is? Why can't we know that when we first step into these relationships? Being in love, even having crushes, is so dazzling, transforming mere mortals into spiritual beings! *I credit Zora Neale Hurston with creating this imagery in* Their Eyes Were Watching God.

During our sophomore year—1959-60—Charles left school, left town. I never knew what happened, or at least I don't remember knowing. Just a few months ago someone put us in touch with each other and Charles told me what had happened over 50 years ago. He said he got into a verbal argument with our English teacher, Mr. Mills, that got physical. He said he jumped out a window of the school, ran as far as he could go, and then took a bus until his money ran out. Ironically, later in his life he became a police officer.

High School Passions

In high school, I was involved in a lot of activities that included male friends, but I never allowed myself to be interested in any of them. I kept pretty busy with being in French Club, drama and choir while following the business track for my general education.

Having years later become a teacher myself, I must share some impressions of one of my most memorable high school teachers. Miss Shipp was my business courses teacher. What an amazing person! She taught us much more than the demands of the curriculum. After having been in her class, I felt confident that I could accomplish anything. She had a way about her that drew in her often-reluctant students.

I know I was not the only one who came out of her class wanting to be just like her. I have to say that I used many of her fun techniques and gimmicks in my years of teaching. I tried to make my subject relevant and exciting. Even when I taught "dry" grammar, I made the lessons into a game with prizes. I am especially proud of the "Mc Jeopardy" game I created for teaching Macbeth. "When shall we three meet again?" "Who are the Three Witches?"

One of the best things I came away with was a sense that the world was bigger than Hobbs, New Mexico. She daily took roll, counting out our rows in different languages. "*Eins, zwei, drei, vier, funf. Uno, dos, tres, cuatro, cinco, seis. Un, deux, trois, quatre, cinq. Ichi, ni, san, shi, go, roku.*" I heard German, Spanish, French, Japanese and, of course, English. She was always so upbeat and encouraging to her students.

It was especially fun that all four of my sisters were taught by Ms. Shipp. A few years ago when I was visiting New Mexico, 50+ years later, we made contact with Ms. Shipp and took her out to lunch. It was so special. She is still going strong. Just being with her again transported us back to her classroom. Even though she is in her 80's, she has the same

Miss Shipp from Hobbs High yearbook in 1960.

Lunch with Miss Shipp. L–R Sisters Linda Kay, Anita, Miss Shipp and me.

spunk. That's what I'm talking about!

From the time I was about eight years old, I dreamed of becoming a teacher. Being with teachers of this caliber fine-tuned my ideals for the profession. I think it odd now that I was on a business track and not the college preparatory one. Looking back, I don't think I had the confidence to be on a college track, which I believed was way above my abilities. I realized much later that I had what it would have taken, but if you don't think you can, you really can't—a word of caution to all parents and teachers.

Actually all of this business training helped me in my path to becoming a teacher, not the least of which was being able to become a secretary to work my way through my undergraduate degree.

Mais Oui!

My other fascination was with all things French. I yearned to study the language while I was in junior high. It was not offered until high school, so I stayed in the same family of languages and studied Spanish in ninth grade.

I was so shocked when I finally got to take French my sophomore year to find that I could not wrap my head around it. Miss Holloway was very encouraging. She wisely advised me to be diligent, to keep up with all the work and homework and that it would eventually fall into place. She was so right, but it didn't happen until the second semester of the first year.

I went on to take French II, but opted to go back to Spanish during my college years, realizing that the college would have required that I take an ad-

In French Club my sophomore year. I am second from the left.

vanced French course. I love French, but I lacked confidence I could move into studying it at the college level. I spent many pleasurable moments in the activities of our French Club.

It was in this extra-curricular involvement that I developed more of a sense of who I was. In my eyes, I was just the middle kid of a family of nine. I always felt that our family was poorer than all my friends. I judged by my wardrobe being very limited when I compared myself to others at school. I was a little embarrassed that my parents argued so much, even though I rarely took home any friends who would have observed this fact. My dad was an accountant after he sold the cafe, but it didn't seem like a very glamorous job and it definitely didn't pay like I imagined other kids' father's jobs did.

In fact, the imagining was the problem. I felt that my family's socio-economic status was worse than my friends', and those with whom I wanted to be friends. I found myself pretending to be better off than we were. In fact, I was not content to be just "as good" as others, but put on airs that I was above others. French Club was one of the places where I could reinvent myself and become who I always wanted to be. French was the language of the elite and I could speak it!

For some reason, I kept finding myself getting embarrassed by my odd choices that revealed more than I thought I wanted to. I still remember dressing up in a black cat costume for our club's *Mardis Gras* party one year. I created a tail to wear with a leotard. A black mask completed the look. The costume was so revealing of my shapely figure. That may not seem odd now, but then it was tantamount to going to the event naked. I embarrassed myself.

Once again, I think my fantasy world got me in trouble. I just didn't think about how I would feel about being so exposed. I wanted to hide and get the night over with. I went home very early without letting on how out of place I felt. Except for that *Mardis Gras* party, however, French was still one of my favorite subjects in school. It seemed to me that my family's "class" was concealed in the atmosphere surrounding this exotic language.

Ever Playing Roles

My longest standing extra-curricular activity was drama. Again, I loved to "be on stage," but at the same time every performance I was petrified almost to the point of freezing up. I was in plays every year from junior high school until I left school at the end of my junior year in 1961. I was in the Dramatics Club every year.

Me as a sophomore in Dramatics Club, second from the right behind Suzy Frier.

In ninth grade I acted in a theater-in-the-round production that was so exciting. I can't remember the play, but it was thrilling to not have a backdrop, but instead being surrounded by the audience. Our props were chosen to represent more than one set. One challenge was getting on and off stage through the audience. Also, without any form of amplification, we actors learned to project our voices, but we also had to be aware of turning our backs to the audience.

Once I was in tenth and was officially in high school, I had access to the state-of-the-art theater our town built. Being an oil town and having only one high school provided a lot of money to put into the schools. Our theater was spectacular, and once hosted the Miss New Mexico Pageant. It was complete with individual dressing rooms, a balcony and a mezzanine outside the balcony that was supported by columns with exotic Italian tiles.

Above the stage was a catwalk that lent itself to many a dramatic flying scene in productions requiring such. The place was amazing to see but especially wonderful for those of us who were fortunate enough to put on the productions.

My specific memories include being in a politically-charged production about Franco in 10th grade. In that one I was alone onstage for the opening scene. I was so afraid I wouldn't remember my lines, but once the curtain went up, the muscle memory of repetition thankfully kicked in. I sweated out my first moment on stage for every play I was in.

My most fulfilling acting role was being a geisha in *Teahouse of the August Moon*. I remember playing several bit parts in this comedic drama. It was thrill-

ing to be Japanese. We wore kimonos and the wooden shoes that were much like stiff but dressy flip-flops. Those of us fortunate enough to have long hair wound it into buns. The makeup took white to an all-new level. When I looked in the mirror, even I was convinced I was a geisha. I was intrigued by other cultures. One of my best friends, Suzanne, was the female lead in this play. She was great.

Our amazing drama coach and director, Mr. Lee Coppick, gave us the confidence to take on some major productions. In 11th grade our class put on *The King and I* in the fall. I did not try out for this show because I was waiting for the spring production, which was scheduled to

Sophomore production of "Time Out for Ginger."

be *The Diary of Anne Frank.* I wanted so badly to play Anne. I am still not sure why her character appealed so much to me. I know the political aspects of the play were over my head. I saw a young teenager falling in love for the first time.

That year would have been about 1961. I remember sitting in the theater downtown when the movie version of *Diary* was released, watching it over and over again. We could do that in those days. Parents often parked their kids at the theater all day for just 15 cents. I studied the part from the movie standpoint, and felt confident I could portray the title role. It was excruciating to try out. I was long on desire, but short on confidence. To my amazement, I won the part.

The set for the production was very simple. The boy playing the part of Anne's boyfriend Peter and I were in all the scenes so our interaction and chemistry were critical to the play. We got along very well and people commented how believable we were being two kids falling in love under dire circumstances.

We were three weeks into rehearsals in the late spring when a shocking thing happened. Mr. Coppick talked to the cast about stopping the production. He expressed concern that there was too little time to do justice to the show since the school year was winding down. I don't know if anyone else was as disappointed as I. Most of our troupe had been in the previous semester's production of *The King and I* and were deservedly worn out, but for me, it was a major letdown. I feigned graciousness, but secretly was very hurt. My insecurities led me to wonder if he stopped the show because I was not good enough. I'll never know.

A thought I had later, especially after having married a Jewish man, was that there could have been some social pressure against our drama troupe performing what was considered a politically controversial production.

Acting was a way for me to get out of myself in a role. I could credit any of my own faults to the character I was portraying, not having to admit to ownership myself. It was very important for my stability, providing a much-needed outlet. Anne was my last drama production.

Later, when my children were quite young and we were living in Santa Fe, NM, I tried out for the city's production of Fiddler on the

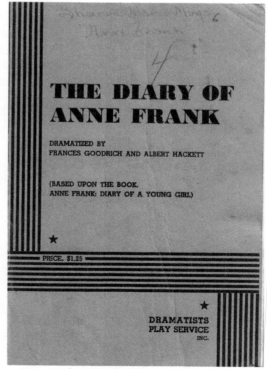

My script from the play The Diary of Anne Frank.

Roof. I passed the singing and dancing portions and was called back to read for a speaking part. I dearly wanted to be Mama. Between the various tryouts, the director released the rehearsal schedule. I knew I could not be away from home that much with three children at home, so did not go to the speaking tryouts.

Diva in the Making

Simultaneously, I was successfully involved in choir. It helped me deal with the disappointment of not playing Anne. This was my chance to get better at singing. When I first tried out for choir my sophomore year, I was supposed to be in the lowest level group, being a novice. That year the beginning choir course was only offered the same class period as drama production. With my junior high drama experience coming into high school, I was eligible to be in the drama class putting on performances.

My beloved drama director spoke to the Music Department Chair, Mr. Freitag, and requested that I be allowed to be in A Capella Choir which was offered a class time I could take it. That was the highest level of the choir program and could be entered only after having completed the earlier preparatory courses as well as passing an audition. The two teachers enjoyed a good rapport and were supportive of each other's programs. Thankfully for my budding passion for both singing and acting, I was able to move into this advanced choir. I couldn't believe it.

I was certainly ill-prepared. The closest I had come so far to reading music was having taken violin lessons in a school strings program in elementary school for a year. Everyone in A Capella could not only read music, but were able to do harmonies, hear individual parts, and were mostly at least a year older than I. I tried not to be overwhelmed, but just paid close attention.

It was a challenge to my creativity to learn each new piece. I made up my own notation for whether notes were high, higher, low, lowest, sustained and for phrasing.

I still use this notation since I have been singing on worship teams for over 40 years. Since that time I have taken piano lessons and helped two of my kids study violin from early ages, but still have not managed fluency in reading music.

Three of the greatest moments while in this choir were poignant and very fulfilling. The first was being asked to be the speaker to introduce our pieces when we went into schools and other venues to perform. I still remember a song we were doing about a train trip. I came up with a catchy way to get the kids' attention, which was thrilling for me. I still recall the first line of my speech, "Do you want to go on a train ride?"

The second accomplishment was performing at a choir tournament and having our choir receive rave reviews by the songwriter himself. We were not told he would be in the audience. Exhilarating! That was the caliber of our choir.

For me the most exciting part was to hear my voice as it twirled in with the others, finding its niche. Since we performed without benefit of any instruments—by definition—we had to be spot on individually so we sounded great collectively. Even though I never fooled myself that I was up to the quality of my choir mates, I know I learned so much and felt such personal accomplishment in trying. Of course, I fantasized that I would become a great diva. Doesn't everyone?

The most memorable performance of that year was our last, when we sang at the 1961 graduation ceremony. The song still rings in my head and heart, "Climb Every Mountain." I was in the class of 1962, but while I was singing to those seniors who were leaving, I knew that I was leaving too, without fanfare nor a diploma. There was no way to stop the flow of tears.

Learning about "Love"

About the closest thing I had to a romance during my early teens was spending many late afternoons talking with a neighborhood boy in his yard or mine. The most significant thing in that relationship was that he taught me how to change a tire. He thought women should know how to do two things for themselves: change a tire and change the oil. I lost interest in him, or vice versa, I don't remember, but it was before I got the oil-changing lessons.

Things began to steam up the summer of 1959 between my freshman and sophomore years on a visit to my Uncle Cecil's family in Seagraves, Texas, where I met Kenneth Herndon. He was about my age. My cousin Betty Mings and I hung out with him since he was a friend of her older sister Pat's husband, Larry.

Somehow it happened that Kenneth and I were left alone at Pat's house. I thought that he must truly love me since it was hard to keep him at bay. On one of my visits he insisted he wanted to marry me and actually gave me an "engagement" ring. I took it, and kept it hidden from my parents, but flashed it to my friends in high school upon returning home after one of my Texas—ostensibly family—visits.

As we were not supervised during our time together, I began to realize that Kenneth's motives for giving me the ring were not loving nor pure. He thought the ring entitled him to take liberties before marriage. I was scared off by his aggressiveness, and had the good sense to return the ring. Thus ended that misadventure.

Meeting Mr. Right

The next summer, I met a guy who seemed to have all of the qualities I wanted in a man. He was impeccably groomed, handsome, intelligent, funny, mature, and he wanted me. What a combo! His name was Bob Ankerholz. He was 22 and I was 16, but I tried to pretend it didn't matter.

In his defense, Bob had good reason to believe I was older than I was. I met him that summer while babysitting my older sister Carol's six-month-old baby

Kenneth, who we called "Buddy." Carol's little house was close to town, and I looked forward to taking Buddy out in his stroller when I window shopped along the main street of town.

On one of these shopping treks, I first encountered Bob when I went into a Kinney's Shoe Store downtown looking for green shoes to put with an outfit I was going to buy with my babysitting money. Being the salesman, he struck up a conversation. He told me later he figured that I was divorced with a baby. We had a good laugh about that. While talking I realized he was the big brother of my friend Judy's boyfriend, Don. He had just completed a four-year stint in the Marine Corps. He wanted to take me out.

At this time, since I was 16, Daddy finally considered me old enough to date. I don't think it was on our first date, but I remember the time Bob came to pick me up to go bowling. I was dressed in slacks, probably pedal pushers, which I considered to be appropriate for the activity. Bob took one look at me and said he wasn't going to take me anywhere dressed like that! I was shocked; Daddy was pleased. Needless to say, I went in and changed into a pleated skirt.

My father had been raised in west Texas, deep in the heart of the Bible Belt. For him it meant that his interpretation of the Bible needed to be aligned with his Baptist heritage. When the Bible admonishes women to not wear men's clothing, my dad and a whole generation of Baptists believed that women should not wear any kind of slacks. I have always wondered how they came to this interpretation since Biblical men would have worn tunics, not pants.

Therefore, women wearing pants in public was still considered by many to be indecent exposure. In high school we were only allowed to wear pants to school once a week, and then there were specific guidelines including wearing a very long shirt (usually our daddy's) that had the effect of covering like a dress. Daddy found it difficult enforcing his strict dress code on his five daughters, so he was very pleased that one of their beaus was like-minded about women's attire.

Dating Bob became a regular thing, usually only on weekends which was the only time my parents allowed when school was in session. When Bob could talk, he called me from his workplace from a pay phone. I had coached all my siblings that they could not answer the phone until it rang more than two times, because Bob would call and ring two times and hang up so I would call him back, thus saving him the dime for the phone call.

Our dates were usually very simple. Sometimes we just "went for a coke" to talk. Riding around in his convertible sports car, the Austin Healey, was thrilling. It was several years old, but still impressive. Sadly, it came to a bad end. Bob let one of his friends drive it once and the guy drove it on a rocky road. The low carriage put the oil pan very low to the ground. He drove over a large rock that scraped the pan and damaged it. Not realizing it, he kept driving and burned up the engine.

One time I was invited to a pool party at a friend's house, which was about a half mile from our house. For some reason Daddy did not let me go. I had already told Bob I would meet him there. I decided to sneak out and walk to the party anyway. I didn't let on to Bob that I had sneaked out. The evening was tense because I feared being found out.

When I got home, Daddy was waiting for me. I told him where I had been, but I don't remember telling him I met Bob there. I don't know what punishment I received, but deceiving Daddy was the number one sin in our house.

I have tried to remember when my relationship with Bob turned serious. In my mind it was when I stood Bob up. There was a guy from school who seemed very interested in me. I was flattered, but not really interested. On this one occasion, on a Saturday afternoon, this guy came over to the house and wanted me to go get a coke with him. I told him I had a date with Bob that night and couldn't. He kept pushing, saying it would only be an hour and he promised to get me back in time for the date. I gave in and left with him.

When we got to the Feastmaster—the drive-in at the end of the main drag—I realized he had no intention of getting me back home for my date. It really scared me that I was apparently powerless to change his mind, but I have to admit I was also very excited and flattered. It's interesting that I felt helpless being in a situation I truly believed I couldn't change.

Bob really had no exclusive hold on me, but I wanted him to be that one. I wasn't in any danger, except for the obvious risk I felt of losing Bob. I was kicking myself for having allowed my ego to put me in such a fix. The guy "let" me use the pay phone at the drive-in to call Bob and tell him I couldn't make it for our date. Bob was put off, as I expected he would be.

I don't know how we got that smoothed over, but I am sure it was after massive groveling on my part, which was the continual role I played in that relationship. I pictured Bob being like a King who deigned to look my way. I was determined to keep him at all cost. Pride wasn't going to keep us apart if I had anything to do with it.

Love, Marriage...Baby Carriage

Bob appealed to me because he had direction in his life, not like the high school boys I was around. He was very ambitious and eager to get on with making his life a success. He believed in my potential and was eager to show me how to have a productive future. He encouraged me to use my business skills and be an apprentice to an attorney's secretary for free in order to prepare myself to become a legal secretary.

So that is what I did during my junior year in high school, all of which time Bob and I were dating. I worked under the City Attorney, Don Hallam's, secretary Lexie Craddock. She was great at training me and often let me go in to take shorthand dictation from Mr. Hallam.

By Thanksgiving of that year, Bob asked me to marry him. I want to be forthcoming about how this decision impacted our relationship. As Bob and I spent more time alone, we were more and more into heavy petting. On our dates he started taking me to his parents' house knowing that his stepdad was out of state working, his mother was at her job as a dietitian in a local hospital, while his only sibling Don was on a date himself with his sweetheart Judy. We were alone.

It was on one of these dates that he said he wanted to marry me. I had heard this from a previous boyfriend, and we know it did not end well. At this point in our relationship, I believed I could not live without this man. My heart was bursting to say yes, which I did. Then his pressuring me to have sex with him began in earnest. I truly believed—and still do—that sex is reserved for marriage. Our petting got more intense, making it more difficult to keep it from happening. At one point he confronted me with a question, something to the effect of, "Who are you saving it for? It's me you are going to marry. I am going to be your husband."

Sadly, I had no one I thought I could go to for advice. I have four sisters and had several very close girlfriends, but I was ashamed to be in such a spot and didn't want to admit it to any of them. My father liked Bob, but I was afraid he might make me stop dating him. My mom was working so hard at the time and she and my dad weren't getting along.

It was not so much a decision but rather the result of petting out of control when it happened. I knew right then that I must marry him. It's not that I had any reservations about marrying him, but there was no way I was going to let the man who took my virginity get away. From that moment, I would do everything necessary to keep him. I was damaged goods. No one else would ever want me. My dad successfully instilled that truth in all of us.

We were about six months from the wedding date that was set for June 4, 1961. I went through the motions of finishing up my junior year. At the time he asked me to marry him I said I lacked another year of high school. He wanted me to try to graduate early.

We both thought I would be able to take a class in night school the second semester of my junior year, which would have given me the credit in English I needed to graduate a year early. I was not allowed by the state of New Mexico to take more classes for credit that year. Bob was pretty upset, but no more than I.

Picture I used for our engagement announcement.

41

He let me know that he wanted to get on with his life and he couldn't be waiting around for a high school girl to be ready. I can't believe my parents actually consented to let me quit school, but they did and I was married right after my junior year, being just barely 17-years-old without a high school diploma.

Bob wanted me to immediately go to work. His personal philosophy that drove him and me was that if I didn't work he wouldn't either. At this point I was already pregnant, having gotten so at the end of our two-week honeymoon during which we drove to Mexico. So now I was pregnant and did not have a high school diploma and was still not 18.

I am amazed that an attorney would hire someone without a diploma, but a new attorney in town hired me to be his legal secretary based on my legal secretary apprenticeship at the City Attorney's office. It didn't last long. That attorney couldn't get his practice going and was only in town for a couple of months.

I then could say I was "experienced" as a legal secretary and felt the courage, with the urging of Bob, to apply for another job with an attorney. I still remember feeling that I was being sneaky in not letting the attorney know I was pregnant and wouldn't be able to stay on very long. I think Bob and I rationalized that we were planning to move to Colorado to make our fortune before I would have to quit due to pregnancy. I continued in that job until Bob and I moved to Denver, Colorado, the end of 1961.

One of the sad experiences I experienced while working for this lawyer, Dewey B. Leach—who was my friend Joanne's father—was when he was hired to represent a lifelong friend of my family. The charge was murder, or at least being an accomplice before the fact. Several of the older boys who were out of high school had been hanging out with a new guy from back east. They got the notion to hold up a local dentist who was known for carrying large amounts of cash.

To this day it seems it was more about the adrenaline rush than the money. My friend never had any money growing up, but the Easterner came from a well-to-do doctor in New York while one of the other guys was from one of the wealthiest families in our town. They all planned it together, allegedly, but my friend had been working the day of and didn't participate.

Unfortunately, they carried a gun. The dentist resisted and was shot and killed in the process of the robbery. The best our office could do for my friend was to get him seven years. If memory serves, the New York kid, who pulled the trigger, got off completely—no time served.

3 chapter

Marriage Maze

Moving to Colorado

Bob's Aunt Virgie and her husband Harold Woods invited Bob and me to come up and stay with them so we could get jobs in Denver. We saw the potential dollar signs by leaving our economically depressed town of under 50 thousand. In Hobbs, it seemed that the only opportunity was with the oil industry, which definitely had its ups and downs. Not wanting to work in the oil fields, Bob and I struck out for greater opportunity.

We arrived in snowy Denver in January of 1962. Being seven months pregnant, I was not expected to find a job yet. Bob set about finding work. He became a clerk at Martin Marietta—a missile industry installation under government contract—south of Denver. We got into a little basement apartment in a residential house in a suburb south of Denver, Littleton, and were finally on our own. We cozied up our nest and Monicqua Suzette Ankerholz "Neek" was born on March 16th of that year.

I have vivid memories of living in that apartment. March in Denver is very cold and often snowy. I washed out diapers by hand and hung them in the backyard on a clothesline. While they were "drying," they became stiff from the cold. I brought them in to let the warmth of the house complete the drying, draping them over every available piece of furniture.

Monicqua as a baby.

Another memory is that there was only the one bedroom, but there was an unfinished area behind a curtain. We set up a cot there for when we had company. This is where my mother-in-law Betty Ankerholz slept when she came to help me after the birth.

There was no way I was prepared for motherhood. Little Monicqua was very colicky and I was clueless how to help her. Betty suggested I give the baby kaopectate. Looking back, that seems to be a pretty strong medicine for a newborn. I suspect the baby may have had a physiological problem, but I also think she was picking up on my stress.

Since I was expected to get a job immediately after recovering from childbirth, I couldn't breastfeed. Thankfully, things are very different these days and moms can often nurse their babies at work. Or they can pump and save their milk for the baby. The pain of not being able to breastfeed was emotional and physical; the method for drying up milk-producing breasts was to bind the breasts tightly. I don't remember how long it took, but it was excruciating in every way.

So, when Monicqua was two months old, I secured a secretarial job at the same company where Bob was working. I was interviewed by an engineer whose previous secretary also had a legal background, so he was inclined to offer me the job even though, again, I had no high school diploma and had just turned 18-years-old.

My job actually filled an important role in the space effort. I was secretary to the propulsion engineers at Martin Marietta's Cold Flow Laboratory. This lab was responsible for testing the various propellants for upcoming space travel, which at that time was the Apollo project. It was an exciting job for anyone, even more for a teenager.

A couple of months after acquiring my job, I also began college work at the University of Colorado (CU), attending the extension division in Denver at night. My early dream of wanting to be a teacher became more real when I signed up for my first classes.

Bob was not keen on my wanting to teach English, thinking PE would be more to HIS liking. In those times wives often were denied higher education, especially once they bore children. I think the only reason Bob was agreeable was that it fit in with his plans. He "let" me go to college because he saw my being a teacher as a kind of insurance against us having to have babysitters for Monicqua. Ostensibly, I would be working while she was in school, and off all the times she was out of classes.

I registered for two or three college classes every semester—including summers—from that time on, which was more than challenging because I was not only working eight-hour days as a secretary, but was driving an hour each way back and forth to work. Our lives just got even more complicated, not the least of which meant continuing to need childcare for our little girl.

In the beginning, Aunt Virgie took care of Monicqua. This babysitting arrangement lasted until the baby was about eight months old. It was such a relief to have my baby in such good hands, if she couldn't be in mine. After Aunt Virgie, having steady quality childcare became something of a nightmare. Many times I was alerted only the evening before that a babysitter would not be available.

On one of these occasions, I went from our recently rented basement apartment in a big complex in Denver, across the street to the home of a person who sometimes was our backup. It was a Sunday evening and the older woman was still at church. I waited with the family. When the woman arrived, she agreed to come over the next day so I went back home.

When I got back to our apartment, Bob was livid, demanding where I had been. My lips curled up in a smile because I thought he was kidding. He was not.

He began to choke me and would not let go. I was gasping for air when suddenly something caused him to release me. He walked out, haranguing me all the way. I was afraid of what he could do to the baby and me.

Weekends were consumed with studies, house cleaning, clothes washing and ironing and in general getting ready to do it all over again the next Monday. It was on Saturday and Sunday that our family dysfunction was full blown. Bob was harsh and demanding of both Monicqua and me. Neither of us could do anything up to his standard. He was often verbally abusive, but it became physical abuse toward me and even our little girl.

These episodes punctuated our lives, but on weekdays we stayed focused to make it all work. Little Monicqua was shuffled between babysitters and whichever of us was home any given evening. Some semesters I was in school Tuesday and Thursday evenings and some, Mondays and Wednesdays. Simultaneous to my college work, Bob entered an evening School of Cosmetology furthering a dream of becoming an entrepreneur with beauty shops. Bob and I drove separately for work since one of us always needed to be at school in the evening. We rarely saw each other between breakfast and bedtime.

After about a year of being employed at Martin, we bought a new home just north of Denver in the suburb of Northglenn. Pride of ownership and a compulsiveness about cleanliness consumed Bob. I was happy to have the house, but the expectations for its upkeep put a new level of stress on us all. Bob expressed his anxiety in dissatisfaction with Monicqua and me while he consumed large quantities of alcohol. There were many nights he came home very late, drunk, smelling of perfume. I was supposed to turn a blind eye and did. I dared not confront him.

Bob's treatment of his daughter was equally onerous. Once when Monicqua was about four years old, Bob took to disciplining her with a heavy hand, or board, or whatever he picked up. It was ongoing. I was afraid to leave them together. Many times I stopped him in the middle of one of his tantrums with her. His reaction was to turn on me and then return to her. Her infraction would have been not doing something fast enough or good enough for him.

Even though Bob's frequent outbursts threatened to push me over the top, I somehow managed to keep my nose to the grindstone and tried to keep my daughter and myself out of his way. His erratic behavior escalated. One night Bob came home drunk as usual, but this time he was ready to commit suicide. He cried and told me how all the kids got BB guns from their dads, but he had to sell pop bottles to buy his own.

I knew that he found out when he was about 12 that the man he knew as his dad was not his biological father. He never got along with the man so it answered a lot of questions for him. On this night he wanted to go find his natural father and kill him before turning the gun on himself. It took all I had to talk him down. He ended up bashing the butt of his BB gun, splintering it. He fell into bed, physically and emotionally spent. I don't know how Monicqua slept through all of this since she was in her bedroom only a short distance from the living room where the drama was unfolding.

That very next day at work, I went to many of the engineers for whom I worked and asked them to loan me money to make a very important long distance phone call. They were all so kind. By lunch I took the money I collected to the payphone outside the building. I had researched that Bob's biological father was in Corpus Christi, Texas.

I knew his story. Bob's mom Betty gave in to a local farmer's son, Raymond Oller, in Sylvia, Kansas, and became pregnant with Bob. The man promised he would marry her after harvest. The baby was due in December 1938. When the crops were in Raymond ran away, leaving his family, his personal farm equipment—including a combine—without a word to anyone. His sisters visited with Betty after Bob was born and expressed shame at what their brother did.

Having this information and having found the phone number of Raymond Eugene—Bob's name was Robert Eugene—I was ready to confront the man. Toward what end, I don't know. I just knew that the pressure Bob felt was all tied to that man's rejection and the resultant poor treatment he felt he got from his stepdad.

I got Raymond's wife on the phone. She said Raymond was not there. I talked to her, spewing out all I knew. She then told me that she never knew but had suspected. She then revealed Raymond was sitting beside her the whole time and would not talk to me.

I am not remembering if I ever told Bob about that call. I was afraid it would do more damage than good. I guess I hoped his father would seek him out and console him. Instead he made comments through his wife that Bob must be a sick guy. There was no compassion at all. We got through that episode, but many times Bob would get very depressed and I assumed he was thinking about his dad.

About this same time, I received an unexpected message from the University. At this point I had completed about two years of college, still in night classes, and was declaring a major. That was when CU realized I was seeking a degree. I was asked to submit records of high school graduation and take placement tests. When they discovered I didn't have a high school diploma, they said I needed to get a General Equivalency Diploma (GED) to be able to seek a degree. Fortunately, Bob's Uncle Harold, having formerly been a professor at the University of Kansas, agreed to tutor me for it.

At that time I was required to take the exam in the state in which I attended high school. New Mexico graciously accepted Uncle Harold's credentials and allowed him to administer the exam to me in Denver. Halfway through college I finished high school! It may seem like a little blip, but the prospect of not being able to continue my college education was shattering to me.

Space Travel

The major benefit from my secretarial job was support for getting an education. I was given permission to work on my classes using the company typewriters (yes, no word processing yet), plus they supplied paper and other materials. I worked on my studies every break and during lunch. I don't know what I would have done to complete my education if I had not had the benefit of this significant support from my employer.

There were many moments that stand out in my memory of my days at Martin, but one occurred not long after I started working there. Americans of my generation can all say where they were when Kennedy was shot. I was working in that lab.

It was an odd day. There was an eerie atmosphere even prior to learning of the assassination. This was never a good sign. When we had a bad day at that place, it could mean a rocket fuel spill disaster.

Word of the assassination traveled quickly among the engineers and staff. I put down what I was doing and went outside to my car to turn on the radio. I could not take it in. We Americans were so smug. Up until that day, I am not sure any of us realized that we could be shaken. That day our world rumbled out of that epicenter in Dallas.

Now we have endured the shock of 9-11, and then the Boston Marathon bombings to all be followed by what feels like a barrage of terrorist attacks. It is one thing to have a personally scary experience. We all have folks around us to console us. Our nation is inconsolable. There is a violation that has penetrated our corporate soul. For me it began the day President Kennedy was gunned down. For a person who tends toward delusional thinking and even fantasy, this was all way too much reality.

On a more positive note, I remember another eventful day at the Lab when some of the NASA astronauts were touring our facility. I got to meet Frank Borman, who was later to become the Commander of the 1968 Apollo 8 Mission. That was thrilling.

It is still difficult, however, to think about Apollo 13's tragedy. Anyone who worked at any level at any time on that project was personally devastated when that ship went down.

All in all, my four years at Martin were full. I was actually very sad when it came time for me to leave to attend college full time. I had made many friends among the staff and got to know some amazing individuals. Probably the most notable was Mr. Lowell Randall. He was in charge of the lab at one point, and I had advanced to being his secretary by that time. He was what others might call a self-made man, but he would argue the point.

He came up as a protégé of Dr. Robert Goddard at White Sands Proving Grounds in New Mexico. Anybody in the industry recognizes the importance of Dr. Goddard as being the pioneer of modern rocket propulsion in the United States. Mr. Randall apparently possessed little or no formal college course work, but was well read, especially in the field of propellants. He was very respected, the results of which brought about his promotion to lead such an important laboratory in our space effort. All of this was on the merits of his experience and knowledge without the seal of any institution of higher learning.

That impressed me for many reasons. Here I was getting an education so I could "become" a teacher. I realized that I had been a teacher since I was very young. I was just formally adding to my experience and knowledge in preparation for classroom teaching.

I counseled many of my students, my own children, and now my grandchildren concerning this truth. It is in us from the very beginning to be what God has called and equipped us to be. That's where we might be accurately called diamonds in the rough. Acquiring education and experience polishes the stone, but the gem was already there.

Spiritual Quest

During all this time, Bob was continually unhappy with everyone, especially Monicqua and me. Even though I was raised a Baptist, and memorized a great deal of scripture, I didn't see how God could help our relationship. Bob and I did not attend any religious services. I often went to work and talked with the engineers about life and God. One man in particular impressed me for his faith. He was a Mormon. I began to wonder if that religion could help me, help Bob.

On one occasion when I was alone at home with Monicqua, Mormon missionaries came to visit. I let them in. They talked a lot. They left me *The Pearl of Great Price* and the *Book of Mormon* to read. They showed me charts of alternate worlds. I was intrigued. Somehow I thought their version of belief was connected to the same Jesus I knew about. I was definitely confused but desperate. I started making appointments for them to return when Bob was not home. I studied. I read both books.

I began to act differently with Bob. I didn't realize that doing the superficial things of a religion is not faith. So, I stopped serving him iced tea or coffee, because of the Mormon doctrine against caffeinated drinks. I would not drink beer with him. He noticed that something was off. One day when he was working on a client's hair, he mentioned what I was doing. The client said, "The Mormons have gotten hold of her." That's what he told me when he confronted me.

When he asked me why I wasn't acting the same way and mentioned the Mormon thing, I stood up for myself for the first time ever. He told me I must stop studying Mormonism or he would leave me. I thought good and hard. I know I was trembling. I responded that it felt like he was asking me to deny God—that's how deep in I was—which I could not do. I agreed that I would not let whatever my beliefs interfere with our lives. He said okay and that ended that discussion. My belief in Mormonism wore off soon after.

College Full-Time

Finally in May 1966, I began college full time on the main campus. If all went well, by June of 1967 I would have my BA in English and speech, plus having a teaching credential. I began driving to the CU campus in Boulder, which is northwest of Denver. It was a difficult commute when the winter snow arrived, but it felt good to be able to just focus on school and family.

The car we got for me to drive was an old DKW, which stood for Das Kleine Wunder, which translated was "The Little Wonder." It was a little wonder – if it ever started! Most days I looked for parking on a hill in Boulder, which meant it was far from the campus. My daily routine after classes was to push the car, getting a roll going, then I jumped in and popped the clutch. It was always stressful to get it moving enough for the motor to kick in. If it didn't start, I was at the bottom of a hill. I must say I was amazed at the kindness of strangers when I got stuck.

The unusual way this car was built, however, was critical to this push-start process. The doors were hung backwards, so I could push the car while hanging onto the steering wheel to make sure I could get back into the car in time to pop the clutch to start it. The door hinges were leather straps that had long since snapped. Going through all of this on a daily basis by myself was tougher with the abundant snows of that winter. It was so hard to get traction in the snow and ice.

We decided at some point we had to get rid of that car, and I was one happy person when we purchased the new turquoise Chevy Mazda. It was roomy and, most importantly, reliable. No more push starts for this student.

Those three semesters seemed like an eternity. I was taking course over-loads each time. I never thought of giving up, but I gave myself plenty of pep talks. When I was on campus, I was all about school. I don't think I made one friend in that year. I never had time to even grab a cup of coffee with someone between classes. It never occurred to me to make any alliances since I was sure Bob wouldn't like it. College people were not his kind of folks.

He himself had tried one of my college classes one summer when I was still going part time. It was a philosophy class with a visiting professor. This teacher told our class that Americans were not true students. I got one of the few D's I ever had in school, but he received an F. The sole grade higher than a D was a C earned by one of the brightest guys in our college. We students appealed the marks, to no avail. This bad experience served to turn Bob off from any college.

Like the DKW I drove from Northglenn, CO to CU in Boulder, CO.

A last hurdle I cleared occurred just before I graduated from CU. I was required to pass the Speech Adequacy Test devised by the Education Department to determine if their future teachers possessed speech that would be effective in the field. I wasn't concerned since I was a Speech minor and was currently in debate classes. I took the test, which was to deliver a speech. Somehow I failed. By then I already had been offered a teaching position at a high school in Santa Maria, California, so I HAD to pass that test. I met with my debate coach. He had suggested the speech I used and didn't understand why I failed. He in turn met with the judge.

He came back to me with this report. The judge felt that there was too much twang in my voice. What else would I have being raised by Texans! She was determined that no one with such a voice could ever be an effective teacher. My coach vouched for me, so the judge relented, requiring one condition. She insisted that I buy a tape recorder to listen to my voice and get rid of the twang.

I retired after having been a successful teacher for 40 years. I confess having never bought the tape recorder.

That June of 1967 there couldn't have been a graduate of CU any more relieved than I. My mother, her new husband George, my sisters Anita and Carol and Carol's friend, Barbara, all came from Hobbs to celebrate this achievement. Five-year-old Monicqua was enchanted by Carol and her friend who collaborated to make her pancakes in the shapes of animals that Neek tried to identify. It was a great time of jubilation. Mine was the only degree in my immediate family at that time.

There was no time to rest on

My graduation from CU with Mother and her new husband, George.

The family when we moved to California in 1967.

Monicqua in the summer of 1967 outside our apartment complex.

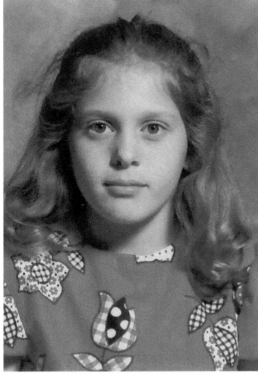

Monicqua with her hair grown out wearing an outfit I made her for fourth grade in Santa Maria, CA 1971.

my laurels because we were busy selling our house and packing up to move to California. Two of us would start school that fall—I would be teaching and Monicqua was beginning kindergarten. We all believed this to be the beginning of a hopeful new chapter in our lives.

Making the Move

When we first arrived, we lived in an apartment. This picture of Monicqua looks a lot like the profile of her sister Sarah's twins who came almost 50 years later. If memory serves, Monicqua had just found a caterpillar that she captured in a jar. She was able to watch the metamorphosis in the makeshift habitat.

When Monicqua entered the public school system she was primarily wearing the clothes I made for her. Girls were not allowed to wear pants, so I made her matching shorts or pants to wear under her dresses. She was forever upside down on jungle gyms!

Bob had already decided to leave hairdressing behind when we moved to California. The prospect of taking another tough state exam to be licensed for a profession he no longer enjoyed sealed the deal. He landed a job selling cars in our new home of Santa Maria. This establishment was the home of the "Hiking Viking" as the billboards still advertise. Bob continued in this job for a while, but the stress of

53

it was hard on all of us. It was strictly on a commission basis. No sale, no pay.

I was earning an income teaching, so there was a buffer, but Bob was working on a bigger plan that required that we both have lucrative jobs. He wanted to amass a fortune while still young and retire to live off the interest. He hated working for others. He had some difficulty with relationships in the car sales work, primarily with the bosses. He was never much for taking orders.

Then he chose to work driving short hauls. He worked evenings and nights picking up crude oil in the fields and delivering it to the refinery. Even though this work gave him the autonomy on the job he craved, it was understandably hard on our family and hard physical labor for him. I got home from teaching just after 3 o'clock and prepared our dinner so he could go to work.

Monicqua and I spent evenings together. We had decided earlier to stop renting and bought a trailer that we envisioned we could put out on a piece of land and either build on to it, or just build a house. The park we were in was upscale, complete with a swimming pool and large recreation center, but there wasn't much else to do for entertainment. Since I was teaching English, I needed to grade many papers most evenings, which kept me very occupied. Neek found playmates among the families in the park.

Bob got in before we woke up and was asleep when we got ready to go to school. It reminded me of when my mother was a night switchboard operator. When she came home from work, it was difficult to maintain a quiet household so she could get her sleep. Even though my "ancestral home" was small, it was not as tiny as our two-bedroom trailer. The most common sound in our house was *shushing*.

First Teaching Job

I don't think I will ever forget my first day teaching. It was fall of 1967. We recently had purchased a new pea green VW to be primarily my transportation. On that long-awaited morning, I set off with my briefcase, a new haircut—thanks to Bob—and the worst case of jitters imaginable.

My first teaching assignment was sophomore English with several different "levels" of students. This school used a tracking system broken into five categories based on the tested academic ability of the students. I taught two of the highest levels,

Me on a California beach summer of 1967 before I started teaching.

two at the middle level, and the only level 5 class of purportedly the least capable 15-year-old's on campus. I still remember how much my mother's graduation gift of a Samsonite briefcase came in handy since I traveled to five different classrooms, but I was 23 and thrilled to have the job. A teacher at last!

The ratio in my classes was typically 36 to me. One of the middle track classes was really tough. Many of my students were from farm worker parents and moved around a lot, which resulted in huge gaps in their learning. My biggest challenge was to get them interested, to spark them on to learning.

Most days, they were able to dampen my little flame from the get go. On one particular day, things got pretty chaotic. It took all I had to get the kids to keep moving in their learning, and to not bicker with one another or even with me. I went home so defeated that day. I pondered all that sleepless night what I could do to turn the situation around. While I was getting ready for school the next morning, a plan began to percolate.

I knew we needed to have a class heart-to-heart. Before I could get class started, however, one of the students sheepishly offered me a very large apple, presumably a peace offering. I accepted it in that spirit and an idea blossomed that I thought would extend the experience to the entire class. It took some doing to scrape all of the desks into a large circle, but that is what we did. I took a seat in a student desk in that circle and began to talk to them.

I told them the apple was symbolic of what our class could be like. I was going to share a piece of that apple with all 36 of them. When they received it, they were committing to try their best to help our learning atmosphere to be fun and productive. I walked around slicing off a sliver at each student's desk. (Yes, I had a knife in the classroom!) We all waited to eat them together, which I realized later, resembled taking communion. We all ate our bit of the "peace" apple to seal the deal. That really changed the tone of the class, and I think those kids became my absolute favorites.

Leaving in the new VW for my first day of teaching at Santa Maria High School.

I remember feeling ill-prepared, not just for dealing with behaviors, but because of my limited knowledge of grammar and literature. Remember, I was the one who never took high school senior English. I had a BA under my belt from a reputable university, but that didn't bolster my confidence. Bob cautioned me that I would not be able to "make them into Hemingways," but that didn't stop me from trying. I knew I needed to know so much more than what I already learned to be able to guide them higher scholastically.

English classes at that time were primarily about grammar with some literature thrown in. Usually the required readings were thematic, so in the sophomore year, the kids were offered world literature. By their junior year they studied American literature followed by British lit their senior year. I was glad that I had already begun a Masters program in English. I wanted to be so much better prepared.

It may seem odd to jump right into graduate school, but my new job in California required that I have a BA plus six units before I began teaching that first year. I started right away taking night classes at the University of California Santa Barbara (UCSB) campus. I have always been program-oriented and thought I might as well go on for the Masters.

That meant back to the grind of evening and summer classes, which I did, at the usual expense to the family dynamics. It took me a few years during which time I transferred my UCSB credits to Cal Poly Technical University (Cal Poly) in San Luis Obispo. The driving distance to Cal Poly was significantly less than to Santa Barbara.

My mind still stings from the comprehensive exams I was required to pass to be granted the Masters in English once I had completed all the coursework. There were three separate tests, each one over four hours long: English and World Literature, American Literature, English Grammar and Language. At the end of my final semester of classwork, I took all three exams. I only passed one of them.

The problem was that I had to wait until the end of the next semester to try the other two again. I did, took two and passed another one. So one semester later I took and passed the last exam. The testing took an additional year. I finally got my Masters of Arts (MA) in English in 1970. Fortunately with my MA I qualified for a Life Teaching Credential in California. That was the last year it was offered for some time.

The Last Act

Those five years were busy with teaching and taking care of family, while trying to adjust to my college classes and Bob's job

1969: Two years into teaching, about the time I completed all the course work for the MA in English at Cal Poly.

of driving truck weeknights. I wish I could say we smoothed out the rocky start to our marriage, but it was far from the truth. Bob was very jealous and suspicious of me. It was almost an everyday occurrence that he accused me of being with another man.

I share these incidents to show the kind of psychological and physical stress I was under. I thought I could fix Bob's life, which would fix my daughter's and mine, but it was not to be.

His mean treatment of us both continued. In about 1970, when he began his driving job and I was still teaching at Santa Maria High, things began to come to a head. He worked nights, and it was a relief for both Monicqua and I when he left for work.

He only worked five days a week and was off on the weekends. That was when all hell would break loose. Usually he accused me of infidelity and griped that neither Neek nor I was doing anything up to his standard. Finally one day I told him I thought I must leave him. He offered the solution that we should have another child.

That conversation went nowhere. I think he believed my unhappiness could be solved by having more children, when I knew I could never bring another child into that environment. In fact, his treatment of our daughter was the main reason I felt I was leaving. I sometime earlier tried to get a doctor to tie my tubes because I feared bringing another child into that dangerous scene. Fortunately, the doctor refused due to my only being 23 years old.

Then Bob said if I would just stay for a few more years, HE would have $100,000 in the bank and then I could leave. We were more than frugal hav-

Me taking students to the park for a lesson.

ing saved all my income those five years and by this time had accumulated almost $60,000. This was 1971, so that was a significant figure. I was hoping we could work on our relationship, not our bank account and I told him so.

It wasn't many weeks later that I tried to force an honest conversation about our marriage. At work there was a teacher—married—who was constantly teasing and flirting with me. I have to say it felt good to be wanted, even if it was just "office banter." It was tempting. That made me angry. I knew that I had to be in a safer marriage or I would continually be tempted.

One weekend morning when Bob and I woke up and were still in bed, I told him I was tempted outside the house. I told him I wanted to save our marriage. He was deathly quiet. He got up and walked the three feet to the bathroom. When he returned to the bed, he was a tornado. We lived in a small trailer with a bedroom on each end so Monicqua was not very far away. Did I mention he also kept a machete under the bed and a .22 caliber pistol in the nightstand?

He screamed at me to give him a name. He kept it up until I finally gave him a fake name. I wasn't sure I would survive, much less our marriage. That was when he began beating on me, choking me. I somehow got to the living room where he threw me on the couch, strangling me. Suddenly, he stopped and clutched his chest. He thought he was having a heart attack. I acted very calm and caring, had him put his feet up on the couch and relax.

While he did so, I moved like in slow motion and told Monicqua to pack up her clothes and a few things. I began to pack mine. I grabbed a few dishes and towels. We started loading things into the 1958 Olds' that was my car at the time. I readied a few things by the back door, including my sewing machine and the portable TV for Monicqua. Bob quieted down but was visibly shaken by the incident. I told him he knew we had to leave. This could not go on.

He suddenly got agitated again and screamed at me to leave. He began throwing my things – even my sewing machine – out onto the concrete patio. I KNEW I must stay totally bland, calm, not show emotion or we would not leave alive. I got Monicqua to the car and that is when she said she could not come with me.

Then I became hysterical. I told her I was leaving for us both. She began to cry and said her dad told her if I ever left, for her not to go and I would come back. I convinced her it was for both our survival and I wasn't coming back. She knew it to be true. We began to drive away. I had no idea where I was going. I think we stayed at a motel that night, but honestly, it is a blank.

There were a number of incidents even after I left and filed for divorce. When we divided the property, we went together to a lawyer Bob hired. We did not divulge any amounts in the three savings accounts we had at that time. We just said this account to Sharon, these two to Bob. Very civil. Still surviving. I was shocked I got any money. My account contained $11,000 in it, his about $45,000.

Shortly after this I went home to visit my family in New Mexico and told them what was going on, that I had left Bob. My father was mad at ME until I explained. Then he was mad at me for not standing up and getting my half of things for Monicqua, if not for myself. I went back to California and filed a suit to get the right settlement. I did win, but it was a legal battle to get Bob to surrender the rest of my half. Instead he filed an appeal.

I was still on a spiritual journey, hoping to find the one that would put my life back together. I found a medium and she read my palm. She was very engaging. First, she "let" me be the special one to buy a new baby bed for her expected baby. I was honored.

Then she convinced me that the spiritual darkness I was in could be broken. Oh, what wonderful words! She said that her candles burned for one month. She convinced me I needed to burn one candle for each of nine months to break the evil over my daughter and I. Each candle cost $500. I did it. $4,500. I noticed after that the palm reader added a new bathroom to her house. I resisted making the connection because I wanted to believe there was spiritual power strong enough to break whatever bad spirits were holding us.

I was still troubled about Bob's soul. The medium said I could do the same for him. She saw a dark cloud over him. So I did. At least I started. My $11,000 was almost gone. I had bought furniture and furnishings for the house Neek and I rented. I got Bob halfway "free" before I ran out of money.

How could an educated person, having two college degrees, having been a teacher for five years do something so stupid? I am reminded that intellect has nothing to do with emotional and mental health. I was looking for help, wherever I might find it.

Once I realized how I was manipulated by that medium, I did not want ANYONE to know. But, it all came out during the trial. That was where Bob made the point that I should not have half of our money because I squandered what he had already "given" me. He actually didn't know if or how I spent my money. I think Bob was just angry that I was trying to get child support from him, which NEVER happened.

My lawyer contended it didn't matter even if I had burned up whatever money I left the marriage with, it being mine to do with as I pleased. The judge insisted I tell what happened to that $11,000. You could have heard a pin drop. It was humiliating—as it should have been—but Bob still lost his appeal and was ordered to give me the rest of my half. My battles with Bob were finally over, even though it was some time before I saw any money.

At this writing Bob is no longer alive. He lived to 80 and had a successful and long marriage to his second wife, Norma. They had no children together, but she brought her three from her previous marriage. I don't know why Bob and I could not make it, but I suspect that my young age gave Bob the false impression that I had no voice.

Alone

I was in my fifth year of teaching high school English when I found myself unmarried in California with my ten-year-old daughter, far from family and friends. As much as I knew I could no longer live with my husband, it was so hard to strike out on my own. I was actually on a bit of a slippery slope. This was the first time I was the adult of the house. I was in charge of my own life, and my daughter's, and it was as scary as it was exhilarating.

I left the marriage with that 12-year old Oldsmobile and not much else. I traded my car for a like-new VW camper with an attachable tent. For about 13 months I rented an oversized house for us. I wanted space—to stretch—after leaving Bob. This new rental was a bright, airy house with big windows in every room, and lots of yellow furnishings. It was what I craved after having lived in such a tiny place for the previous six years under such frightening and stifling conditions.

Our home on wheels had felt encapsulated, even cocoon-like, a controlled space where I did as I was told. I was never an equal adult with my husband. My new home—this oasis—filled with strands of the music of Carole King, defined both my emotional angst and my yearnings. I felt like a newly emerged butterfly.

After I re-established myself, I began to spend more and more time with some of my fellow high school teachers who were leaning toward counter culture. Our gatherings were punctuated with wine and smoke, mostly of the toke variety (marijuana smoking). I was making alliances outside my family for the first time. I was a bit adrift but was actually reveling in not knowing what came next. We called it "going with the flow," and flow I did. I even began to smoke cigarettes, which I swore I would never do in reaction to my mother's smoking.

Two years later when I quit all smoking, I admitted that my smoking was to cover my toking.

My looser philosophy flowed into my child rearing. I tried to be more of a friend than a parent to Monicqua. It sounded good—it was the thing—but I grew to know it had scared my daughter. Children were just little adults, after all, or so I had come to believe. It was rare for me to force my opinions on my young charge. In the back of my mind I knew this was a reaction to my own father and the heavy handedness of my husband. Bob controlled our daughter while he ruled me.

Simultaneously, as a teacher, I began to question how learning was taking place. I wanted to elicit more from my students instead of lecturing them. My very selective reading and research indicated that if you left young people alone and did not force learning, they would take to it naturally. I placed couches in my English classroom. I remembered the thrill of helping create a new English class, "The Literature of Social Protest." That course title summed me up. I also began to spend several afternoons a week after school teaching students who had either dropped out or were expelled from school—a "continuation" program set on the high school campus.

When I got the word a separate campus for a continuation high school was forming, I transferred to be the English teacher for it. At Delta Continuation I put the final touches on my educational views. I wanted to teach children in a much freer space, a total environment. To its credit, it was effective to have the students work out of self-directed packets to earn their credits. We teachers were there to coach and guide them through the process. That was 1972. Continuation schools are flourishing in California today—2019—and are alongside equally effective charter schools as alternatives to "comprehensive" public schools.

Set Adrift

I became so convinced that mandatory education was killing what I began to believe was children's natural desire to learn, that I was contemplating leaving my teaching job to help start a "free school" after the fashion of the Summerhill School in England. The teachers who were just beginning this were friends of some of the Santa Maria teachers I knew. I set out to visit them before making up my mind to leave my public school teaching.

The group was calling the school *Helios*, which is the name for the sun god, and it was ironically located in a section of dark wooded area in the Big Basin area—which is actually a mountain basin—above Santa Cruz, California. They seemed to be living the dream I had of education: teachers befriending, coaching kids who appeared eager to learn. I returned home, still not having decided if I would join them. I realized I was making a choice that could greatly affect both my daughter and me.

The choice to change the course of my life was very difficult. By that time I was involved in many alternative ways of interpreting and guiding life. I consulted them all, seeking a clear message to go or to stay. I threw the *iChing*, consulted a medium, and pored over my astrology books. In retrospect, I find it peculiar that I never revisited my early experience with Christianity as a source for direction. In spite of all my resources, there was never a clear message of what I should do—go or stay.

During that time, two of the *Helios* teachers came to visit me to see if I was suited to what they were doing. I was a little taken with Murray who was their apparent leader. He was totally oblivious to my charms, and thus the more intriguing. I have to admit that I let the chemistry I felt for him sway me to move with them. In my muddled state I took it as a sign.

I got rid of pretty much everything, but could not bring myself to get rid of my daughter's things or furniture. The only things I brought from my early childhood were three dolls I adored. I brought some dishes and several small appliances, but mostly these got destroyed by the teenagers who were often in charge of cleaning up our communal kitchen. They seemed oblivious, or might have even been stoned, when they put the blender, base and all, in the dishwater for clean up.

I also hedged a little by taking a leave of absence from my teaching job, thinking I could come back in a year if things didn't work out. I had no savings, and no plan for income. I used much of my savings just getting resettled. It didn't bother me at the time. There was this perhaps marijuana-induced sense that everything would be okay. I still continued in this dreamy haze after several months at Big Basin.

While all of this earth-shaking change was happening, I had not talked to my parents about it at all. They were 1500 miles away so not likely to know what I was going through. When I did talk to them, they were understandably concerned for their granddaughter and me.

My marriage to Bob lasted 11 years, but it felt to me like a lifetime. At this point it had only been one year since we had been separated so I had no desire to conjure up the images that led to the marriage's failure to update my family. I tried to assure them that I knew what I was doing and was finally happy. Suffice it to say, I had a ten-year-old daughter, two college degrees, a good number of battle wounds and a move to California to show for that union.

Communal Living

My move to Big Basin was in early Fall 1973. The school planters I was join-ing had purchased a different property several miles farther up the mountain from the one I visited that summer. All of the previous owners, who essentially comprised another commune, left the property by the time we moved onto it, with the exception of the "boat people."

It was the most incongruous sight imaginable, a 46-foot-long catamaran perched up on that mountain. The boat builders were essentially one family, which consisted of a dad and mom— "Beau" and Wanda—and her eight-year-old girl, Gabby, and their two-year-old boy, Toby. There was also a second man, Rube, who was helping them. I later learned Rube threw in with the boat people after his wife Mary left with the previous owners of the property's son—and Rube's best friend—Jeffrey Becker.

The vessel's construction site was close to the road for ease of transporting when the time came. The whole operation was under the spread of a big old oak tree. Unbeknownst to all, there was an underground stream under the tree. That previous spring a vicious storm eroded the earth around the roots causing water to flood out, which in turn led to the tree roots losing their grip on the earth.

Once the storm abated, Rube and his three-year-old son, Jacob, had come on deck just when the tree lost footing and pitched directly across the bow of the almost completed boat. The miracle acknowledged by all was that neither father nor son was hurt at all. They were spared when the two huge branches went to either side of them.

The catamaran did not fare so well, however, having sustained a major breach of one of its hulls. The boat people had been on the verge of moving the boat to the Monterey Bay for launching. The damage would take several more months to repair, during which time the boat people occupied the land with us, living on the boat.

I often think of what a friend that tree, that storm, that spring was to me. Had the giant oak not fallen and damaged the boat, I would never have met Rube.

Building Our Home

I didn't dwell on the plight of the boat builders because I had my own set of troubles. About that time I began having trouble with my VW bus. Roger, one of the men of the new group, was a mechanic. He used one of the buildings on the land for his garage and was committed to taking care of the vehicles. My van spent more time with Roger than with me!

I detached the tent from the bus and put my only vehicle in the shop for him to fix. That little tent—which was where Monicqua and I slept—was quite vulnerable to the elements, which quickly became an issue when the rains hit. Every fall there was a deluge, with rampant flooding all down that mountain. Most of our energies were spent trying to keep warm and dry.

The main structure on the property was called the "Great House" which was only an A-frame house with a great room, small bedroom and a bathroom. Above the living area was an open staircase to an open-air loft. On this property there was another small, very rustic building dubbed the Copper Kettle pre-

sumably because there was one there, which I never saw. Many of those in our group camped out in this building.

Other than that, there was one very tiny cabin. Each of us had the responsibility of building our own house. We also were asked to help our students build their residences. Parents of our same ilk had already begun to drop off their kids for us to "educate" and take care of. It was a pretty impossible situation, but somehow none of us noticed, or cared, or wanted to be uncool by exposing it.

The present owner told my son Joshua – who visited the Big Basin property while in the area for a training program recently – this is the original garage, but it looks like the building we called the Copper Kettle. Either way, it is still standing 45 years later.

We got word that with some labor we could get used lumber and building materials for our house building projects. When the weather permitted we all loaded into a large flatbed truck to salvage building materials at a local Boy Scout Camp that was being torn down. I don't know how many days it took us, but we pretty much dismantled that camp, board by board. We worked carefully because we needed to reuse the materials, even the nails if possible.

Energy and idealism we had much of, money almost none. Most of us were getting some kind of government subsidy such as Aid to Dependent Children.

Two of the smaller cabins that still stand. I don't remember these being built when we lived on the property.

Plus many of the parents of our students basically turned over their Aid checks to us to take care of their kids

Little House by the Falls

I chose to build my house on a tent platform within view of a small waterfall. This "foundation" was the remains of a simple square structure of a half wall upon which a tarp was spread fashioning a tent. This was the dwelling place of the boat people before they were able to move onto the vessel for its final stages of construction. This site was situated in a remote area of the narrow 10-acre parcel by Blossoms Creek.

I calculated that I could put up a 14-by-16 foot cabin on that platform. I even planned for my house to have a bay window. I scavenged windows from our dismantling project. I knew there would be no electricity, but I planned to have at least a series of connected hoses bring water into the structure. It was to have a small "living" area that spanned the width of the structure so was about 14 by 6 feet and then two 7 by 10 foot bedrooms off that room. Each part of the three living areas could accommodate only a single piece of functional furniture appropriate to its use: we owned only two twin beds and a table.

For any casual observer—of which there were none—it might seem that I knew what I was doing. *Au contraire.* I hauled planks by day and read carpentry books by night. It just all seemed logical to me. If you can cook using a cookbook, why not build a house by reading a carpentry book. And that was what I set out to do.

I was forgetting a fundamental truth. I was educated—however meager it seemed—in Home Economics classes in high school for cooking so I was not reading cookbooks blindly. I had no such training for construction, assuming we can't count the 2-by-4 chicken wire cage I made for the injured hawk I rescued as a kid.

House building was grueling work. Where do people get the idea that hippies were lazy? I had never worked so hard. After helping sort out the scrap lumber, it was a grunt to get all of those supplies down the narrow path along a hillside that led to my building site. From time to time some of the other "teachers" and even some of the students helped haul the loads.

My endeavors began to resemble an old-fashioned barn raising. I built a frame for one side of the building on the deck of the platform and then enlisted the help of any hands available to stand it up to nail it into place. After the four walls were secured, I began to worry that the rains might hit and stop my work so I decided to put on the roof next. It was a plywood, tar paper and rolled-roofing job.

About the time I completed the roofing on the wooden framed roof, another problem developed. The roof was so heavy that it began to skew the frames. I was working on the roof when I heard the nails creak at the same time the structure beneath my feet began to sway and lean. That was when I found out there was a way of bracing the four frames together that I had neglected. I immediately took care of it, and my fellow travelers made themselves available to help. Once braced, with the roofing on, I felt fairly confident I could proceed in spite of weather.

It was then that a carpenter friend alerted me that the platform could never bear the weight of the finished cabin. It was built for a light tent structure. Once again, I backed up and began learning how to reinforce the foundation under the platform with the help of that carpenter.

My son was told by the present property owner – who has been there most of the time we have been gone – that what might have been my cabin was leveled by the 1989 California La Prieta earthquake that was centered in the Santa Cruz Mountains.

With all that was going on, I never expected Monicqua to do the labor with me unless she wanted to. As I said, I was not into requiring anything of her. I feared she would leave me if things were too hard for her. Consequently, instead of working with me, she was thrust in with the odd mix of "students" who were flocking to our school. The daily routine of these students was to imbibe some form of drug—the most popular being acid (LSD) and marijuana—and then to hang out with little or no effort toward building their own places to get out of the impending wet weather.

Monicqua later shared that she experienced a close call with one of the 13-year old boys while he was under the influence. It scared her enough that she became determined to live with her dad, but I initially thought she just wanted to go visit him.

Monicqua Goes to Her Father

It was on me to take Monicqua to her dad's. It was a 210-mile trek south from Big Basin to Nipomo. My van was finally out of Roger's shop. Rube's son was back with his mother, so I asked if Rube would accompany us for several reasons, not the least of which was to have strong arms in case Bob resorted to his historical aggressiveness. It was a wrenching separation. I was fearful for Monicqua being back

This is either my cabin or one very similar. Mine was built on a platform that had pylons under it as it extended over a chasm. It had the same slanted roof. We can't see the front which would have had my bay window.

in that environment, but was torn when I learned of my daughter's near miss back at Big Basin.

It did not go over well with Bob that I had brought a man with me. The transfer was abrupt, then we were on our way back to what was now home. Stopping for the night at a Santa Cruz beach, we dropped acid together and spent the night in the van.

While I was still "high" on LSD the next morning, I sought out the community bathroom situated farther down the beach. It was while in that tiny facility that my hallucinatory state totally freaked me out. Suddenly I was convinced I could not get out of the toilet stall. I actually envisioned that somehow I would die there, leaving people wondering how it came to be.

Mustering all my mental strength I fought against the drug and was finally able to return to the van.

There were signs all around me that I did not do well with drugs, including marijuana, but especially LSD. This was only my second "trip." I wasn't remembering the specifics of the first time I dropped this drug, but remembered some bouts of anxiety then, but nothing so seemingly life-threatening and terrifying as this one. This was, however, not to be my worst experience with this hallucinogen.

With Monicqua at her dad's, I began to pay more attention to Rube's son Jacob, who had just turned four and had come to stay on the boat with his dad. On many occasions, I took Jacob with me into town to do wash or to shop, just giving him some energy. It also felt good to be around a child, since I was missing my own.

Jacob became attached to me and on one particular occasion when he and his dad did not see eye-to-eye, he stood out on the deck of the boat calling out across the land to me, "Cherry." He was left with a slight speech impediment caused by a cleft palate, and that was the closest he could come to saying Sharon. His nickname for me stuck. I spelled it Shari.

Momentous Beginning

It was during this unlikely phase of my life that I was beginning to realize I had met the love of my life, Rube, which was a name he took on, primarily because friends in college addressed him by shortening his last name, Rubinstein. *In some parts of this memoir he may be referred to by Dick, which was the name his parents used for him.*

I was around Rube's son Jacob a good deal. Rube was busy with his boat building and I with my cabin building. A few times he let me borrow his old GMC truck – "Jimmy" – to go into town. On one occasion he went with me to a teahouse in Boulder Creek. I was definitely being drawn to him, but I couldn't tell if he felt the same way. He was always a man of few words, and even fewer actions – of the romantic type that is. He was a very focused, hard worker.

The pivotal scene was the morning after I had dropped acid and gone to the

"Dead" concert with some girlfriends from my newfound teacher group. The concert lasted until quite late. For some reason, the next morning I still woke up early. I was in the open loft area of the Big House looking through some of my stored boxes when I heard the screen door open and "knew" it was Rube. I looked down at him at the same moment he looked up at me.

Jolting. Tender. His radiant, twinkling blue eyes cut me to the quick. The effect was heightened by his ample "fro" being transformed into a halo by the early morning rays from the screened-in doorway. From my vantage point up in the open loft, I could not perceive any distance separating us. The connection was visceral, unshakable. It was as if we both were receiving the very essence of the other through the portals of our eyes. Cosmic. That was the word we all used.

It was not exactly the "stranger across the crowded room" experience. Of course, he had not been a stranger for a few months since I had landed here in my VW van. There was no crowd at this early hour in our A-frame hub. Most of our fellow inhabitants were of the sleep-in type, especially considering we all were late-night tokers and trippers (LSD users). At this moment, we could have been surrounded by huddled masses, but we were only aware of each other.

He did not drop his gaze. Rube stood transfixed, framed by the door jamb. It was the look for the launching of ships. I knew in that instant that we would always be together. I knew that somehow we had always been together. It was a reunion unlike any I could have imagined. It was at once ancient and newborn.

We exchanged some kind of greeting that did not reveal the depth of emotion, the electricity. But we both knew. I was sure of that—as sure as anyone could be still buzzing from tripping at a Grateful Dead Concert.

I learned later that Rube's former band once opened for the Dead. I learned just a few years ago from Rube's oldest buddy, Eitan, that their band couldn't be heard since they didn't realize they were to bring their own sound equipment. The band did, however, smoke dope with Jerry Garcia.

What was he doing there, anyway, at this hour? I knew I was there to sort through my hastily stored belongings from my former life. I probably had more stuff crammed into the loft than most of my fellow travelers, because my break with the materialistic former life had been wrenching even though carefully planned for—and longingly awaited—for over a year. I later came to know Rube was an early riser, often at the Big House before most of us were awake. This moment heralded a new chapter in my life, and his.

Moving On

In the meantime, I believed my daughter was just on a visit with her dad. When it was time for Monicqua to come back, she refused. I had been awarded custody and could force her but didn't feel right about invoking it against her strong repugnance for my lifestyle. I also didn't feel I could leave what I believed to be my life's work. I just hoped she would come to her senses, and I buried myself in finishing up my cabin.

About that time Jacob's mother Mary came to get him for her turn with him. She observed that Rube was interested in me and expressed relief to me that he had someone. In my fogged up mind, she was giving Rube to me. She was approving of our relationship which was important to me.

She was now with Jeffrey, but he was also with his own wife, Gwendolyn. On the new property Jeff's parents purchased outside St. Helena, Jeffrey occupied the main farmhouse while Gwendolyn and their son Jesse lived in a little cabin close by and Mary and Jacob were in a similar cabin on the other side of the main house. Jeffrey's parents—who also sold us the Big Basin property—owned a home at the front end of that new property.

I did not focus on their arrangement, because my relationship with Rube was intensifying. I continued to work on my house and also began helping Rube on the boat, both with renewed effort in the absence of our children. We would often talk at night. Again, I consulted astrology to confirm that we should be together. I noted that I was Aries and he, Leo. I also noted that my mother was Leo and his mother was Aries. These little clues seemed to fuel my case that he was the one for me.

By this time I had all the walls up in the cabin, the salvaged windows installed, including the bay window, and had fully insulated the whole house. The next step was to put up interior walls or sheetrock. It was at this point that my life took a drastic turn.

Rube and I were a couple, except for our necessary separation while each attended to our specific building projects. When the annual rains began to engulf the basin, many a day we wandered the property looking for a dry spot to be together. The big house was full of everyone else trying to stay dry and warm.

Mary, Jacob and friend Angela about the time Mary and Rube split up.

We ventured out to The Copper Kettle where most of the teachers lived. Invariably we were not alone. There was another small cabin we sometimes went to where we built a fire to sit and talk. The drive to stay warm and dry was stronger than any other.

The main house was still the hub, and the location of the only bathroom for about 20 people, even though there was at least one outhouse on the property. I felt guilty if I spent too much time in the bathroom. If I was just washing up, I would leave the door open so I could get out if someone needed to use the restroom. On one of these occasions, I washed my face and was poised at the mirror applying mascara when Rube's face appeared in the doorway, inches from mine.

All he had to say was, "What are you doing?" It was truly just inquisitive, but at that moment I thought to myself in an accusatory tone, "*What WAS I doing?*" I had given up wearing a makeup foundation, but I felt very insecure without my eye makeup. In that moment I knew that if it didn't matter to my love, why do it? All makeup was out of the picture from that day for the next 20 years. The reason I started "using" again is another story.

We occasionally got the chance to go into the Santa Cruz Bookstore. Our custom was to each find our reading material and settle into one of the many overstuffed chairs. On one such occasion, we both dropped windowpane LSD prior to going to our favorite reading spots. The thinking was that the hallucinogen heightened the reading experience. For me it became another frightening event. As I sat reading I was incrementally becoming overcome by jealousy. There was no rational reason for that emotion. Rube was never one to have a wandering eye, but I knew how deeply he had loved his wife Mary and how devastated he was when she left him.

I could not tell Rube I was suffering. I left the bookstore and walked to the telephone booth in the parking lot to call my friend Sally who was back at Big Basin. Fortunately I was able to catch her at the Big House where there was the only phone on the property. Sally told me I was to focus to fight the forces of the drug. Sally kept having me repeat something akin to a mantra where I repeated something about the three points of a triangle.

Sally counseled, "Go from the top of the triangle, trace it down to the right point, now go across the bottom to the bottom point, and then trace back up to the top again. Keep repeating this and your mind will come back to you." It proved an effective way of forcing my mind to not focus on the out-of-control jealousy emotion. After some time, it worked. I went back into the bookstore to my reading, not telling Rube of my battle.

I hated being so insecure, but I later reflected that the negative, insecure emotions in me were the ones the LSD seemed to target and blow out of proportion. My earlier bad trip experience at the beach was all about fear, especially of dying. This was about my own insecurities in feeling that surely Rube could not love me, but instead was secretly still wanting Mary.

By the middle of November of 1973 it was obvious to both of us that we were to stay together.

November 23rd was a nice weather day so we decided to go on a trip together. That is, an acid (LSD) trip. We crossed the street to a large open national forest area and just hung out there all day together. By the time we returned, we knew we were really "together."

My friend Sally met us when we crossed the highway returning to the land. She took one look at us and she also knew. She had been making corn and seashell necklaces. She proceeded to put one on each of us. We wore them for "wedding rings" for a long time and I still have them in my jewelry box. At some point, we substituted turquoise rings as our marriage markers, but none of this was "sealed" by an official marriage license or ceremony until much later.

Joining the Boat People

Things moved quickly after that. I was determined to join Rube on the boat, so I turned my almost completed cabin over to the teenage boys of the school. It was with mixed emotions and a few admonitions that I surrendered my little house, but I felt I found something, someone, far greater. I was completely smitten with my new man, Rube, and he apparently was with me.

Hard to believe that just six months prior I swore I would never marry again. I was done with all of that. In fact, I did my back door thing again even in this relationship. I didn't think I wanted to take his name, or at least not completely. I toyed with the sound of Shari Rubin for some time before finally admitting to myself I was going to totally commit. It was a scary thing to do—to put myself into another man's hands. I grew to believe that where he went was where I wanted to go also. That was the only way I could be. I was in or out. Totally.

An early visit to Rube's mother Marjorie and step-fa-ther Jeff in the Fall of 1973 after we became a couple having "declared" ourselves married. We are wearing our corn necklaces that were our wedding "rings." R to L: Marjorie, an unknown family friend, Rube and me, and Rube's step-brother Eric with son Jacob in the foreground.

As I moved onto the boat with Rube, I began to understand more about the marvels of its creation. It was made without any plastics. All of the blocks for the tackle were hand-made by Rube and Beau. We were all involved in applying the much-needed linseed oil every-where. It was tough to construct all of the masts knowing that we didn't have the true test until we launched the boat and began to rig it. It was all a labor of love in every way.

Perhaps the hardest thing we did was to construct a skiff. This was necessary since there was no motor on the boat—nor any intention for one—and the only way to get on or off the boat once it was launched was to have a small craft for rowing to and from shore. Everyone hated ar-tificial things, but the decision was made that the skiff would be constructed out of fiberglass – awful, prickly, lethal, stinging stuff. It felt like a million pins were sticking in any part of my body that came in contact with the spun glass type fiber.

But it was a necessary evil. This skiff would be the only way we could get to shore when supplies were needed. Due to the boat's large size, there would be no sailing into any port on the western coast of America.

Mistrust Arises

Things were going very well between us when a situation arose that caused me to have doubts about Rube's love for me. This brought back the same intensity of jealousy I'd experienced earlier, but without inducement from a drug. Mary had left her sheep at the Big Basin property and asked for them to be brought to her at her new home. Rube took them. He did not want me to accompany him.

I do not remember when I learned that Rube slept with Mary on that trip, but it was devastating since that was my greatest fear. But, then, he did return to me. There was that, and I noted it at the time I discovered what I felt was a betrayal, but it was considered the norm in our community for folks to accept their loved ones sleeping with others. I never got the knack of that. I felt that I truly did not belong because I could not conquer jealousy the way everyone around me seemed to be able to do.

As Rube set off on this trip, I went with him just as far as his friends Billy and Andrea's homes in San Francisco. It was a fretful night in which Billy tried to reassure me that Rube was committed to me. When Rube returned, we took the opportunity to attend a conference that we all believed enhanced our spiritual beings. It was called Erhard Seminars Training, or EST. For me, that was another freakout.

The experience was constructed in such a way that the attendees not only took responsibility for every tiny detail of their behaviors—with the attendant shame and despair—but also learned to use their minds to control all aspects of their lives and that of others.

While I was in one of the sessions, I needed to go to the restroom to take care of my monthly occurrence. I was confronted by one of the trainers who insisted that I created the situation so I could step out of the training. I honestly don't remember how that ended up. All in all, the experience made me realize I was truly a spiritual being, but also physical, and I also was aware that the spiritual realm EST presented was pretty dark.

From the Mountain to the Sea

At that point we were still in the catamaran perched on top of that mountain. It took many months to repair the boat. When the day finally came to take it to water, we dismantled it and loaded each hull onto a separate semi to be transported down to the coast at Monterey Bay. There it sat in a parking lot by the launching area while we re-assembled it and rigged it for sailing. It was a complex procedure. The mast was to be raised and the junk sails put in place.

The site for the reconstruction was the small fishing community of Moss Landing. We negotiated with people who owned some small businesses at the tiny wharf to park the boat in their parking lot for the process of re-assembling it. Rube had contacts in this town since it was where Mary's family still lived.

So by day we rigged, and by night we read Michener's *Hawaii* to each other in the belly of that snug vessel. We chose to read that novel because that was the first destination of our voyage. We were to sail there and then take the Trades to British Columbia where Beau owned some land. The plan was for both families to settle there.

The salt spray of the ocean was cooling us while we worked to rig the boat. The process involved reconnecting the hulls, which involved restoring the platform and its nets fore and aft. This structure was built so as to allow for independent movement of each hull, making for an unusually stable catamaran.

Once the hulls were attached again, our sights were set on the mast and the rigging. We had to launch the boat into the bay before setting up the masts. Junk sails were raised on the mast as the main form of locomotion, there not being any other method of propulsion intended for this vessel. This was mostly due to a purist view of sailing being just that, having no "safety nets," not even a motor. Organic. Natural.

Most of our daylight energy was spent physically getting the boat ready for launch. There were days, however, that Rube and I walked around the wharf and visited the various seafaring shops. We acquired personal items needed for the trip including foul-weather gear.

This is where we also purchased our "Acme Thunderer" whistles which were essential to our communications, shore to boat to shore. When supplies were needed, we planned to ferry someone in to shop using the skiff. When they were ready to return, they were to stand at the end of the pier and blow their whistles. We usually set a scheduled time for those on board to expect the return.

Sometimes Rube and I spent some quiet moments in a local eatery there in Moss Landing. By evening, we returned to the boat where our only light was from oversized candles made for that purpose. That was our time for reading, talking and loving.

The whole process of moving the boat to the shore, reassembling and rigging it, and preparing it for launch took over six months. During all this time the

Our boat in the water at Moss Landing. The tires tied to the sides provided buffers for when we moved the boat down the ramp into the water.

boat was our home. That parking lot was our "yard." The salty air was our constant companion. Fog was our warm blanket. These were the spring months so there was always a chill in the air. Layers of clothing were the norm for dressing.

"Spit baths" were our only way of cleaning up. We lit the little Primus-stove and heated water with which we bathed without ever submerging. Occasionally we found showers on beaches or in business establishments or in friends' homes.

We sometimes took day trips or overnighters to visit places and people. It was spring of 1974 when we went to see Rube's brother Eric who was attending the University of California Santa Cruz (UCSC). It was before the boat was launched, but after getting it to Moss Landing for rigging.

On this visit Rube and I took a walk around the campus. It was also Rube's alma mater. We decided to drop acid. For me, it was probably my fifth time. Rube counted his hits in the 100's, having probably topped 500 times he had dropped acid in the previous ten years.

While stoned, I distinctly remember that Rube and I were standing on a hilltop overlooking a long valley on the UCSC campus. It seemed to me that we were a Prince and Princess at that moment. Years later I realized that this was an offer being made to us, to be those persons. It was not from the Father, however, but an angel of light—the wrong spirit.

Launching the Flying Cloud

At last the boat—we dubbed The Flying Cloud—was ready to be put into the water. We positioned logs under the hulls and used Rube's old GMC truck driven between the hulls to push the boat from the parking lot 60 feet to a small concrete ramp used for launching boats. You can imagine the process this took to figure out, including getting the logs and calculating the move. We attached old tires to the one side that might bump the small piers to be buffers against damaging that hull. It was a nerve-wracking process in very tight quarters, but the jubilation of finally launching far outweighed our concerns.

Once the boat was afloat, the plan for getting it out into the Monterey Bay was next. Before moving forward, literally, the mast, sails and rigging had to be set in place. This portion of the work took as much creative engineering as it did brute

Our fully masted and rigged catamaran is towed out of Monterey Bay by a much smaller boat.

strength. Once the boat was fully rigged, our ship was ready.

Prior to actually taking the boat into the bay, we purchased a lot of supplies so we would be able to go a long time without having to send someone ashore. Not having any electricity, therefore no method of refrigeration, we chose foods that did not require cooling: carrots, cabbages, apples, oranges, raisins, eggs, oils, spices, various beans, brown rice, canned and powdered milk, soy beans, whole grains to make flour and cereals, and some cheeses.

There were many friends who had come to be part of this momentous event. There must have been 15 of us on this relatively small vessel waiting for the motorboat that was to tow us out past all the breakers and into the protected harbor. Mary and Jacob were among those who came for the launching. Rube's friend Billy was also present.

As we felt the lurching stop and go of the small boat struggling to pull our large craft against the incoming waves, I was surprised to find that I was seasick. I was not the only one, but for sure Rube was never seasick. I couldn't fully enjoy the entry into the bay until the sickness passed. There were several of us with our heads hanging over the hulls that day. It was my first and last time being sick on that vessel.

Once we were safely anchored in the bay and the high of the moment began to wane, our guests departed on the towboat, leaving us alone. The first order of business was to get the crab pots lowered. Our stores were full of all our recent purchases to complete our meals. We were planning to live on the bay for some months to check out her rigging and to practice sailing before setting out to cross the ocean.

Life on the Bay

We fished daily. Our crab pots were the most successful means of providing protein. We developed so many crab dishes. Our mainstay was crab salad that included carrots and cabbage. It is hard to believe that someone could become weary of such tasty fare, but I think I gained an appreciation for the Israelites who complained about the manna. I would like to note that at this stage of our spiritual walk, we did not yet view crab as being *treif* (Yiddush for non-kosher).

Many a squall came up in that body of water. When that occurred, we weighed anchor (pulled up the anchor) and sailed the boat to a more protected part of the bay, but always within short range of a pier of which our favorite was Santa Cruz. Rube and I rented post office boxes in several communities around the bay so we could get our mail sent wherever we were anchored at the time.

When I was trying to keep custody of my daughter some time later, the fact that I rented so many post office boxes was used to discredit me as being a transient mother.

As happens in anyone's life, we worked out our routines around the necessities of this kind of existence. We fished and crabbed for food, shared cooking and cleaning responsibilities, learned to sail while basking in the spray and sunshine most days. The little Primus-stove was also how we cooked our meals.

There were times we entertained visitors. We arranged visits by letters and at the appointed time, a couple of us rowed the skiff ashore to pick them up. My daughter Monicqua came for a visit, as did Jacob and his mom. We did not always have a pier to row to, so we sometimes beached the little boat.

Once when we were returning Jacob and his mother to shore intending to beach the skiff, we hit the waves sideways and almost capsized the boat. We all got plenty wet but were otherwise safe. There was an extra scare because Jacob had surgically implanted tubes in his ears and was not supposed to get them wet. Somehow he stayed dry that day.

Rube and I liked to be the ones to row ashore since we took "shore leave" at a movie theater and usually also a café. Mostly we walked around whichever town we happened to have rowed to and enjoyed each other's company. We also took care of any shopping that needed to be done. At the pre-arranged hour, we went to the farthest tip of the pier and blew our Acme Thunderers. Usually it was Beau who rowed the skiff to pick us up.

A Frightful Mishap

One time after Rube and I and the kids rowed Beau and Wanda ashore, a terrible thing happened. When we got the skiff back to the boat, Gabby, the eight year old, was assigned to tie off the little boat. She was an unusually responsible child, as was even Toby, the two-year-old, so we were aghast when we realized the skiff seemed to be floating away from the boat.

Rube was suffering from a cold at the time so I decided I should be the one to dive into the water and go after the skiff and row it back. Thankfully we always kept the oars in the boat! I will never forget how shockingly cold that water was. I swam toward the little boat, watching in horror while it kept getting farther away. At one point I realized that it was too far away, evidently caught in a current, so I realized that I needed to get back to the anchored boat. There was a moment or two when I actually feared I could not make it back due to hypothermia setting in.

We didn't know what to do to recover the skiff. It was no exaggeration that little boat was our lifeline, so we had to get it. Rube decided to jump in and try to swim for it. He quickly realized that was futile and climbed back on board. The only thing to do was to sail for it.

We weighed anchor, set the sails and began to tack – steering the vessel into the breeze – in the almost windless bay angling toward the drifting craft. It was a successful mission, not without moments of doubt, when we were finally able to snag the rope hanging from the little vessel. Once the skiff was secured, Rube and our small crew sailed back as close as we could to where we had been before and dropped the anchor.

You can imagine our relief. And Gabby learned a scary lesson. The boat was back in what we thought was the same spot before Beau blew the whistle for us to come to get them. Rube rowed to retrieve Beau and Wanda and I stayed on the deck with the children.

No one told Beau anything. He knew exactly where the boat had been and was aware it had been moved. After the story was told, it was an unhappy dad who chided a contrite little girl. I think, however, Beau was pleased to know that in a pinch Rube and I could handle the boat. So the experience was a bit of a test for us all that we felt we passed.

5
chapter

*Out of
the Haze*

Yearning for a Home

Rube and I had several occasions during those months to be the ones to go ashore. It was during some of this time off the boat that we began to discuss our future. A restlessness was growing. We both wanted to have our children with us. We knew it would be impossible to set up housekeeping with our two children on the boat—it just wasn't big enough. Already the other couple had two children.

Prior to the catamaran leaving for its first ocean voyage, Rube had written a letter to his old friend Andrew Shishkoff – who later became known by his Israeli name Eitan when he moved to Israel. *For clarity's sake I will refer to him as Eitan throughout this writing.* The Shishkoffs were then back in New Mexico at the old commune. Rube respected Eitan as a spiritual man and asked him to "bless" our voyage. His friend's reply was something to the effect of, "I would rather you were a fisher of men." The Shishkoffs had fallen "prey" to the wave of Jesus Freaks who invaded the otherwise content counter culture folks. Rube heard that his buddy Russ and his wife Jane had also turned to "The Way."

This occurrence was especially grievous to Rube who was Jewish. Both of these friends, who were also Jewish, essentially did the worst thing conceivable. They joined in with those who called on the name of the One who the Jews believe was behind all the heinous things that ever happened to their people. Rube was aware that I used to believe the way the Resniks and Shishkoffs now did, but I had put aside those leanings some years back.

In spite of the potential danger and discomfort of being around our "enchanted" former buddies, the urge to have a place for our family was so strong that Rube and I decided to leave the boat just prior to its maiden voyage and go to where Rube once lived with his friends on that commune in New Mexico – aptly subtitled the "Land of Enchantment" – smack dab on the Continental Divide. The commune was also well named by its occupants "Stone Mountain," double entendre intended.

Camp Joy

Anticipating the move to Stone Mountain, we realized that we would be trying to do subsistence farming on that remote piece of land, but had no real skills at growing things. We had friends living in the Santa Cruz area at a large "teaching" garden that had been established just three years earlier. We stopped at Camp Joy to learn about gardening. At least one of Rube's oldest friends, Billy, had become part of this group. We knew we would be welcome there.

With some angst we left Beau's family and the boat which would give us a few months to learn at Camp Joy before heading to our new home in time for the growing season.

We learned that Beau and his little family did make the trip to Hawaii as sched-

uled, and then on to their home in British Columbia. It must have been very hard on them not having more adult backup, but Beau was an excellent sailor, so we really didn't worry about them.

When we arrived at Camp Joy, we were temporarily given a little cabin. We worked with everyone all day, breaking now and then for a little nourishment. We were learning French intensive gardening, which was about preparing the soil by working the dirt from the lowest level where it was clods to a fine silt by the time we hit the top layer. We planted garlic. It flourished in that rich soil.

Each evening we joined in with all the others to prepare our common meal in the large barn. We ate, drank, toked, laughed, danced and were satiated by food and fellowship. When the merriment wound down, we adjourned to our little cabin to a beautiful cast iron bed. This frame had been painted in the most brilliant colors. It was then we learned that it was painted by Billy and others of Rube's friends when they were high on the psychedelic psilocybin. When we left Camp Joy heading to Stone Mountain, the residents gifted us with that bed.

We slept on that bed for over 25 years, renewing the mattress from time to time. We never painted over that frame. One of our granddaughters—Raina, daughter of Sarah—wanted the bed frame a few years ago. Her paternal grandfather Don Whitley sandblasted it and painted it white. It now graces Raina's bedroom. There is something special about its remaining in the family.

We carefully packed our bed into Rube's GMC "Jimmy" truck along with our newly acquired tools for gardening, cooking and living in the rustic environment of the Continental Divide territory of New Mexico. I had cashed in my teacher retirement money—which was only for six years of teaching so barely $4000—in order for us to purchase all the things we needed. We also used my funds to buy a loom for Mary. Rube felt he owed her something she would value and had always wanted. That door seemed to close and our adventure began.

Historical pictures of Camp Joy about the time we were there. I don't believe any of our lifetime friends were in this particular picture, but it accurately reflects the mood of this garden.

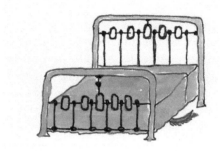

Rube's drawing of our bed with our dog Rado's tail peaking out. Taken from a children's book Rube and I wrote together, "Rado Red Dog Pursues Patience."

Stone Mountain

The winter Rube and his wife Mary and baby Jacob had lived at Stone Mountain some three years earlier, the temperature had dipped to 40 below. That might not seem too awful, but this little family was living in a teepee they sewed themselves. There was just a little open fire in the center of the teepee to keep them warm. The smoke escaped at the peak of the structure where the poles and canvas were left open. Rube said they were always freezing. It was actually that winter that convinced them to return to California.

It was this piece of property that Rube and friends occupied after having fled California some years before. I say fled because they truly believed there was an Apocalypse coming and wanted to be in a remote place away from civilization, which this property was. In our minds—and theirs—we were homesteaders, never mind the fact that the property belonged to someone already—our friend Andrea's parents. It fit right into our romantic view of the world.

At this time, however, there was none of the original group still living on the land. The main building—Adam's house—was still standing and unoccupied. This became the destination for us to settle down and have a home. Rube and I determined, however, that we would stay away from those "Jesus Freaks," as we began to think of Rube's old friends.

The journey was over 1000 miles, ostensibly 16 driving hours. Driving the Jimmy was definitely a slow go. We camped out at least one night at a roadside rest stop in the high desert. It is still scary to think that we spread his old sleeping bag and our blankets behind some rocks in an area teeming with venomous critters.

Iconic picture of Jacob, Mary and Rube in front of the teepee they sewed at Stone Mountain.

We had already decided we wanted to have a baby so I had my IUD removed before the journey. We were using the basal thermometer method of practicing birth control. We were happy to get pregnant any time, but wanted to know we knew a healthy method of preventing pregnancy afterwards. In that rough terrain it was not a surprise that the thermometer was shattered. That was the beginning of the pregnancy of our firstborn together, Joshua.

When we arrived at the old commune outside of Lindrith, NM, it was like landing on another planet. The terrain was undulating with arroyos and hills vegetated by sparse scrub brush. This was high desert land. In order to reach our destination, we navigated through about five gates that were separating other peoples' property. We were still in a playful mode and excited to finally be "home." I jumped out at each gate to let Rube drive the truck through before I got back in. Sometimes he would jokingly try to drive off without me. We were hyped by the thrill of setting up our new home. Stone Mountain was at the top of a dirt road that wound around the small mountain.

I was seeing the commune for the first time. There was the hogan Connie and Eitan built and lived in. The beams, having been covered with dirt, had all fallen in. The windmill stood in the garden spinning in the gusts of hot dry wind. Rube and his friends hand dug that well. An ancient iron bathtub sat expectantly with its clawed feet mired in the now hardened soil in the garden at the base of the windmill. By building a fire under the tub we heated the well water for lavish baths—a real treat having come from no access to full immersion. This garden was where we would take our baths and plant both our vegetables and marijuana. By the end of August 1974 we were harvesting from our garden.

The structure to the side of the garden was an attached goat and chicken house. Fortunately they were still standing; we planned to raise goats for milk and chickens for eating and for their eggs. I believe there were goats and chickens already there

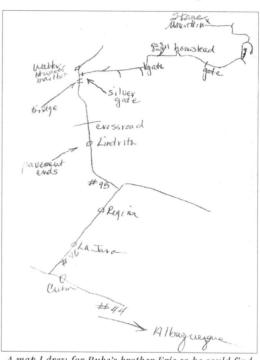

A map I drew for Rube's brother Eric so he could find us when he came to Stone Mountain.

What's happening here now is that we are starting to harvest from the garden. The squash is plentiful and the tomatoes are just beginning to get red. We plan to can some tomatoes, and make relish and catsup. We will be doing sauerkraut as there are about 90 cabbages. We are drying squash and will be drying the blue corn too. It's getting really close to time for the first freeze so we're getting a little anxious — the corn, some cabbages & the tomatoes & peppers need more time.

Excerpt from a letter I wrote to Eric telling him about our garden.

because a guy named Keith was still living on the property. It was Keith who was raising marijuana as well as poppies for the dope. Keith made a gift to us of small marijuana plants so we could have our own crop.

Adams' house at the top of the property seemed to tower over the other structures. It was two stories, but probably only about 10 feet by 20 and with low ceilings. It was wider than it was deep. The back wall was actually the side of the biggest hill. Someone had carved out a bread-box-sized shelf in that wall over which there was a hinged wooden door. That served as our cooler where we kept butter, milk and cheese.

There was already a 55-gallon drum with a spigot at the house. We rigged up a system of hoses to bring water from the well to that drum, *voilà* running water. Thankfully there was a wood cook stove someone left behind. The whole front of the structure was windows, some of which were broken. Replacing the windows was one of our first tasks. This required a trip to the closest town, Cuba, NM.

We had all the modern conveniences, even an outhouse, which was located between our house and the garden. The previous occupants built it earlier. I was so grateful for it. The structure was a small shed with room for two holes. It would have been an added luxury for it to have been a two-seater rather than just a two-holer.

In the daytime, it was very usable, but at night was another story. Since I was pregnant, frequent urination was my lot for the duration. There was no way I was going to go outside to the outhouse in the dark. This was wild terrain where any kind of creature could be lurking. A large tomato can served as my chamber pot.

The dirt floor of the first level of the house, which was a crude kitchen and living room, was covered with a large rag rug. Thick, rough hewn stairs led to the upper level, which provided room enough for our bed and clothing. We stored our five-gallon buckets of marijuana we had harvested that summer in our bedroom.

As soon as we got settled we traveled out to Cuba, where we bought repair supplies as well as food for our present needs including large quantities of wheat, beans, soybeans and rice that could be stored for what we believed would be the Apocalypse. We kept our doomsday rations in tightly sealed five-gallon buckets.

Our meals were simple fare. For breakfast we typically used our grinder to crack wheat before we toasted it in a skillet over the wood stove, followed by boiling it until it was a hot cereal. With a bit of honey and goats' milk it was sumptuous fare! We consumed eggs from the chickens and used the goats' milk to both drink and make cheese. We were great fans of fried rice with eggs and cheese or homemade tortillas with beans, rice and cheese. We ate whatever veggies we could produce. We were never hungry.

Our life settled into a routine. Get up with the light, smoke a joint (a marijuana cigarette). Drink a cup of coffee while we were making breakfast. After we ate, our day was consumed by tending the animals and the garden. We also chopped a lot of wood for our use and to sell to the local Native Americans. They valued our piñon for cooking their bread.

When we had the cook stove going for cooking or canning, there was bread to be baked as well as any pastries such as cobblers from berries we found growing on the land. By evening, we were usually quite exhausted from our labors and "went to bed with the chickens," that is as soon as it was dark. Since we had no electricity, we saved on candles by being up with the sun.

On very rare occasions, we drove into Lindrith where there was a gas station, a bar and a post office. Rube would always tell people, "You could get a beer and a hamburger in the bar." It was a rare treat that we relished. Rube was always ready for a cold beer. This gave us the opportunity to pick up any mail that might have come in for us, which was our only communication with the outside world.

We rarely dropped acid, as it was a luxury to have a trip when there was so much work to do. Actually it became more difficult to smoke dope since it kept us from producing. Our lives depended upon our ability to lay in food before winter. Knowing I was pregnant, I chose not to smoke dope or drop acid for fear of harming the baby. Rube often toked alone.

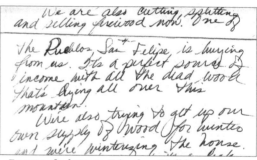

Excerpt of a letter to Eric where I tell him about our selling firewood to the local Pueblo Native Americans.

Garden Bathtub Baptism

When we arrived in June of 1974, Rube's friends had already moved to another property—the Mesa— some miles away from the original commune so there was less danger of encountering his newly "converted" buddies. At the same time, however, Rube genuinely missed his friends and wanted to see them again. We received Russ and Jane and Eitan and Connie and their growing families that summer on several occasions.

None of our friends ever directly chided us for any of our behaviors that ran counter to

The property at the Mesa where the Shishkoffs and Resniks lived.

what they now believed to be true from the Bible. They said nothing about our living together without being legally married, nor about our drug use. They instead just poured out abundant affection toward us.

On at least one occasion we went to visit Russ and Jane when they were hosting a Christian teacher from Santa Fe. Don Compton of Shalom Ministries came up and held meetings with any who would listen. When he was called into ministry, the Lord impressed on Don that there were many of God's people—Jews—who were among the lost hippies. He felt it was his personal mission to bring Jesus to these lost sheep.

I remember having a conversation with Don after one of his teachings about tithing. I was flabbergasted that Believers would give 10% and even more to God's work. We talked about the ministry of the famous TV evangelist Billy Graham, and I expressed my belief that he was a scammer just trying to get people's money. Don did his best to convince me otherwise.

Don gave Rube and me a battery-operated tape recorder and many spiritual tapes featuring teachers I later recognized to be giants in the faith, such as Derek Prince and Bob Mumford. Once we came to the realization that Jesus was who He said He was—the Jewish Messiah—it was these taped teachings that solidified our faith.

Satan was not going to stand still for this interference in the souls of two people he was claiming for himself. At this time some people from a religious cult—Jehovah's Witnesses—made their way to the commune. As I explained, it was no small feat to get to this remote enclave. This property was a 40-acre piece far removed from roads and behind about five gates as you can tell from the map I inserted earlier.

These interlopers spouted their philosophy to us, but I had actually memorized a good bit of the Bible as a child, and I was aware that they were twisting the meaning of some very significant teachings. I shared this with Rube who decided to investigate.

As it happened, Rube owned his maternal grandfather Ralph Moore's Bible. Ralph was a Methodist. Rube saw it solely as

Portion of the letter I wrote to family explaining about the various visitors we were having.

a family heirloom until then. We began to look for and read the very passages that were being misinterpreted. In the reading—and probably because our friends were heavily praying for us, as we learned much later—Rube and I began to understand and accept the Gospel.

After some weeks of such study, we got word to his friends that we were ready to be immersed as a symbol of our new faith. Eitan and Russ, dumbfounded that it could actually be true, came to the little commune to baptize us.

Just a week prior to this we had some friends hitchhike to see us. They came when we were gone taking Monicqua to the airport to fly back to California as school was starting for her. We were just about to have Jacob with us. He was being brought by Mary.

Mary and Jacob were there when we were baptized on September 8, 1974. Mary had come in on the train from California to bring Jacob to spend some time with us, which was the agreement she had with Rube. When we picked her up from the station, we stopped by a wellness clinic on our way home to pick up prenatal vitamins. That was the first she heard we were pregnant. Neither of us knew at that time that the real reason for her visit was to get Rube back again.

Rube and Mary ended up having a long talk one evening. She was asking him to come back to her, while he was asking for a divorce so we could get married. I only learned of her intentions after that meeting. He did tell her he wanted to marry me, and she agreed to a divorce.

Everything changed for us. We were raising some funds by selling homegrown marijuana to locals, and realized from interpreting scripture, that would have to stop. We tried to still sell dope one time after coming to the Lord. We took some of our best product to the University of New Mexico (UNM) in Albuquerque and we practically couldn't give it away. Literally, everyone had just bought some "good" Mexican weed and no one was in the market.

We did sell one lid – being the equivalent of a sandwich baggy full – which gave us enough gas money to drive to Santa Fe where Eitan's family had moved. Rube asked Eitan to pray with him for his drug addiction. He prayed for Rube to be set free from the "spirit" of marijuana and, honestly, something left him that day. He was set free and NEVER AGAIN desired any kind of dope, after being a heavy toker and tripper for over 10 years.

At this writing, marijuana is being legalized all over America, for medicinal purposes and for adult recreation. Knowing as I did that a "presence" left Rube when he was set free of drugs, I have pondered if the spirit that left him that day was of marijuana or of something even more sinister - addiction perhaps? I don't have to know its name. What I do know is that marijuana is still a gateway drug that cripples its users from getting anything accomplished.

We also knew that winter was approaching and, Dear Reader, I have already expressed how harsh the winters could be on that commune. We needed a way to make an honest living somewhere less hostile.

A Near Miss

As I mentioned earlier, when we first came to Stone Mountain, a hard core doper named Keith was the only hippie still there. He routinely saved all he made from selling what he grew to get a roundtrip ticket to Afghanistan where he could stay doped up until his money ran out. At that time he would literally crawl back to the airplane to return to the States. His homegrown poppies were the major source of his personal drug use.

Wickipedia 2019: Afghanistan first began producing opium in significant quantities in the mid-1950s, to supply its neighbor Iran after poppy cultivation was banned there. Afghanistan and Pakistan increased production and became major suppliers of opiates to Western Europe and North America in the mid-1970s...Afghanistan's opium poppy harvest produces more than 90% of illicit heroin globally, and more than 95% of the European supply. More land is used for opium in Afghanistan than is used for coca cultivation in Latin America. In 2007, 93% of the non-pharmaceutical-grade opiates on the world market originated in Afghanistan.This amounts to an export value of about US $4 billion, with a quarter being earned by opium farmers and the rest going to district officials, insurgents, warlords, and drug traffickers.

Prior to our leaving the property, we decided to get rid of our dope. I actually boasted to Keith that Rube was planning to destroy it all. Keith fairly freaked out and confronted Rube in our house. Rube told him that he felt it was his duty to destroy it, believing the Bible on a couple of levels specifically to not taking drugs and also to obey the laws of the land.

Keith stood up, walked up the rustic steps to our loft bedroom and grabbed a five-gallon bucket we had stuffed full of all the marijuana flowers from our plants. He promptly stepped out the window on the opposite side of the room that opened onto a dead tree and was able to get down with the bucket. He set off for the deep canyon that ran the length of the property.

I was aghast for several reasons. First, it was I who "leaked" the information to Keith that Rube intended to get rid of all our dope. Second, I felt it should be Rube's decision to deal with our crop in the manner he believed God was leading. And lastly, I had fallen into a pattern in my life of bragging and it was a boast when I told Keith about Rube's plan. I felt great shame for my poor character deterring Rube's determination to follow God as he saw fit.

Without hesitating, I left the house, and followed Keith. We all knew that Keith buried a lot of his crop in that canyon but didn't know the exact location. I waited on the sparsely vegetated precipice at the edge of the canyon, hoping to see where Keith had gone. Actually, I really didn't have much of a plan. It became crystal clear when Keith came out of the canyon without the bucket. I tried to hide behind some scrub sage thinking when he left, I would go down to the canyon to find our dope. For a moment, I thought I was clear, but he suddenly stopped in his tracks, spun around and headed right for me.

By this time I was several months pregnant, my belly bulging in my overalls.

I was still driven by my having botched everything so I stood up and told Keith that it was okay for him to keep our dope because now I knew where his was hidden. That did it. He swelled up like a lion. Fear seized at my heart. Keith was the man who had beaten up his former lover to the point she suffered broken arms and heavy internal injuries.

In that moment, I believe God got ahold of me and I realized I needed to come clean. I blurted out that I did not know where he hid his stash, but that I was just trying to get him to return our dope so Rube could be the one to deal with it. He was visibly stunned by my confession. I took that little window of opportunity to slip quickly past him back to our house.

Later that afternoon when I was down the hill from our home, milking the goats, I saw Keith going up the trail to the house carrying our bucket of dope. I quickly finished up and headed there. When I arrived, Rube and Keith were sitting across from each other at our little booth table. Rube seemed calm but Keith was very agitated while he explained how heinous it was for us to consider getting rid of the dope. He argued that it was fine if we didn't want it, but we should give it to him so it could be enjoyed.

Keith thought it strengthened his argument to attack belief in the Bible. He said it was God's people who encouraged a man to sacrifice his son to God, referring to Abraham and his son Isaac. Rube realized that even though Keith returned the dope, he was going to continue to try to change his mind about disposing of it. Abruptly Rube stood up, grabbed the bucket and emptied its contents into our fireplace, poured kerosene over the lot of it and struck a match. Keith was horrified, but finally defeated, left our house.

It was becoming clear that we needed to leave Stone Mountain. First, we no longer had a way to make a living since dope sales and selling firewood to the Native Americans nearby had been the only options. Second, we would never be safe around Keith. Dope was a religion to him.

Rube spoke of his maternal uncle in Colorado who might take us in and help us get a fresh start. The plan was developed, long distance calls made from the bar in Lindrith and we gave away our goats, packed up our geese, chickens and other belongings into Jimmy and set off for what seemed to us like the Promised Land. Fortunately Rube's uncle lived on a farm, so we knew the three geese we brought would also be received.

Going Straight

It was winter of 1974 when we arrived at Uncle Don and Aunt Bridgit Moore's farmhouse in La Junta, Colorado. Two more nurturing folks you will never meet anywhere. I have to say, upon reflection, we were a scruffy pair. It was amazing they could see through all of that to even be able to trust us. They gave us a landing place when we came to their 360-acre farm outside this small community. They put us up in their own home where we stayed for a few months before getting our own place.

Uncle Don got up with the chickens—literally—every morning and went out to plow, weed and otherwise run farm machinery prior to going to his main job. He was an amazing mix of intellectual and gentleman farmer. Having retired as a PHD of Nuclear Physics at a major company, he was now the Dean of Faculty of the local community college. Once he came in from the fields, got cleaned up and headed to the office, Bridget continued whatever Don had been doing on the farm. What a duo.

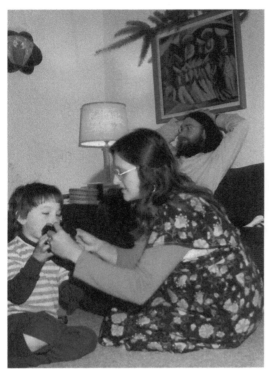

Rube's four-year-old son Jacob, me pregnant with Joshua and Rube at a Christmas visit with his mother and stepfather in San Jose, CA, shortly after we moved to Uncle Don's farm. I was wearing one of the many dresses I made on my treadle machine.

And they were still raising Bridgit's two kids. William and Sarah Lynn Anson were teenagers. Don's three children—Beth, Ann and Jim—were grown and on their own. Sarah seemed captivated by our presence. I was never able to get a read on William's view of our "invasion."

Many years hence Sarah Lynne told us how mesmerized she had been by us. She was at an age to put people on pedestals, and somehow she looked at us as some kind of folk heroes. We saw ourselves as broken rebels that God was healing from all our misdeeds and were oblivious to her adoration.

We threw ourselves into life on Uncle Don's farm. I was about six months pregnant and not as capable of helping, but Rube began farmhand work. Don grew several cash crops, mostly onions, sugar beets for the sugar factory, and flowers for Burpee's Seeds. At the same time Uncle Don kept his own cattle for beef and had several milk cows. He and Bridgit always kept a very large garden just for family use. Rube ran equipment, hauled hay, and we both milked the cows. We

A later picture of Uncle Don and Aunt Bridgit – far right – when they had come from Washington state to attend Jeff's memorial. Also pictured, left sitting, Rube. Standing: a family friend and Marge.

also helped tend the family garden.

We possessed three college degrees between us, so were equipped to get jobs as needed. Due to my late-term pregnancy, I wasn't able to work, but Rube quickly secured a job that proved to be a great transition from the hippie life-style to a more straight life. He was hired on as the blacksmith for the reconstruction of historic Bent's Old Fort in the Southeast corner of Colorado on the Santa Fe Trail. His History degree was what recommended him for the job.

During the first several years we were in La Junta, Rube continued to work at the Fort. He was trained there to be a blacksmith, which was a joy to him. He learned to make all kinds of hardware from nails to chandeliers, all of which were used in the reconstruction of the fort.

The fort project began with only two-foot high adobe walls, the bricks having been taken throughout the years by locals for their own building projects. Rube was hired as a Living History Park Ranger and made 95% of the hardware builders used to restore the fort. He was also given the job of planning and equipping both the blacksmith's shop and the carpenter's shop. He was very proud of this accomplishment. We were there for the dedication of Bent's Old Fort.

One of the first homes we had after leaving Don and Bridgit's was a farmhouse on a parcel someone else worked. This property was just down the county road from Don's farm, which was also the same road to Bent's Old Fort where Rube worked. It was at this place that we lost our geese—Gus, Gertie and Lucy Goose—to some kind of predators, probably the coyotes that roamed that river valley. Ja-

Richard Rubenstein is a blacksmith in the replica of the original shop. The bellows are actually in use and most of the tools used at the fort were made in the blacksmith shop.

Newspaper article about Rube being the blacksmith for the reconstruction of Bent's Old Fort outside La Junta, CO on the Santa Fe Trail.

Bent's Old Fort outside La Junta, CO after it was restored.

cob was coming every summer for a few weeks to visit and did so while we were in this house.

As a testimony to the harsh winters in southern Colorado, that first winter a blizzard hit. Even though our house was a stone's throw from the road, we could not see it. We began to realize that there might be people caught in the blizzard on the road. We used a rope to tie ourselves to the house porch so we could go help them. Before long our house was full of stranded folks, mostly those who worked at the Fort. We fairly emptied our fridge getting them all fed, but we took care of everyone until the storm broke. We got word later there were some people who died in that storm, some just a few feet from houses. Thankfully none died by our property.

Rube and I got legally married at Shalom Ministries. Rube was given the shirt and tie by one friend and the suit by another. I made my wedding dress.

It was an amazing feeling when we finally were able to have a real wedding ceremony. This picture shows my 8-months' pregnancy figure.

When I was eight months pregnant with Josh, Rube and I were given the chance to get legally married. Ironically, his divorce was final on Valentine's Day 1975. We took a trip to Santa Fe where Rube and I were married by Pastor Wade Pope of Capital Christian Church on February 16, 1975. The little ceremony took place at Shalom Ministries with the help of founder Donald Compton, who I mentioned was instrumental in so many "hippies" coming to faith in Jesus, including us.

Russ, Jane, their kids and her mom came from Albuquerque. Eitan and Connie and children, along with numerous other friends, all joined in the joyous celebration. Jane's mom was taking pictures. I made my special "maternity" wedding dress out of polished tan cotton. We enjoyed cake and lunch at Connie's table at their home in Santa Fe afterwards.

With the birth of Josh imminent, we moved into a newly-built apartment complex in La Junta, which constituted the projects for this little town in Colorado. We got settled into our basement two-bedroom apartment just before the baby was due. Even though we had left Uncle Don's farm, we still kept connected to our family. We shared their large garden and still were given fresh milk, homegrown beef and eggs and occasionally homemade ice cream. Yum!

Baby picture of Josh. If memory serves, Don's daughter Beth Moore made the quilt.

For our part, Rube and I continued to help with the farm. Most notably we took over the chores, including milking cows and feeding the future hamburgers when his aunt and uncle went out of town on their infrequent breaks. One of their favorite destinations was to take the train south to Santa Fe to enjoy the outdoor opera.

It was while we were taking care of the farm that spring that the baby came. Rube and I fed the beef cattle and were heading to the milkers when we were aware that a gate must have been left open because the cattle were getting out and heading toward the river where there were no fences. The bovine critters could have gotten pretty far if not chased back.

I was helping round them up, jumping bar ditches and the like, when I went into labor just as the last steer was locked back in the field. This was good news since my due date had come and gone two weeks previously. Little Joshua entered the world the next day on March 27, 1975.

Once I was on my feet from giving birth, I took a part-time job at the local college teaching English in a learning lab, while

Our little family outside the blacksmith shop of Bent's Old Fort outside La Junta, CO. Josh was about seven months old. The picture was taken in October 1975 by Darlene and Rodger Young when they came to visit us with their daughter Rhoda Beth. For some playful reason Darlene and I always referred to each other by our children: Rhoda Beth's mom, Joshua's mom.

Aunt Bridget and a neighbor, Mrs. Wagstaff, shared babysitting little Josh. This was the same college where Don was the Dean of Faculty, BUT there was no hint of favoritism. Even though I had earned both a Bachelor's and Master's in English, Don insisted I jump through many more hoops than the usual candidate to avoid even the appearance of nepotism.

chapter

6

HIS
Ways

Sharing Jesus

After the fort was constructed, Rube was kept on as the resident Blacksmith. In our spiritual lives, Rube and I began working in a field more closely connected to our newfound faith. We met other Believers who wanted to participate in ministry, as did we.

We were one of three families who founded Maranatha Ministries there in La Junta, which consisted of a coffee house ministry run by Sally and Laverne Johnson – who I believe had seven children, a Christian school run by Rube and me, and a worship team led by David Jiron. David and Becca had four or five children at the time. We named our music team "Listen Christian Crusade." It was from this base that we set out to minister to others. Rube and I sang and played instruments as part of this band.

Another of our believing friends, Angel Ramirez – married to Gloria – became the preacher for our outreach team. We regularly traveled to Buena Vista State Reformatory to sing and worship with the incarcerated men. We also ministered in county jails. It was a very fulfilling time for us all.

It was during this time that Monicqua, then 13, came to visit us for the summer, just after Josh was born. During her stay, she too accepted the Lord, but still returned to her dad's at the end of the summer. We stayed in close communication, however, and by the end of that school year, she came to live with us.

By that time we had bought a home inside the town of La Junta. It was a house that was created from an old carriage house. The walls were stone and two feet thick. It was smallish, probably about 1200 square feet, but we were so excited to finally have our own place that we didn't fret the size. Its front room ran the width of the house having been a porch that was later enclosed. One end of the room was a massive stone fireplace. We learned that the stones were locally quarried. From this room through a door that once was the front door, there was a large room we used for dining. On the side of this space was a staircase ascending to a low-ceilinged loft that was our bedroom.

Under the stairway was a small bedroom that was Neek's.

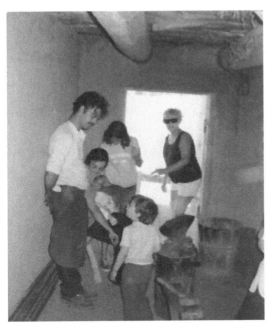

My mother Jean Berryman, Monicqua and Jacob visited us in La Junta in the summer of 1975 when Joshua was a few months old and Rube was still operating the Blacksmith shop.

The dining room opened into the very small galley-type kitchen, a corner of which had been carved out for a tiny bathroom, and on the other wall of the kitchen there was a door leading into what had been probably a rather large tack room that became a bedroom for three-year-old Josh.

It sounds a bit rustic, but it was quite comfortable. The structure was well-plastered and obviously well-insulated making it very cozy in winter or summer. The previous owners put in rose bushes and fruit trees, which were a delight to our senses and our palates. We were situated adjacent to a park with a tennis court on one side. Monicqua and I both loved to play tennis. Another larger park was a few blocks away in the other direction. This park was complete with a baseball diamond. We won't talk about what a bad sport Principal Rube was when we played baseball with our students. What happened to the kind, sweet person when he hit the field?

Also a block away was the town's junior college, Otero Junior College, where I had previously taught. I used the college's music practice rooms to take piano lessons and for practicing since we did not own a piano. Rube once gave me a birthday card with pull-off tabs for ten nights of his washing dishes so I could walk across the street to the college to practice. Best present I ever received!

Our home housed the Christian school. Our front room was our "learning center," the dining room was where kids graded their work, and upstairs was

1520 Belleview Ave. in La Junta, Colorado with our Volvo station wagon alongside. It had been converted from an old carriage house. It felt like a mansion to us.

the reading laboratory. An older lady from the Assembly of God Church we attended, "Sister" Madsen, volunteered to run our reading program. Pretty much every square inch of the home was dedicated to this school. In fact it took over our home so much that I found it difficult to shut down when school was over for the day. It took a wise Rube to walk up to my desk, close whatever I was working on and declare, "School's out!"

It was almost impossible to

Our narrow "living room" – that had been converted from a porch prior to our buying the house – became the learning center with individual student "offices." I circulated to help them with all subjects. They signaled for help by putting up either the American flag for academic questions or the Christian flag for a personal need.

make a living running the school. We enrolled about 20 students, but we could not take in enough tuition to live on. We did not require our fellow ministers to pay for their children to attend the school, which constituted about half of the student body.

Once we even employed a young woman who lived with us in little Josh's room in one of the twin beds. It was she who taught the one kindergarten-aged student, who was the Johnson's youngest daughter. We pretty much just fed her and gave her a place to live, so it didn't last long. Rube took two other jobs to try to keep us afloat. He drove a school bus mornings and afternoons for the local public schools and also worked several nights a week in a recovery center for substance abusers.

During that time I had a crisis of faith. Monicqua was now living with us and it seemed permanent, but there were issues in our relationship. In hindsight, perhaps they were the typical disconnect that happens with a mom and daughter about that age. I took it very personally, having almost lost her in the events surrounding my hippie years and coming to faith in Jesus.

I really wanted to re-establish the bond we had when she was younger, but she seemed more drawn to the Johnsons who were the coffee house part of our ministry. All of the teen kids spent as much time at the coffee house as their parents and the Johnsons would allow. I felt rejected by Monicqua in favor of the Johnsons. I developed a deep bitterness toward them. This is horrible to admit on so many levels. Not only were we all in ministry together, but we were 100% dedicated to the Lord's work.

I was experiencing a growing grief at what I perceived to be the loss of Monicqua again. One day I became distraught and withdrew to our loft bedroom. I had it out with God. I practically yelled at God that I couldn't take the bitterness any longer, but I needed for Him to make me willing to be made willing to let it go. I had no faith that He would or could do such a thing but my black heart was so heavy.

In the INSTANT after those words left my lips, I was transported into His presence in such a tangible way. The heaviness was replaced with the purest peace and love. I was so transformed in that moment that all I wanted to do was go find the Johnsons to give them big, deep hugs. I am not sure what I did right then, because I had never told the Johnsons how much I resented what I saw as their interference in my already troubled relationship with my teenager. I know that I did become much more demonstrable of my new love for them for as long as we lived in La Junta.

To this day I would love to see them, to hug them again. God is SO GOOD. If they had ever picked up on my earlier animosity, they never said. Having this angst disappear cleared the road for my daughter and I to interact in a more normal course. It took many years for her to trust me again.

By the spring of 1978 I was pregnant with our daughter Sarah. I had assumed that we just wanted one child together since we each had a child from our previous marriages. We both realized at the same time, however, that we had one "waiting in the wings," so to speak. We somehow knew she was a girl that we felt God already called by the name of Sarah. I had always hoped to name a girl after my beloved Aunt Becky, but it seemed God had other plans.

We finished out that school year, but knew financially we would not be able to keep the school running. So, when we closed the doors that summer, it was for the last time. La Junta Christian School was no more. We needed to make a living wage. Rube continued working for the recovery center during the nights but that and some public school bus driving constituted our meager income.

We managed to continue our yearly visits to Rube's mom in San Jose. We all enjoyed many side trips to the numerous educational settings in the area. We especially loved Marge's cooking for us.

Trail to Santa Fe

Early Fall of 1978, before the baby was expected, Rube was told he had been recommended by our friends in Santa Fe to Christian Life Church that had just begun a new Christian school and who needed a principal and a high school learning center teacher. Another couple had been put in charge since the school was just established that fall, but due to a difference of opinion they left. It was all set for us to take over, but we were waiting for our baby to be born. We got in a visit to Rube's mom's house a few months before Sarah was due. Grandpa Jeff and Marge loved to accompany us to the beach.

Rube, Monicqua, me pregnant with Sarah holding Joshua outside our Belleview home in La Junta, CO.

It was on a freezing morning in mid November, when Rube had just returned from his night job and crawled into bed, that my water broke. He got no sleep that day. Some friends were pre-arranged to take Monicqua and Josh so we delivered them and headed to the hospital in the neighboring town of Rocky Ford

Summer 1978 in San Jose, CA at Boehm house: Rube, Marge, Joshua and me pregnant with Sarah. I assume G'pa Jeff took the picture.

for the birth. We used the medical facilities in Rocky Ford, not La Junta, because we could access "indigent funds" at this clinic to pay for the birth. It is also where Joshua had been born. We were calling the baby Sarah Lee Shortcake, in faith she was a girl. Joshua was almost four and Neek was 16. Jacob was about nine and was at home at his mother's in St. Helena, CA.

Rube and pregnant me walking at the beach near San Jose, CA.

A bright-eyed Sarah at about 11 months.

We barely made it to the hospital in time. Lying down in the back of our VW camper while Rube drove, I was practicing the Lamaze breathing I learned in birthing classes. The pain got intolerably intense. Rube told me to shift to the next phase of the breathing, but I was afraid I was going to run out of stages and would really be in pain. I didn't know that I was probably fully dilated at the time. I took his advice, escalated my breathing and got immediate relief.

I do believe I received a special blessing from God at that time. In the intervals between contractions, I felt God's presence so palpably that I began to look forward to the next contraction so I could experience that beauty again. I was transported to a heavenly place. This lasted until I gave birth.

In the meantime, we got stuck at a railroad crossing that bisected that little town. The clinic/hospital was on the other side. Rube quickly got on a frontage road to try to get over the tracks ahead of the oncoming train. He narrowly made it.

When we got to the hospital they rushed me into a room where I was examined by the Head Nurse—who happened to be a Believer in Jesus—and all she said was, "Don't Push! The doctor is not here yet." It was probably 15 minutes before the doctor arrived and little Sarah joined the family. We added Ruth for her middle name in order to honor Rube's mother, Marjorie Ruth. Now with the naming of this memoir, it is even more significant that we loved the name Ruth. Sarah Ruth Rubinstein was born in Rocky Ford, CO, November 14, 1978.

Since Rube had been already hired to take over that Christian school in Santa Fe, we began making plans to make the move. It was when Sarah was eight days old that Rube and the three kids and I set out in our two vehicles to Santa Fe. Rube was driving the old Volvo station wagon ahead with three-year-old Josh, and I was following in the VW camper with Neek and infant Sarah.

We first caravanned to Pueblo, CO to put Rube's mom on an airplane back to California. She had been with us to help after the birth. I was following Rube to Santa Fe to look for a house. Rube was going to start work while I returned to Colorado with the kids to sell our house.

It was an icy road—actually black ice—we encountered just outside of Walsenburg, CO, as we headed south. While Rube kept control of his car, Monicqua, the baby and I were not so fortunate. I had let newly licensed 16-year-old Neek drive so I could take care of the baby. Neek began to slide, losing control of the vehicle. Just prior to this, I had taken the baby out of the little cardboard crib we wedged between the little refrigerator and a back seat, since I was afraid Sarah was getting cold. VW's of that era were notorious for having poor heaters!

When Neek hit the ice, I foolishly thought I could help her by unbuckling my seat belt, which I did. Almost immediately we spun around and flipped the vehicle onto the driver's side. I was thrown into Monicqua, while still clutching the baby. My seat popped loose and hit baby Sarah in the head. Our not being killed was a miracle. We realized that my having brought the baby out of her crib, however, saved Sarah when we watched in shock as the heavy refrigerator crushed the bed she had just been in.

There were many cars off the road that evening due to the unexpected road conditions, but Rube was able to pull over and was horrified at what he saw in his rearview mirror. He watched our camper's lights spinning front to back and then going sideways when we circled 180 degrees around then flipped the vehicle onto its side. As the camper came to a rest, Monicqua sprang into action and climbed up through the passenger door. I handed her the baby and then pulled myself up. Passersby helped us down.

We were all banged up and the VW was askew, but we were helped setting it right so we could continue to drive until we got somewhere we could get a motel room and rest for the night. We were all shaken and Neek and I were very stiff. I was worried about Sarah having taken a hit to her head, so we took her to a chiropractor when we got to Santa Fe.

We were a grateful family when a month or so later we sold the La Junta house and could complete the move to Santa Fe. For the actual trip, Rube was towing an open trailer covered with a tarp. I was following in the VW camper. A few hours into our journey, I saw a box fly out of that trailer and off into a field. I couldn't stop to get it for fear Rube would not have seen me stop and continue on. I told him about it the next time we stopped. For years when we missed something, we would always say that it must have been in that box. All that angst would not have happened if we were in the era of cell phones!

Our VW van with the family about that time with three of the David and Becca Jiron family, our previous ministry partners, who were visiting from Colorado. R–L: Jiron's oldest daughter, Rube holding baby Sarah, Joshua front middle, me and Jacob and young Jiron.

Baby girl and her dad.

Our Growing Family

It was late fall of 1978. We purchased a doublewide trailer already set up in a mobile home park in Santa Fe. Our living situation kept changing, however, as the size of our family grew. Our dream of buying land and building an adobe house was set in motion by buying this mobile home, but it would have to be moved out on property when we were able to buy land. Sarah was a baby and Josh only three. Monicqua was sixteen. Jacob was just nine years old and still living with his mother in California.

Rube always had such a close bond with the children. Little Sarah was his first experience at raising a baby girl, since he had only started raising Monicqua when she was already a teenager. Sarah was into sucking her two middle fingers for comfort. Sometimes she would be in such a dreamy state that her daddy would have to get forehead to forehead with her to get her attention.

Likewise, Rube had been interrupted in his parenting of Jacob since he and Mary were separated when he was just four. Jacob's visits were short and infrequent. Rube felt he had a second chance at parenting with

Josh and Sarah.

There was so much coming and going during the twelve years—1978-1990—we lived in Santa Fe. Honestly, it is difficult to get the timeline straight, so if you are reading this and were part of those years, you will have to forgive me if I get times, places, faces, events different from your memory. It has been a process to piece this all together, especially since I have no one to corroborate but our children and some friends and other family. I hope to faithfully capture the spirit of the times if not the exact details.

No matter what was going on in our lives, we drove down to see my family in Hobbs, southern New Mexico, every summer. Most of that time my siblings were in the general area of my hometown so I was able to visit with all of them.

Mother's house was always the gathering place when we visited. This is how the cousins were able to spend time together. Our yearly visits were usually for less than a week. It was rare for anyone to come up north to see us.

I will say here that we made every effort to spend the two-week Christmas break each year with Rube's family in California. His mother Marge was great at taking us to check out many historical and literary exhibits in the San Jose area. The highlight of these trips was going to the beach.

Joshua and his dad looking at a favorite picture of G'pa Jeff Boehm.

On a visit to see stepfather George and my mother at the house where I grew up in Hobbs, NM. Sarah is about three and very interested in mother's poodle that is half hidden behind George.
I am standing and Rube is seated. I believe we are watching Josh play with his cousins.

Joshua, Rube, me and Sarah preparing to leave my mother's house after a visit in 1981.

Live and Learn

For the first three of those years—1978-1981—Rube and I ran Christian Life School. The curriculum we used was Accelerated Christian Education (ACE), which we also used in our La Junta Christian School. Just as our students in Colorado had done, these children completed all of their subjects individually in little offices that consisted of desks in small cubicles.

The teachers circulated helping as needed. Kids completed booklets, called PACEs, then tested on them. It was very similar to the booklets I used at Delta Continuation School in Santa Maria all those years ago. This program consisted of 12 PACES or booklets per subject per year where Delta's required only ten per school year. Also, of course, Delta's curriculum was purely secular where the PACEs had a Christian foundation.

In the beginning, newborn Sarah was often strapped to my back in a carrier while I walked around helping students in the large sanctuary-convert-ed-to-learning-center. Josh was in a K-4 program that year and the next year officially in kin-dergarten with beloved teacher Evelyn Craig. Monicqua was 16 and in high school.

Rube with Sarah celebrating her second Christmas in 1979 when she was just one.

When baby Sarah needed a nap I put her in bed in the nurs-ery that adjoined the sanctuary. After the first year when Sar-ah started walking, she was in childcare and that was when our good friend Connie Shishkoff took care of her while I taught.

During the time we taught here, Rube was the Principal, while I headed up the Language Arts programs. I taught small writing classes for the older stu-dents and also created a year-book documenting the school's students, staff and varied ac-tivities, *The Saint Express*. Jacob came to live with us and attended this school. Monicqua completed her last two years of high school at Christian Life, graduating in May of 1980.

The 1979-80 school picture of our family at this time at Christian Life School. Me holding Sarah, Monicqua, Joshua, Jacob and Principal Rube.

By 1981, 19-year-old Monicqua had become a governess for a family who owned one home in Santa Fe and another in Palm Desert, California. She lived with them taking care of their adopted daughter—who was actually their blood granddaughter. They traveled a great deal and Monicqua spent a month with them in Hawaii, as well as visiting other sites. She made some connections while they were at their Palm Desert home and after a short stint at the Santa Fe Junior College, moved back there on her own.

The four graduates that year. Monicqua is to the far left and her best friend Ginger – Pastor Conley's daughter – is beside her. I am two rows behind her in the center wearing a blue dress with a corsage. Principal Rube was conducting the ceremony.

While we were still living in the smaller trailer and before I began my three-year teaching job at the penitentiary, I spent about six months homeschooling Joshua. I used the ACE curriculum and got him through first grade. Our friends—Bob and Cindy Harris—were also homeschooling their two children. We teamed up. Sarah turned three while we were living there.

I taught all academics four mornings a week and Bob worked with the kids in his woodshop on projects one or two half days a week, while Cindy helped with hands-on science projects for them and we teamed up to take all four of the kids on field trips one day a week. By the end of the school year, Joshua went to a public school for second grade. He had completed two grades in one year.

Monicqua at her high school graduation reception at Christian Life School. Seated next to her left is Norma Ankerholz, her dad's second wife, and her father Bob.

While we were still living in La Junta, having heard about the Suzuki method of teaching violin to very young children, we began Josh and Sarah's musical path. Our old friend Rodger Young, himself a clarinet soloist in the Army Band, pointed us to Dr. Su-

Sarah on her third birthday morning with Josh looking on. The curtains on the window were ones I made on a treadle machine while we were living at Stone Mountain.

zuki's book, *Nurtured by Love*. After reading it, Rube and I were convinced that this would be the way to introduce Joshua and Sarah to music.

Rodger went on to set up his own music studio and instrument repair shop in the D. C. area. They came out to visit us with their younger daughter in 2009. She plays violin.

By the time Joshua was four, just after moving to Santa Fe, we found a teacher there who used the Suzuki method. We were fortunate that the classes were held at the local junior college. Being group sessions, we were able to afford to start Josh then. By the time he was five he was involved in yearly recitals as well as performing at special events. This progam required that the parents attend each weekly class and practice every day with the students. Rube got Joshua up before breakfast each day for their practice sessions.

Rodger Young, the friend who inspired us to begin violin lessons for the kids.

Rodger, Darlene and daughter with me and Rube for a rare visit in our home in Elk Grove, CA, 2009.

As soon as Sarah was two, she also joined the violin classes. I became the main one to attend her classes and practice with her daily. Her first "instrument" was a cigar box attached to a ruler. The students were taught respect for the instrument before being allowed to have the real thing.

Even though this method does not advocate teaching the children to read music when they begin, they were taught a lot of music theory. Sarah's first "recital" was about making the movements of a pendulum clock which was about rhythm.

Once Sarah graduated to a real violin from the cigar box, she played the 1/16th size violin. Rube and I both worked with her. A favorite picture is of Rube trying to get his fingers on the strings of her little violin.

It's hard to characterize our

lives during this time, but suffice it to say, lessons continued, but our other life events were intertwined. We had a number of good friends in Santa Fe. Some of the closest, in addition to the Resniks and the Shishkoffs, were the Northways. Terry and Sheilah were attenders at Christian Life Church while we were there.

Our children were close. They had an older boy, Michael, and their second child, Rachel, was born one day before I had Sarah. Of course, we were still living in Colorado, knew the Northways as fellow hippies who had come to the Lord, but had no close association until we moved to Santa Fe. When we realized our girls were a day apart, it began a tradition of sharing their birthday parties for many years.

As I mentioned, I had always wanted to name a daughter after my special aunt, Becky. One day I was in the parking lote of Christian Life and encountered Terry Northway going up the long outside staircase to the church offices. I knew Sheilah should be delivering their younger daughter any minute. I asked him and he responded that she was born. I then asked, "What did you name her? Rebecca Marie?" He turned, startled, and replied, "Yes, how did you know?"

I really don't know, but I had a flash that they had named her that. I had never shared with them my desire to use the name Rebecca. My middle name of Marie held a lot of significance

Five-year-old Joshua deep in concentration playing his violin.

Sarah and I performing the pendulum swing at the recital.

Josh on the same recital stage as a young violinist at about seven years old, circa 1982.

Rube playing Sarah's first violin from when she was three years old. Background pictures to the right show Sarah at her third birthday party above and below, Rube with Jacob at Rube's mother's house a few months before I met them.

Rachel Northway and our Sarah celebrating their fourth birthdays with Strawberry Shortcake cakes made by their mothers, Sheilah and me. Note the matching dresses! We are in the Northways' dining room.

for me as well. As a child I used Marie like a surname for all of my dolls: Sylvia Marie, Rebecca Marie etc. I am glad both names finally found a place since I was not planning to have any more children.

As of this writing, I have three granddaughters who bear Marie as their middle names: Sarah Annemarie Busch, Hannah Marie Whitley, Ava Marie Rubinstein.

Life went on. We continued Josh and Sarah's violin lessons, recitals and other performances throughout their lives into their high school years. During the early years while we were still in Santa Fe, their music school was invited to perform in the rotunda of the New Mexico State Capitol.

When Joshua was ten, he and a group of Suzuki students got the opportunity to tour in Mexico. He was staying in the home of state officials in Chihuahua on his tenth birthday. They tried to make him a German chocolate cake which was his favorite. That was an unknown dessert in their culture, but they tried. It was a great opportunity, but I could tell it was hard for Josh to be so far away from home.

Joshua (center) playing at the NM State Capitol.

We also had access to a music camp through our teacher's acquaintances. Each fall we drove to the mountains by Santa Fe to Hummingbird Music Camp. The young musicians all lived in two large, separate boys' and girls' dormitories. Rube and I were two of the rare parents who got to attend the camp with our kids because we supervised all the kids in their dorms. It was the only way we could afford to have them attend, but it was a rare treat for us to be around all the expert teachers the camp brought on board for the weekend.

It is hard to imagine now how we were able to keep the children participating in their mu-

Josh, second from left, with his Suzuki touring group when he was ten.

sic, athletics and school activities while our lives were so busy with running a private school. During this same time period I was asked by the Pastor/Superintendent of Christian Life School to troubleshoot the new computer for the school office. During that time we worked at automating the school records. Rube, who was already a computer geek, found it difficult to keep from peeking over my shoulder. We felt we were able to deliver a quality education at this school and were in it for the long haul.

There were other dynamics in the church, however, that soon impacted our livelihood and our spirits. In the spring of the same year, the pastor of the church, who was also the Superintendent of this Christian school, began having trust issues. One of his key leaders seemed disloyal on a matter I won't go into. Unfortunately the pastor got a bit paranoid of everyone in leadership, fearing a takeover. He didn't know Rube very well, or he would have known that being disloyal was the furthest thing from his mind.

It didn't help that Rube had contracted walking pneumonia that spring and was having a difficult time fulfilling his principal duties. The pastor asked Rube and I to leave at the end of the school year, which we did. The parents of our students and the church members were told Rube was too sick to continue, nothing else.

To the pastor's credit, however, a year later this man went all over town apologizing, stopping at all the homes of persons he felt he offended during his siege of fear. Rube and I appreciated finally being vindicated, but it did not immediately heal the damage the dismissal caused.

"Pen" State

Being let go at Christian Life began a difficult time especially for Rube as he was devastated by the distrust. He applied to teach at the Penitentiary of New Mexico (PNM) and was accepted that fall to be in charge of the Basic Education Program, primarily helping inmates secure high school diplomas. He was hired to come in just after the horrible 1980 riot. One of his more danger-

ous assignments was to teach on Death Row. Rube said he did not feel intimidated, but rather saw it as an opportunity to share the gospel with those needy souls.

During Rube's six-year teaching stint at PNM—1981-1987—the most memorable thing that happened was that during lockdowns – which happened on occasion – he was reassigned to milk cows, which he loved, given his recent farm background.

Sarah (center) at a performance at Hummingbird Music Camp. Her violin teacher's daughter, Maddie, is far left.

Fortunately, nothing as bad as the previous riot ever occurred while he was working there; however, there were many occasions when rumors reached a point that protective measures were taken.

This same year, I too was hired to teach at PNM, albeit through a business college that brought its program to the inmates. While both of us were teaching there, we were pursuing graduate degrees at UNM, he in educational adminis-tration and I in educating special students with behavior problems.

I focused my Masters thesis on a study of inmates' pre-prison—high school—inappropriate behavior interventions. My finding was that at that time almost none of these persons had been identified nor helped by special education measures while they were still in school, which I hypothesized might have cir-cumvented their acting out to the extreme of being incarcerated.

I experienced several instances while working at the prison when my safety was jeopardized. One of these times, just as I arrived at work one morning, I was met by officials at the entrance and told there was credible intel that a woman hostage was going to be taken. At this time, there was the main facility and an adjacent women's facility. The only place the male and female inmates could see each other and interact was in the education programs.

The officials didn't know if the intent was to take a female teacher, inmate or guard. They left it up to me whether to teach that day. I weighed it carefully but believed we could not cower every time a threat was made. The reality of working in a penitentiary is that threats are constantly in the air.

I agreed with their offer to have guards take me around to the educational wing via the lawn without having to go through the cell block. Most of the class-es were in trailers that were added outside the education wing after the recent riot. My class that day, however, was in the block itself.

I was escorted in through the back entrance, my students were released to come to class and then I locked that door. It wouldn't have stopped anyone, but it might give those of us inside a little time to react. Yes, I was locking myself up with inmates. I believed I had a good rapport with my students and was safe. For whatever reason, nothing out of the ordinary happened that day.

I did, however, often find myself having to be firm with my incarcerated scholars. Many of them were in for murder, but I took authority as needed. A couple of my accounting students argued with me on a Friday about not want-ing to take their books back to their cells, which I insisted they needed to do to be ready for a test on Monday.

These guys were both in for murder—one for killing his best friend while high on drugs and the other for cold blooded murder. I don't know whatever possessed me to insist, but I did. After the rest of the class left, these two lit-erally got in my face before leaving—there were no guards in the classrooms—accusing me of getting a double paycheck for being a teacher and a guard. I stood my ground. They were pretty unhappy when they left the room with their textbooks.

It seems that my two students had planned a prison break for after class that day. They hid under the classroom trailers—as evidenced by their textbooks found there—before climbing under one fence and then over another one as soon as it was dark.

They were caught at someone's home in Santa Fe eating pizza and came back peaceably. They lost the privilege of going to classes, so I did not see them again. I got some feedback, however, from others in the class.

My students razzed me that I assisted the escape. Since we were learning about prepositions, I was using my usual metaphor, that you can find prepositions as they are related to a fence: *over* the fence, *under* the fence, *through* the fence, *to* the fence, etc. The class told me those escapees just followed my teaching. Ha, ha...

During all the time I was teaching at the state penitentiary I was taking classes from UNM in Albuquerque toward a Masters degree in teaching students with behavior disorders. I was allowed by the administration at the pen to do my masters thesis research in the "jackets" of the inmates. I was looking to see if there were a "significant" number of them who would have qualified for the current special education category of Behavior Disorders, and might have benefitted from special education intervention, possibly keeping them from committing the crimes for which they had become incarcerated.

It was very illuminating. I am not remembering the actual percentage of inmates who might have been helped by such intervention while they were still minors, but it was significant. I discussed my project with the inmates in my classes. When I completed the degree in 1983, my inmates sent me with their blessings to teach at Santa Fe High School. Their sentiment was basically, "Go see if you can catch any of them so they don't end up here!" It was a tearful parting.

Family Detour

In about 1982, we realized we needed to move from the single-wide trailer we purchased as we did not have enough room for the kids. We had downsized to this trailer from our double-wide one when we realized it was not just too large to move to property, but also it was not constructed well enough to survive such a move intact.

Monicqua was living with friends and was fully moved out of our house soon after graduating, but with Jacob moving in, we still needed more room. Sometime after Monicqua left, we sold the trailer and rented a four-bedroom, two-bath home in a neighborhood in the same part of Santa Fe where Jacob, Sarah and Joshua each had a bedroom.

While we were still in the rented house, in 1983, we experienced the second and final visit from Rube's father, Herbert, who was living in East Lansing, Michigan, with his second family: wife June, son Kevin and daughter Kathleen. He came to celebrate Rube's getting his Masters in Educational Administration from UNM. At the same time as Rube was getting his MA, Josh and Sarah had their violin recital, which Grandad Herb Rubinstein was able to attend.

During Herb's couple of weeks' stay he was having to do dialysis on himself. It was not his kidneys, per se, that he succumbed to, but it was his heart just a few years later. He had a heart attack in the recovery room after having surgery to restore blood flow to his legs.

Herb worked most of his career in hospital administration, but when he was about 60, he decided to go to nursing school. Herb's father was a medical doctor and Herb had intended to follow in his footsteps. As a young man in premed classes at Berkeley, Herb and his lab partner and soon-to-be wife Marjorie got waylaid by left wing politics and both dropped out of school. Neither went into the field of medicine as both intended.

Herb was never reconciled to not being a medical practitioner, even though he had become a hospital administrator after earning a Masters Degree in the area from Yale University. By becoming a nurse, he was at last in hands-on medicine. He worked as a nurse for several years before he died.

The same spring I completed my Masters in Educating Students with Behavior Disorders, also from UNM. This degree gave me the opportunity to return to

L-R: Jacob, Joshua, Grandpa Herb, Rube and Sarah.

teach in a high school. I had found it difficult to secure an English teaching position in Santa Fe. I often expressed it that English teachers were a dime a dozen at that time. I was hired as a Special Education teacher at Santa Fe High's Technical School. I continued in this subject for a couple of years, but it was stressful for me and my family that I was constantly interacting with overwrought teenagers. I was successful at helping these students incrementally become part of mainstream education, but it was very intense. When an English teaching spot opened up, I jumped at it.

Getting my MA in Special Educaton from UNM with friend Russ receiving his MA in Counseling.

The Promised Land

Our mobile home on our ten-acre property twenty miles outside Santa Fe, NM.

Jacob in his karate uniform, Rube, Joshua, me and Sarah proud of being on the land. We are posing in front of the shed that just about blew away as we were assembling it. You can see how young our "helper" children were at the time.

The family in Santa Fe before attending a music concert.

About 1983, we finally were able to buy a ten-acre piece of land where we hoped to build a home. It was located about 20 miles outside of Santa Fe. We purchased a well-constructed single-wide mobile home from our friend Shelley Finkelstein, who was moving out of it to marry our friend Bob Devore.

We had to develop the property. There was electricity to the property line, but we brought it onto the land, dug a well and put in a septic. This all sounds so easy to say now, but each of these activities was very complex, expensive, time-consuming and exhausting. We also planted a grove of olive trees. Building a tool shed looked easier than it was. The day we put it up there were high winds. Mostly all of us were needed to hold the structure against the wind while Rube put it together. The kids were young, but enthusiastic helpers.

We settled in with the three kids—Jacob, Joshua and Sarah. Even though it was hard to have to drive so far to any civilization, we felt we were closer to our dream of building an adobe on land. It was more difficult to continue the kids' violin lessons, Sarah's ballet, Jacob's karate and Josh's baseball living now 20 miles ouside of Santa Fe, but we made it happen. We made sure we included excursions to cultural events such as local symphony performances.

We had Sarah in ballet during some of that time. She was a mouse in the Nutcracker one year. We were not impressed with the tone of the ballet she was learning other than the classical performances. They seemed a bit provocative. She was not happy, but we stopped her lessons.

Josh loved playing baseball every year. As a family we spent many an hour watching him practice and play games. It wasn't Sarah's favorite thing but she did enjoy playing with the siblings of the other players while her brother played ball.

We did, however, have a big mishap one Spring. I had just picked her up from ballet and met Rube and Josh at the ball field. She was in her leotard, but had on tennis shoes, not her bal-let slippers. She decided she would do a *grand jete* over the heavy chains that enclosed the ball field. Her tennis shoe did not clear the chain. That was an ER visit where she received stitches for having bitten through her lip.

Josh and Sarah definite-ly loved the wide-open space of our new property. On one side, there was a ranch that ran the entire 20 miles to Santa Fe. When it snowed each winter we were there, the kids went sled-ding on the hills on that ranch. They were often joined by their new friends and neighbors who lived on the adjacent 40 acres, Dominick and Kinberly Ruvolo.

During this time, we helped another Santa Fe congregation, Capital Christian Church (CCC), begin a school. Rube headed up their Finance Committtee for the new school while I worked with the Curriculum Committee. This school was going to be more traditional, but would be using Christian textbooks. CCC also became our place of worship. This church was led by Pastor Ed Viser and was where most of our

Josh on the very successful Sargents team.

Josh's 7th-8th grade combination class at CCC. He is the tallest in back, flanked on left with Principal Dar-lene Cole and his teacher Ms. Bea Johnson to the right.

longtime friends attended.

About this time, Jacob expressed that the property was too isolated for him. Also there was a lot of physical labor we all performed to make the place fully functional. He was resistant to taking on his share of the duties.

Jacob and I remember the final time he ran away differently. I remembered it being on Halloween, that he did not take the school bus home, but instead had previously taken whatever money he found at our house to buy a bus ticket for California. I remember the occasion because our family had made cookies and were looking forward to decorating them after school so we could attend our neighbors—the Ruvolo family's—party that evening. Once again we abandoned everything to look for Jacob.

Jacob and Monicqua think the time Jacob actually left was in the spring of that school year, which could have been true. Each time Jacob left without our knowledge, it was traumatic as the whole family dropped everything, even long-planned activities, to go look for him. We were never successful at getting at why he was so unhappy. We put him in counseling at Capital Christian. Mostly he seemed disturbed that his mother and father were no longer together.

In any event, Jacob did not finish ninth grade in Santa Fe with us. He took a bus and landed at his maternal grandparents, and finally at his Uncle Mike and Aunt Patsy's house in Truckee, California. It was only after this we were told by his mother that Jacob had run away from her and Jeffrey many times which made them decide he was to come to live with us. They did not take him back in.

There were many adventures while living on this property. One of the scariest was when there was a brush fire. Sarah was sick and I had a bad back ache, so I stayed home from work with her. I became aware of the smell of smoke. Upon going outside to look, I saw a fire spreading across some of the neighbors' property about 40 acres away from us. The wind was whipping the fire through the brush causing it to spread. Several homes were in danger, including our own.

I grabbed some old Levi's and drove myself and Sarah closer to the fire line. Having her stay in the car away from the fire, I helped sling wet pants on the fast moving flames. It was grueling, back breaking work. Most of our neighbors were involved in the fire fight. We gradually got the flames put out.

Joshua, Rube and my Daddy,
who was wearing a "#1 Dad!" badge.

We were told that a neighbor's welding caused a spark that started the fire. Due to high winds that day, fire equipment was working elsewhere so it was good that there were sufficient neighbors at home to snuff out our fire.

In the lull—oh, I jest—between such excitement, we continued to drive from Santa Fe to southern New Mexico and into Texas as far as Kermit to visit my family every summer. My daddy was the one living in Kermit with his wife, Daphne. On one such visit, we snapped a picture of three generations of "my guys."

Mother was still living in Hobbs, New Mexico. As indicated, her house was the hub for our sibling get-togethers. Most of that time Elaine was living in Colorado, where she still resides. Anita has lived in the Midland-Odessa, Texas area all her adult life. Dwayne was a Border Patrolman in southern New Mexico and the two youngest, Linda Kay and Michael have also stayed in the surrounding Hobbs area.

Both Rube and I being teachers, we took advantage of the two-week break each winter to visit Rube's family in California. His mother and stepfather were still living in San Jose for most of our visits. Jacob would come over from where he was living with either his mom or his uncle to visit. On this occasion in about 1988, Jacob was sporting a perm that made him look like a young Bob Dylan.

Animal Lovers

We brought to the land with us the two Springer Spaniels—Sadie and Princess—we had purchased while renting the house. We decided to breed them for puppies so located a male with a good hunting blood line in California—Duke—and flew him into Albuquerque, our closest major airport. We bred both our females, built a dog kennel and began having puppies a couple of times a year.

In about 1988, when we had been on the property for five years and Rube and I were still teaching at SF Tech, we learned from a colleague that she was selling a horse. At that time Sarah was needing something. She seemed to be struggling, not in her schoolwork, but in general. She got very excited at the possibility of having a horse.

We negotiated with our friend, who lived on a section of land—one square mile or 640 acres—and owned seven horses. She was selling her three-year-old Palomino mare, which was bred as a cutting horse. We didn't plan to have cattle needing to be cut from a herd, but were excited at how smart the horse was.

Amarilla Roseburn "Marilla" joined our merry band. The family built a corral for our new addition. The ten acres was fully fenced but lacked a gate at the road coming on the property, plus some of the fencing was of questionable strength. Marilla was never let out of the corral unless we were working with

At Grandma Boehm's house:
Back: Jacob, Grandma Marge, Joshua, Rube,
Grandpa Jeff. Front: Rube's sister Jo's boys, James
and Sean Thorpe, and Sarah far right.

her. Sarah was especially enamored with Marilla, as with the dogs and puppies. She declared at the grand old age of eight that she was going to be a veterinarian when she grew up.

I don't know why we didn't put up a gate—priorities, I guess, but also we could not be sure of the state of any of the fencing that separated us from our two neighbors and the big ranch. Fence mending was a huge project, certainly not on our radar.

By that time we owned our horse, four Springer Spaniels – Duke, Junior, Sadie and Princess – and a part Persian cat named Cyrus D Smudge. With eleven-year-old Sarah's love for critters, we also had a tarantula living in a terrarium in her bedroom. Evidently our property was on their migratory path and this one lost a leg and couldn't keep up. Sarah eventually turned it loose outside to hopefully rejoin its cluster.

Joshua loved our dogs, but was intimidated by the horse, which anyone should be. We were very ignorant about the needs of horses, but operated on a theory that teenager Josh should be able to hop on Marilla and ride her around the property to get the "kinks" out. We later realized there is a real way to do this, called lunging which is done safely from the ground, not on the critter's back!

We were pretty nuts to not realize Josh would get thrown and how dangerous that was. Marilla got spooked at most anything, and we didn't know yet how to desensitize her. The worst was once when she encountered a rattlesnake, many of which were all over our property. Josh is still not keen about getting on a horse. Both Sarah and Josh can tell stories of Marilla taking them to one of the many cactus plants on the property, stopping short, and dumping them onto the thorns. Ouch!

Rube continued teaching at the penitentiary for four more years before joining me at Santa Fe Tech in the fall of 1987. His second year at SF Tech, he and I joined with a drafting teacher to create some interdisciplinary courses there that combined Rube's computer skills, my English and journalism, and a colleague's drafting and graphic design abilities. We produced a creative writing magazine, newspapers, yearbooks and other publishing projects with our students. It was this experience that prepared us for employment on the next part of our journey, which would take us out of state.

Our Palomino mare Marilla in the corral we built on the Santa Fe property circa 1988. This was the beautiful way the sun would often make the land appear at dusk.

The last summer before we moved, I was hired to work in the JTPA program through one of my bosses at Santa Fe Tech. I am not remembering what the acronym exactly stood for but the thrust was to advance marketable technology skills of young people of the local Pueblo Native Americans. This entailed traveling to several of the farflung villages weekly to deliver paychecks to the students of our program. Many of these young people were being paid to learn office skills so that they could hopefully secure gainful employment. I especially remember the generosity of the Santo Domingo Pueblo people on my visits.

Normally I would not have been worried leaving teenage Josh and eleven-year-old Sarah at home on our land to go off to do this job, but that summer there was a recent prison break at the State Penitentiary, which was just down our county road, and the inmates were still at large in our "neighborhood." Josh and Sarah were not pleased, but they went with me for those JTPA visits that summer. In my view, what our kids lost in free time, they more than made up for in cultural awareness of the local Native peoples.

Josh once asked why we bought him such large eyeglass frames when he was a kid. We told him that it was the style. I find it personally funny that Josh chose equally large frames for Eitan, as well as all of his kids who wear glasses.

Joshua at 12 when he began "lunging" Marilla. I wanted to include this specific picture so Josh's son Eitan David realizes how much he favors his dad. Eitan is 12 now.

Eitan - Josh's mini me - also at 12 years old.

Rube Comes Home

While we were teaching and raising the children, we were reconnecting with Eitan's family in Santa Fe and Russ's in Albuquerque. They all had begun to realize they could stay Jewish and worship the Jewish Messiah, Jesus. Rube was especially intrigued since he was never able to adjust to the rhythm of worshipping on Sunday. We began meeting in Eitan and Connie's home with others like-minded.

Not long after establishing this meeting, Eitan was called to Maryland to run a Messianic Believers' school. It was sad, but we knew that was what Eitan wanted. We helped them pack up their two kids and their belongings for the long trip. They still owned an old wood cook stove, a remnant of their hippie days, that I admired. I traded them for it by painting the interior of their house after they moved.

I was torn, trying to understand why it was so important for Rube to worship as a Jew. Frankly, I was raised in churches where the assumption was that the Jews, having blown their relationship with God, lost their "chosenness." The teaching was that the "church" took the place of the Jews and all the scriptures directed to Jews now belong to Christians. I needed answers.

I was thrust into studying my Bible. It was shocking to realize how "well-meaning" Christians blinded us all to the Jewish foundations of the Bible. Jesus was a Jew! Now I became like a second class citizen, which is where most Christians relegated Jews since the death of Jesus. This was the point at which I felt the Lord spoke to me that my house could not be divided. I was to follow Rube in his journey back to his Jewish roots, which was also the beginning of the Christian faith.

Rube and I both felt that God fulfilled the Ruth calling in me that day. I wasn't sure what all that meant, and all these years later, I am still working it out. I have studied with Rube and on my own. Our home is a Messianic Jewish home. Wherever the road took me, I knew I was in.

Rube's desire to worship in a Jewish style was intensified after we attended the yearly conference of the Union of Messianic Jewish Congregations (UMJC) the summer of 1988. At this event, Rube and I both were impressed – while each was in a separate break-out session – that we were to start attending Adat Yeshua, our old friend Russ's Messianic congregation in Albuquerque.

We loved attending CCC, where we were both singing and playing instruments on the worship team, and this was where we helped start a Christian school where both Sarah and Joshua attended. The only issue was that Rube yearned to worship the Jewish Messiah—Jesus or Yeshua, his Hebrew name—since having come to faith in Him back in 1974.

We went to our then-pastor of CCC, Ed Viser, and shared that we felt called to leave the church to attend a Messianic congregation. His reaction was that he couldn't understand why a Jew needed to worship Jesus in a Jewish setting, but that he trusted us in the Lord. He allowed us to share with the congregation on a Sunday evening. We were released to attend Adat Yeshua.

The transition was not without its bumps. The kids still at home—Joshua 12 and Sarah 8—were SURE we were not supposed to change our place of worship! They had built up great friendships, especially as they were also attending the church's school. Most of their friends were at CCC. Josh and Sarah were devastated until they started reconnecting with our friends' children at the Messianic congregation in Albuquerque.

Many of the long-time "hippie" buddies in summer 1988
at the Northway home in Santa Fe, NM: (front) Terry Northway, Eitan Shishkoff.
(back) Richard "Rube" Rubinstein, Don Aaker, Ed Berman, Russ Resnik.

Some of their wives at the same time. Jane Resnik, me,
Sheilah Northway, Debbie Aaker. Connie Shishkoff was taking the picture.

Once we made the move to Adat Yeshua, it seemed there was an explosion of joy in Rube. So many of our old hippie-turned Believer friends were worshipping here. We were put on the Adat Yeshua Worship Team so also drove over in the middle of the week for practice sessions. Josh was part of the team playing his violin. Sarah would often wander around in the back of the sanctuary when we were practicing, playing her own violin having picked up the music by ear. We all were transitioning. Rube was finally at home.

Under the umbrella of Adat Yeshua, we later worked with another Jewish Believing couple in Santa Fe—Michael and Ann Rothman—and their two girls to start a Messianic work there. As it happened, we did not stay in New Mexico long enough to see this ministry off the ground.

Five of the sons: Luke and Danny Resnik, David Shishkoff, Michael Northway, Joshua Rubinstein.

California
Rays

Rumblings of Change

As much as we loved being out on the land, it became obvious that we were never going to be able to build the adobe house we yearned for. First, we were very underpaid as teachers in New Mexico—at that time this state was 48th in the nation for how low their teachers' salaries were—so we could not afford to build.

Second, we were too busy with teaching, taking the kids to their various lessons and athletic competitions, while driving such long distances to work and twice a week to Albuquerque to worship that we had no energy for doing the house-building labor ourselves. On several occasions we optimistically worked at making adobe bricks only to see them wash away when the rains came.

We had many reasons to want to move back to California. Josh and Sarah both wanted to attend California colleges. Also, both Monicqua and Jacob by this time were firmly entrenched in California, albeit Jacob was in the northern part of the state and Monicqua, the southern. We were also convinced we needed to be closer to Rube's family, few of whom knew the Lord, which was a growing concern for us.

In the spring of 1989, Rube and I attended a job fair at the University of New Mexico in Albuquerque and were able to both get offers to teach at Florin High School (FHS) in Elk Grove, a school district just south of Sacramento, California.

FHS was especially interested in Rube's technology experience and skills. At that time he was working out of the NM governor's office helping bring computers to schools across the state. Rube was very knowledgeable about setting up technology. This new school was to have a TV studio and needed Rube to develop it. We presented ourselves as a package deal.

When we discussed this offer with our current principal, Dr. Paul, she asked if we would be willing to delay leaving by one year so we could implement the new interdisciplinary courses we just developed. We stayed until the end of the 1989-1990 school year.

The school district in Elk Grove, California offered us jobs to teach the first year of FHS, which would have been 1989-1990. Florin's principal, Bill Huyett, was willing to wait for us to join them in its second year so we could fulfill Dr. Paul's requests for us to leave after starting the courses we helped create.

One of the hardest things to leave, however, was our Messianic synagogue. We researched and there was not one anywhere in the greater Sacramento area. What we didn't know, but soon learned, was that there was a small group of Jewish Believers meeting weekly to experience the more Jewish aspects of their faith in their Messiah. Julia Schley, the sister of pianist-composer, Alyosha Ryabinov, whom we knew through the Union of Messianic Jewish Congregations (UMJC), was our contact for this group.

Finally, we rented out our SF property, loaded up what belongings we thought we needed and started the journey to California. We moved in August of 1990, just in time to get settled before the fall semester began. Sarah was beginning seventh grade and was enrolled to attend our neighborhood Galt Middle School. Josh was a sophomore and came to FHS with us.

California Dreamin'

Grapes of Wrath travelers had nothing on us. By the time we moved, we were quite a caravan. Rube drove most of our belongings in the longest U-Haul trailer, with Marilla in a horse trailer in tow. Josh, having just received his driver's license at 15, drove our old BMW. I followed in an Isuzu Trooper towing a flatbed trailer with much of our accumulated equipment and tools. We tried to keep the cat and dogs partially sedated to help them travel. By this time Sarah was the only real passenger and we shared her by having her shift from vehicle to vehicle when we took rest stops. She was great at keeping us awake.

We necessarily made many stops to accommodate the animal, as well as the human, critters before we reached our destination. We found pet-friendly mo-

tels where we parked our horse trailer when we needed to rest. The trip took three full days. The house we bought was located ten miles south of Elk Grove in Galt. The night we pulled off Highway 99 at the Simmerhorn exit, the moon was HUGE and FULL. What a welcome.

We were so excited until we found that we did not have the key to our new house. We called the realtor. While we were waiting for the keys, we drove the horse trailer into the half-acre pasture that made up the back section of our new property and turned Marilla out. She immediately ran to the fence where there were two neighbor horses and began to spin around. Free at last!

This could be Cyrus D Smudge (the part Persian cat) with one of the abandoned kittens we raised and found homes for. Cyrus loved being outdoors, which led to his untimely demise. We never knew if it was coyotes or even owls. This might be the other white cat – named Chumley – Sarah got from her friend Karin.

Marilla's exhilaration at having arrived was not any greater than ours. To pick up and leave, traveling a couple of thousand miles, was exhausting but thrilling. This was a new chapter in all

Galt property where we lived for 15 years.

our lives.

Our rhythm of life in Galt was only partially rural. The front part of our acre provided space for an expansive lawn and a comfortable 3-bedroom, 2-bath house with a large swimming pool enclosed in the fenced-in backyard. Our pool was frequently the site of baptisms.

Behind the pool was what had been at one time a three-car garage, probably for farming equipment. When we purchased the property, this garage had already been converted to two-thirds workshop and one-third "mother-in-law" quarters with a bedroom and bathroom. What was left of our pared-down tools and equipment found ample space in the workshop. When we moved into this house, Josh was 15 and Sarah almost 12.

Our backyard pool with Rabbi Rube baptizing several congregants, under the watchful eye of our dog Sadie.

Our formal family picture after moving to Galt in 1990.

Josh and Sarah had always loved winter sports, for which we had to drive a bit north of our home in Galt. Rube and I preferred to do cross country skiing. We took family trips to the mountains where we did our cross country and Josh and Sarah did downhill skiing.

From our home base in Galt, we made even more trips to see Rube's parents in the San Francisco Bay area while visiting my parents in Texas and New Mexico at least once a year. By then Rube's mother and stepfather had moved from San Jose to Santa Rosa. We visited the Boehms just after we completed our move to California.

Beginning Beth Yeshua

Even before we got settled in Galt, we were concerned about where we would worship. Believing as we did that neither the traditional church nor the traditional synagogue was the right fit, we were concerned that we had no options in the Sacramento area. One day, within two weeks of our arrival in California, our UMJC friend Jody Ryabinov, wife of Aly-osha, called to remind us that her sister-in-law Julia was close by and that she was recently widowed with four small children.

When we contacted Julia we learned that she was part of a group of Jews and mixed Jewish-Gentile married couples who were believers that Jesus—or Yesh-ua, his Hebrew name—is the promised Jewish Messiah. This is the way we were worshipping in New Mexico. We began to meet with this group on Friday eve-nings in Sacramento.

At first it seemed that we were all like-minded. In short order those of us who had already been part of a Messianic Synagogue in other states—which included Julia who was formerly from Adat Hatikvah Messianic Synagogue in Chicago—were anxious to have our own congregation. When we began the planning, it became obvious that our group was split between those wanting a con-gregation and those wanting to continue this weekly Messian-ic fellowship with their actu-al allegiance still to the varied churches they attended. We even had a large Christian church in Sacramento offer to take us in as a paraministry under them during this time. We have nev-er believed we should be under a church, but a congregation in our own right.

For those of us who had all come from Messianic congre-gations, the desire for a true Messianic work of our own was very strong. We began orga-nizing it with mixed blessings from our small band of Messi-anic Believers. We first began meeting in Julia's den. We real-ized we needed a place where we felt comfortable for strangers to also attend. We were reluctant to subject Julia and her four small children to whoever might come through the door.

Rube revealed—even for the

Sarah and Josh on one of our skiing trips.

1990 Santa Rosa visit with the Boehms. L–R front: cousins Sean and James Thorpe. Back: Sarah, Jacob, Joshua, me, Marjorie and Jeff Boehm. Our 1987 Isuzu Trooper is parked at the curb.

first time to me—that he believed he was called to lead the group. The key people wanting us to form a ministry agreed with Rube. That summer of 1991, he went to an international Union of Messianic Jewish Congregations (UMJC) conference to meet with the Planters Committee. He was put in place as the spiritual leader of the new congregation. This was the same oversight organization under which our long-time friends Russ and Eitan—also hippies turned Messianics—were leading congregations and other ministries.

We had been attending the yearly UMJC conferences since before founding Beth Yeshua under their umbrella. We have continued attending these conferences each summer.

We found a community-center type facility to hold our meetings and began conducting services. It was a bit rocky as there was some concern by a couple of people about our direction and who should be our leader. When the dust settled, Beth Yeshua—House of Jesus—was born. Rube always believed this name was given by the Lord.

A visit we made seven years later to see the Boehms in 1997. Our son Joshua, Rube's brother Eric, and my daughter Monicqua's family were also there. Sarah would have been in college at the University of California Davis (UCD). Rube was taking the picture. Back Row L-R: Joshua, Eric Boehm, me, Rube, Ryan, Aaron and Monicqua with Grandma Marjorie and Sarah Annemarie in the front.

The work of planting a congregation began in earnest. With Rube and I still teaching full time at FHS, it was all a juggle. Not only were we planting the synagogue, but Rube was taking Yeshiva courses toward *Smicha*—ordination as a Rabbi. He was always an avid reader, but now his focus was split between computers and ministry within Messianic Judaism.

Rabbi Dr. Michael Schiffman directed him through the coursework, which was daunting given the circumstances. Rube was a full-time high school teacher of computers and mathematics while also serving as the school's Technology Coordinator. If that were not enough, he and I were the key planters of Beth Yeshua during the same time period. Rube was taking the prescribed yeshiva courses primarily offered at the summer

Rube and I at one of the yearly UMJC conferences we attended.

conferences.

When he returned from the conferences, he was plunged head first into the school year beginning and the continuing ministry of the congregation. He worked on his coursework as best he could, but by the time he had taken all the required courses for *Smicha*, he was missing many papers from several classes. His mentor, and our dear friend, Rabbi Schiffman, graciously worked with Rube to complete all the missing assignments.

Rube studied for thirteen years before receiving Smicha as a Messianic Rabbi. He is being recognized at the UMJC Conference in 2003. Rabbi Schiffman is facing him, praying for him.

At this time we had moved our new congregation to rent from Landpark Church in south Sacramento. We didn't feel we had as much use of this facility as we needed, and we also were concerned that we needed to be in a more central location in Sacramento.

We asked Capitol Foursquare Church on O Street in midtown Sacramento if we could rent from them. They had a new, young man leading their church – Pastor Mark – who was not sure what we were about but felt that his denomination was compatible with Messianic Believers.

Early Beth Yeshua at Landpark Church with our family: Aaron, Monicqua and baby Sarah Annemarie, me, Sarah, Rabbi Rube and Joshua. In the foreground is co-founder Julia Schley's younger son, Dan.

I had been studying along with Rube and attended some of the same courses. He often recommended books for me to read that were part of his ordination program. During that time I was given the opportunity to have a Bat Mitzvah ceremony. At the time I was not sure what it made me, being married to a Rabbi. I was definitely in and helped my husband begin and maintain this

Elders Al Kushner and Rabbi Rube officiating for my Bat Mitzvah Ceremony. I read from the book of Ruth.

ministry.

My husband believed I had fulfilled the Ruth calling and that since I had also studied Hebrew and knew all the prayers that I should have a formal ceremony. He believed that I was Jewish because I was following him in the faith.

We enjoyed the use of this facility until 1996. At that time Rube and I and Elders Al and Patty Kushner took a trip with a local church that was going on a tour to Israel. We were celebrating Sarah's graduation from high school, but all of us had always wanted to visit the Land.

Picture of our worship team when we shared a facility with New Hope in Sacramento. Front at keyboard: co-founder Julia Schley. L to R: Josh on violin, Rosemary, Sarah and me singing, Rube leading on guitar.

When we returned from the journey, our trip hosts, New Hope Church, wanted us to join them in their facility they were renting. They were then located in Sacramento adjacent to the State Fairground.

Early on Rube decided that we were to bring in the Elders' wives to serve with their husbands. The group included all but Nick Hanson of the original founders: Leanne Maddox, Julia Schley and Rube and I. At this time both Leanne and Julia had married. Some years later Rube and the Elders – including the wives – agreed that scriptually Elders should be men. All of the women stepped down.

Earliest Beth Yeshua Elders and wives: Patty and Al Kushner, Leanne and Alan Gold, Rabbi Rube and me, Julia and Richard Blalock.

While we were still using the New Hope facility for our congregation's meetings, Rube took the opportunity to fulfill a lifetime goal of having a Bar Mitzvah ceremony. He had been interrupted from having this event which marked his "coming of age" when he was twelve years old and his parents divorced.

Elders Al Kushner and Alan Gold preside over Rabbi Rube's ceremony. Rube is wearing his father Herb's Bar Mitzvah tallit and kippah. Our Hebrew teacher, Rachel Roubin, and Joshua look on.

We enjoyed our relationship with New Hope for four years

until in 2000 they decided to buy their own facility. The new property was farther east along the Highway 80 corridor. We felt it was too far away from Sacramento proper, so began to look for another facility.

At this time we found some commercial property in the industrial area off Bradshaw Road in Rancho Cordova. It was a lot of work to convert the warehouse space into a sanctuary, classrooms and an office, but that is exactly what we did. We were there for 13 years at which time our Elders believed the Lord wanted us to leave. It had been getting increasingly more expensive and we did not have any way of expanding our use of the larger building to better accomodate our needs for all the parts of our ministry.

Two years prior to this the Elders were beginning to believe we should be moving on, so they wrote the new lease for two years instead of five. In those two years, they did not decide to move until the week before our lease was up. Once they decided, we told everyone to come to the Shahkrit service in work clothes the next Saturday. We asked various ministries to come during that week to pack up their things. After the service, we fed everyone kosher hotdogs and we moved until after dark that night.

We only learned where we would move a couple of days prior, but we had rented a storage unit in midtown Sacramento to accomodate as much of our things as we could. We moved into a facility that served as offices for various ministries, but could also be expanded to create a sanctuary space on Saturdays. We only "owned" our small office there and rented various rooms for our children's ministry and Hebrew classes on a week-by-week basis. We knew it was an interim location but were there for almost three years until our present location became available.

We now share a church property with two churches where we are considered partners and enjoy full use of the facility. Since both of the other congregations meet mostly on Sundays, we have access to not just our own private office every day, but all classrooms, the kitchen and fellowship hall as well as the sanctuary on Saturdays. We have other meetings during the week as needed.

Earlier this year – 2020 – we have found ourselves in the position of not being allowed to hold our meetings as we choose. First, there are strict government regulations in place due to the "pandemic" of Covid 19. We have not been able to use our facility for three months now, going into the fourth.

Now the government is "allowing" faith communities to start up again, but the conditions are very contrary to being

We often took our Holy Day Festival of Sukkot to the state Capitol grounds.

a faith community. We are not only limited as to how many can worship at a time – basically 63 for our size facility – but we have to take temperatures, not sing or pray out loud, as well as keep a six-foot distance between any families.

Secondly, the church who owns the facility we use has decided to go by the Health Officials recommendations which are even stricter than those the government is imposing. Our leadership seriously considered leaving this location, but recently had a heart-to-heart with our landlord's pastors, Dan and Babs of Journey Church. We had given our six-month's notice, but withdrew it.

For several years, even before the Pandemic, we had been livestreaming our Saturday morning shacharit services. We moved the service to Josh's living room when we were forbidden to meet at our sanctuary, but continued for several months before recently getting word from our Governor that faith communities could open up with adherence to health protocols for social distancing and safety.

We had a business meeting and one service back in our sanctuary before we were shut down again. For the time being, we have been livestreaming the Saturday service from the sanctuary and are using zoom for Hebrew classes and other leadership and business meetings.

I should add that this change is not just about the virus, but also about fulfilling our Calling, hence Vision for Beth Yeshua. We have found ourselves for almost 20 of our 30 years ministering primarily to Gentile Believers who want to know more about the Jewish foundation of the Gospel than to our original charge of reaching out to Jewish and intermarried families concerning their prophetic covenantal destiny.

Josh has led this charge. It is not easy. The mantle rests heavy, but he is determined to obey what he believes the Lord is asking of us. The present leadership and congregants have for the most part been very understanding of the need to refresh our original vision. It is fitting that we will be celebrating Beth Yeshua's 30th birthday this year. It's a new season.

Teaching in the Sacramento Area

Rube was teaching math and computers, as well as serving as the Technology Coordinator at FHS. Since this school was only in its second year when we arrived, he was instrumental in making sure we had the latest in technology. Rube established their TV studio from which he personally taught and broadcasted Geometry lessons that were picked up by the local middle schools for its advanced math students.

At FHS I taught various levels of English, but mostly favored teaching freshmen and seniors. I also began their school newspaper named for the school's Mascot—*The Panther Press*. I was the formal journalism teacher for the school as well. I loved being a coach to these kids. Teaching journalism actually helped me develop a similar coaching method in all the classes I was teaching. My main drive was to guide all my students into being well-read and becoming good writers.

During my 17 years at FHS—1990-2007—I collaborated with some amazing educators. Since the school was in its infancy when we arrived, much of the staff was very involved in developing the curriculum. It began with freshmen and sophomores the first year. During my first year there I worked with a team who wrote the curriculum for the senior English program. Again, I was working on interdisciplinary curriculum not too dissimilar to that I helped create at SF Technical High School. At Florin, the English and Social Science teachers made connections between their subjects.

During the summer of 1994 I signed up to teach summer school. For the most part the students were freshmen who had failed freshman English, so were repeating. There were a few students who were taking the summer course so they had more room for electives during their upcoming freshman year.

Some of my "cool" students just hanging, watching folks go by. Of course, I joined them!

I used an "AA" strategy that summer. We began by saying, "Hi, my name is... and I failed freshman English." The effect was that we were not just going to survive the course the second time around, but that we were going to thrive. Since we had four hours together daily, I devoted a portion of their time to publishing a creative writing magazine. They developed all the categories, wrote the pieces, took pictures and drew art. Their title was *TAZ: Teens Against Zummerschool.*

I continued working with creative writing and in 1995 joined with four fellow English teachers and six of my journalism students to begin a creative writing magazine for the school. What began as a combined senior project became a yearly publication.

For several years at FHS I branched out to teach remedial English to non-native speakers

Inside cover of the 1994 summer school creative writing magazine TAZ.

as well as students with major gaps in their ability to use the language using a program called *Language !* I primarily taught freshman and senior English and Journalism most of my time at FHS. My journalism class met for one period in my regular English classroom.

Joshua was a student at FHS from his sophomore year, when we arrived in California. He opted to be part of my Journalism program from his first year. By his senior year he was sharing Editor-in-Chief duties with another student. He was definitely one of my most innovative journalists and especially good at this style of writing, but also took us into the next century with his computer skills. I liked to have two persons share the responsibility, but it was especially important so that I was not perceived as giving my son special honors. The staff would have risen up against me if I had held Josh back. During that time Joshua graduated from Florin High in 1993 and went on to UC Davis.

At Beth Yeshua, we always celebrated our graduating seniors. Rosemary McCrea – Josh's future bride – graduated the same year from El Camino High School. Josh and Rosemary are two of the three graduates being recognized at a Beth Yeshua service.

Josh always lived in Davis during those college years but came home on the weekends for our services, some home cooking and to get fresh laundry. During three of those years, he roomed with several of his high school friends who were also attending UCD, Kenny Baird and Mike Vu. Josh, having married his sweetheart Rosemary just before his senior undergrad year, moved into an apartment. They were both very grateful when he fin-

Inside cover of 1995-1996 Volume I of Roars & Whispers, the voice of Florin High students.

The board reflects our brainstorming for the next upcoming edition, being led by Editors Paul Duval and Dustin McCurdy. The rest of the staff look as if their brains had been fully picked out.

Josh receiving his high school diploma from Principal Dr. Odie Douglas.

Joshua showing his appreciation for his dad when he graduated from UCD in 1997.

Rabbi Rube presenting BY's three graduating high school seniors with gifts. Joshua is far left, fellow graduate from different high schools, Art, and Rosemary McCrea.

ished his degree and they could move back to the Sacramento area. Their love story is in the next chapter.

A unique thing happened while Rube and I were both still teaching at Florin. Once Josh got his degree, he became a long-term sub at FHS. On the first day of classes one of Josh's first period students came up to him to report a problem with his schedule. The student couldn't figure out why he had "Rubinstein" listed as the teacher for three of his classes.

Josh had fun informing him that this kid managed to get Josh's mom for English and his father for math, and Josh for history. Josh reported that a wide-eyed kid ambled back to his desk. I am sure Josh let him know that we all had eyes on him.

Me outside my classroom at Florin High School.

During my last few years at FHS, Josh began to teach there full time as well. He was primarily a social sciences teacher but his experience and education helped him branch out into other areas. Having been in my journalism program as a student, now as a teacher he was able to take over that program from me. With a strong background in electronics, computers and graphic design, he also took on the yearbook production from a grateful colleague.

Another enjoyable aspect of having Josh teaching with us at FHS was that he and I shared some of the same students. Many of my senior Advanced Placement (AP) Literature students were also in his AP Government. At graduation one year some of our students recommended Josh and I to call out their names at graduation. Great fun!

Rube and I kept all the teaching and ministry up for twelve years, at which time Rube retired from teaching in 2002 to lead the

Josh and I in cap and gowns as faculty at a FHS graduation ceremony.

WELCOME
David W. Gordon
Superintendent

LUNCHEON

INTRODUCTIONS

Dr. Odie Douglas

PRESENTATIONS

Cheryl Hollis
President, EGEA

Carl Woodbury
Executive Secretary, EGEA

CLOSING REMARKS

Mary Helen Fitch
*Director for Certificated Personnel
Human Resources*

✳ HONORED RETIREES ✳

Adult Education
Manuel Jauregui - 15 years

Maeola Beitzel Elementary School
Tamara Wilson - 22 years

Harriet Eddy Middle School
Barbara Haase - 15 years

John Ehrhardt Elementary School
Carol Bogovich - 13 years

Elk Grove Elementary School
Esther Gajarian - 39 years
Dawn Jones Brown McVay - 24 years
Thomas Nelson - 32 years

Elk Grove High School
Matthew Fitch - 28 years
Dave Kent - 35 years
Dan Risley - 33 years

Florin Elementary School
Janell Born - 23 years
Sydney-Suzann Ingram - 15 years

Florin High School
Daniel Johannes - 14 years
Robert Lipoli - 20 years
Robert River - 33 years
Richard Rubinstein - 13 years
Sue Thomas - 25 years

Florin High School/James Rutter MS
Sue Gage - 32 years

Isabelle Jackson Elementary School
Karen Norberg - 37 years

Joseph Kerr Middle School
Dianne Cadwallader - 27 years
Howard Jacobson - 32 years
Shirley Peters - 22 years
Ron Schaan - 35 years

Anna Kirchgater Elementary School
Yvonne Del Biaggio - 11 years

Charles Mack Elementary School
Orene Dunzweiler - 22 years
Peggi Gossett - 35 years

Florence Markofer Elementary School
Kay Moreau - 13 years

Prairie Elementary School
Nancy Myers - 19 years
Maxwella Smith - 18 years

*Rube's retirement luncheon for
Elk Grove School District, Florin High.*

*My "school" picture for the
last year I taught. I was 63.*

*Some of my sophomore English students in 2006 read-
ing an adaptation of Oedipus.*

*Some of my senior students
the year I retired.*

*Retirees from Elk Grove School District in 2007.
I am on the back row, near the center, two to the right of the lady in the aqua top.*

congregation full time. He still maintained a home office for the ministry and his personal study.

I continued to teach AP English at the 12th grade level for the three years before I retired. I occasionally was assigned to teach sophomore English.

My last year of teaching – School Year 2006-2007 – I taught AP Literature at FHS half day and the other half I taught AP Literature and English 12 at Bradshaw Christian School (BCS). I helped that school develop these courses which embodied their new 12th grade English curriculum.

Josh had already left Florin to teach at this Christian school, so once again, we were on the same faculty. He developed their AP Government and Economics programs, as well as took over their journalism program which produced both a magazine and a yearbook.

I retired from teaching in 2007. There was a small ceremony in the Commons for those of us leaving that year. I received a plaque commemorating my 17 years at Florin High School, but I had been teaching altogether for 40 years.

Josh Joins the Family Businesses

During our 15 years in Galt, Joshua and Sarah were pursuing their educational, athletic, musical, spiritual and romantic paths. Both met their beloveds during these years. Monicqua and Jacob were adults, fully on their own by this time and did not live on the Galt property.

Josh was introduced to Rosemary through mutual friends and got better acquainted the second summer—1991—we were in Galt when he was 16. They both served as junior counselors together at a Jews for Jesus annual retreat—The Ingathering—held in the mountains in the San Francisco Bay area.

In the ensuing years, Joshua didn't seem to have a clear idea of what he wanted to do "when he grew up." He excelled in the social sciences as well as in language arts. After playing football his sophomore year—the results of which was two dislocated shoulders—he pursued baseball as his primary sport and performed well at it. He could pitch side-armed and was feared by batters on opposing teams. He was on the high school baseball team and continued in Big League Ball in the summers.

One of his friends got him acquainted with some guys who were rowing crew, primarily team rowing. Josh got up very early to meet these guys at the Sacramento River to pursue this activity. If memory serves, they often rowed against athletes from UCD, this being a popular sport at that university just across the river. I believe Josh continued in this sport during some of his time attending UCD later.

Musically, Josh still played his violin and continued some private lessons, but even though his love for the instrument did not wane, he really had no time for the lessons. He did get to play with the FHS jazz band as their first-ever violinist. He also played violin on the Beth Yeshua worship team.

By the time Josh was attending UCD, Josh and Rosie weren't really dating.

She was also attending UCD, but did not have a car so often asked Josh if he would give her a ride to Sacramento to Beth Yeshua for Shabbat services. He did not seem to like doing this and by his own admission was very rude to Rosie. Rosemary and Joshua were both singing on Beth Yeshua's worship team, so they were thrust together. This went on for several years.

By 1995 when Josh was in his first semester of his junior year at UCD, Rosemary gave up on Josh wanting to be with her. Rosie didn't know that Josh had a conversation with me lamenting the fact that he thought he had lost her. He was very upset for what he then saw was his fears having kept him from acting on his feelings. Rosemary even had another boyfriend by then, but she was perplexed that nothing had ever come of what she believed to be a positive connection between them.

She asked him to go for coffee with her. At this time she confronted him and asked what happened, not expecting that there was any interest on Josh's part for a relationship with her, nor her with him. Josh replied something to the effect of, "God told me I was going to marry you back when I was 16, so I ran." She was surprised by his admission, having had a similar Word from God about their being for each other. They decided that they should start seeing each other to see if anything was there. The

Josh and Rosie at their Tena'im—Engagement Party— at Beth Yeshua's Landpark location in Sacramento.

Josh and Rosie's wedding at California State Capitol rose gardens with Josh's family. L–R: Sarah, Jacob, me, Joshua and Rosemary, Rabbi Rube, Monicqua pregnant with Ryan, Sarah Annemarie, Aaron.

flame was kindled. They became engaged shortly after, both being 20 years old.

Rube and I made our first trip to Israel that summer of 1996, taking a newly graduated Sarah for a graduation present. When we returned from our three weeks in Israel in mid-summer that year, Josh informed us that he and Rosemary wanted to get married in the winter and not wait until he got his degree. He proposed that he go to work right away so they could establish their home and proposed he would go back later to finish his degree. Since both Rube and I were in education for so many years, we were aware of the dangers of leaving school. So many did not return.

Josh needed some classes to fully complete his junior year. We proposed that he take them right then, as the summer session of UCD was about to begin. We also proposed that right after he finished summer school that he and Rosie get married prior to his starting his senior year. They agreed. They had just six weeks to plan the wedding, which fell heavily on Rosie since Josh was in classes.

Josh and Rosie's coming together was such a remarkable story, enriched by the fact that Rosemary's parents had come through a journey similar to ours. They were a type of northern California hippies who also were a Jew and Gentile coming to believe in Jesus. Our common life experiences have always forged a bond between our two families. Martin and Susan McCrea just celebrated their 50th wedding anniversary while we are all still rejoicing in being family with them for almost 25 years.

A strong family bond exists between our family and Rosemary's. L-R Rabbi Rube, me, Joshua and Rosemary Rubinstein, Martin and Susan McCrea.

My favorite picture of Rosie and Josh at their reception sitting in chairs waiting to be hoisted up by their guests for the traditional Jewish dance in the air. They were actually petrified they would be dropped!

Prior to the fall semester of Josh's senior year at UCD, Josh and Rosie married on the second day of the Jewish New Year, which corresponded to September 15th, 1996. It was a lovely ceremony by the rose gardens on the State Capitol grounds. They held a reception at a nearby ballroom. For such little time to plan, it was amazingly beautiful and very well attended. Rosemary is to be credited for that.

In the midst of trying to keep track of all that was happening in our family, I was still very much entrenched in my English teacher responsibilities at Florin High. I was teaching primarily senior English as well as Journalism, publishing *The Panther Press*.

The board reflects that my students wrote daily short journal entries. We were studying *Macbeth* at the time as evidenced by the topic concerning the three witches. My student – whose face I totally remember, but not his name – and I were probably discussing an essay he had written.

December of 1996, in my classroom of almost the entire 17 years I taught at FHS, J-8.

Meanwhile, Rosemary took on several jobs during the time Josh was in his senior year at UCD to help keep them afloat financially. She was a nanny for a family and also did house cleaning. Josh received his degree in Political Science in May of 1997.

The young couple continued being part of the worship team at Beth Yeshua, while also serving as youth leaders. When they were recruited to tour with Jews for Jesus's Liberated Wailing Wall, they left these posts. Their new ministry adventure was being part of a group of seven Jews living on a bus crisscrossing the continental United States ministering in song, drama and the Word in a different church almost every night. At the end of that 18-month tour, Josh and Rosie were asked to lead the next tour of 18 months, so they were traveling for about three years.

UCD graduate Josh with wife Rosemary at his side being prayed over at Beth Yeshua by Rabbi Rube and Elder Alan Kushner.

While Josh and Rosie were traveling the country, they realized they would be close to Kermit, TX where my father Monroe was bedridden fighting cancer.

Josh and Rosie with the Liberated Wailing Wall team and the Jews for Jesus bus as they left on tour.

The team decided to go to Josh's granddad's home and serenade him as he lay in bed. I was visiting my dad at the time.

When Josh and Rosie got off the road in 2001, they gradually became more involved with the congregation. Almost from their return, Josh took over leading the worship team and meeting weekly with his father on spiritual matters related to Messianic Judaism. Both Josh and Rosie were on the worship team and picked up working with our youth ministry.

Me, Daddy's wife Daphne, Daddy, Rosemary, Joshua and their fellow Liberated Wailing Wall team members. The Kermit newspaper picked up the story.

Rosemary received her RD degree at Sacramento State in 2005. Pictured seated center with her fellow graduates.

Josh doing face time with their firstborn, Eliana.

Rosie had been working on her Registered Dietitian (RD) degree at Sacramento State University, which she completed in 2005. Rosemary has been working in her field at a local dialysis clinic. She has also started her own business of life coaching called "Real Food Rosie."

The couple did not have children until after nine years of marriage. Josh and Rosie surprised Rube and me one day not long after our move to Elk Grove from Galt. They called and said they needed to talk to us. It was very ominous sounding. When they got to our house, we watched their arrival from Rube's home office that was off our front entryway. They seemed very shaken up and a little detached, maybe even "out of body." When they entered Rube's office, they lifted their eyes, both looking firmly at us and said they were pregnant! Honestly, they looked like they were deer caught in the headlights. I know I shrieked with joy!

Eliana Rose joined the family March 17, 2006. She looked then and still does today to be a mini-Rosemary, except for her lighter coloring including red hair. She has her mom's speech patterns, same facial structure and demeanor. I find myself calling her Rosemary without thinking.

We knew that Josh would be a good father. Kids were always drawn to him and he loved interacting with them. He had the ability to step into their world without condesending or becoming a kid himself. Watching him with his firstborn was a joy.

Once they got into the baby making mode, it continued. Two years later Eitan David was born on January 15, 2008. It was interesting to watch this little one. There was something so familiar about him. I realized that he is the spitting image of his father. It was like watching Josh grow up again. I sometimes call Eitan by his father's name!

Big sister Eliana was very affectionate with her little brother Eitan.

Both Eliana and Eitan have had a great love for Torah from an early age.

Josh and Rosemary's story continues with three more children, but I want to backtrack and share where Sarah was during all of this.

Sarah Gets Her Dream

Sarah is a diligent person in all that she does. Her goal of becoming a veterinarian never faded. She is a faithful friend of all animals, as she believes they are to their humans.

In the early years, Sarah and

Eliana Rose as a toddler at the State Fair with me and g'pa Rube.

Daddy Josh with Mother Rosemary reading the Hannukah story to Eliana and Eitan.

Eliana and Eitan at play. The little fire truck was passed down in the family from cousin Ryan Busch.

Eliana kisses Torah as Eitan walks it around the sanctuary at a Simchat Torah service at Beth Yeshua.

At the co-op camp with the Boehms. Front row from right: Sarah is 4th. James 5th and Sean 8th. Jeff and Marge Boehm are in 3rd row up from bottom, 3rd and 4th from left.

Sarah at her 8th grade dance.

her two younger cousins, Sean and James Thorpe, took various trips with the Boehm grandparents. Marge and Jeff attended a co-op camp every year. One year the three kids joined them. What Sarah specifically remembers was how hot it was traveling in the dead of summer in a car without air conditioning. The Boehms did not "believe" in air conditioning in cars, calling it decadent and frivolous.

Sarah's academic progress continued in California at Galt Middle School for just her 7th grade year. This facility was being replaced by a newer model, Greer Middle School, from which she graduated two years later. Her eighth grade year brought many celebrations.

We had always planned for Sarah to join the family at FHS as a freshman, which she did. Most of her coursework in high school was focused on the science and math needed to prepare her for continuing in a pre-vet path.

She allowed for some diversions in her studies. While still in high school, she participated in volleyball one year followed by running cross country, and was in choir all four years. In her junior year, she was the only Florin choir member to audition for and win a spot on the California All State Honor Choir. She had been in choir since 7th grade and continued singing in the choir at UCD when she went to college. She also sang on the worship team at Beth Yeshua.

Sarah participated in her Bat Mitzvah ceremony when she was 16 instead of the customary age for Jewish girls of 12 or 13. We had begun the congregation Beth Yeshua when she was 12 so we were not really ready to help her prepare any earlier.

Sarah - 3rd from left - and her friend Karin - far left - and two other friends at 8th grade graduation.

She continued her violin lessons throughout most of high school. We found a very special violin teacher, who held first chair of the violin section of the Sacramento Orchestra and was the daughter of our previous violin teacher in Stockton, CA.

Somehow in all of this, Sarah did not neglect her horse Marilla. For her high school senior project Sarah worked with a horse trainer. It was long overdue. You've heard the stories! Sarah was optimistic and loved learning how to train her. There were some scary moments, however.

Sarah being presented for her Bat Mitzvah ceremony by father Rabbi Rube with me at Beth Yeshua Messianic Synagogue in Sacramento, CA in 1994.

The one I remember best is when Sarah was working on turning the horse in a rather small fenced-in arena. As Sarah and Marilla came to the corner of the arena, Marilla didn't understand the cue Sarah gave so she just stopped suddenly, throwing Sarah onto the ground. Sarah was unable to catch her breath for what seemed like a long time. The project itself was a great success and deepened the bond between girl and horse.

Sarah was great about helping our then-two grandchildren, Sarah Annemarie and Ryan, ride her horse. Our property became

Sarah's senior portrait with her violin.

Sarah with Marilla on our Galt property.

Auntie Sarah taking Ryan for his first ride on Marilla.

Sarah Annemarie and Ryan being coached by Auntie Sarah on the fine art of making a spoon stick to their noses. Ryan, that's a fork, little man!

the site for many family gatherings. At that time we still just had Marilla. Monicqua and Aaron's family lived 40 minutes away in Roseville but often made the trek to give the children a chance to ride the horse and visit with family.

Sarah took on a very special role with niece Sarah Annemarie and nephew Ryan. She taught them all kinds of tricks, such as how to make a spoon stick to your nose. Her niece seemed to master it, but nephew looks convinced he can do it with a fork.

Sarah's senior year also brought her beloved into her life. Rube and I never were keen on our children dating. We leaned toward kids going out in groups instead of with one person alone. During this time a young man presented himself to Sarah and asked her to "hang out" at the mall with him. We allowed it, after meeting this high school student one day after school in my classroom. He professed Christianity so we felt somewhat assured Sarah would be safe.

Josh and Rosie, who were at this time engaged, went with Sarah and her beau to the mall. It was pretty much a disaster. Sarah reported that the guy was kind of "hands on." That ended that misadventure.

Not long after that, I became aware of a young man—Michael Whitley—who frequently came to my classroom before school with one of my editors of the school newspaper, Paul Duval. I remember once looking at this boy and wondering why Sarah couldn't be interested in a clean-cut guy like that. Her mall friend was a bit scruffy in attire as well as manners! Little did I know that Michael and Sarah had already been making connection in the only class they had together, economics. Michael invited Sarah to the Senior Ball which began their relationship.

Sarah and Michael graduated the same year, 1996. He had opted for the business track at FHS, hoping to have his own business, while Sarah chose to take courses that would help her do well as a pre-vet student in college. Mike and Sarah stayed a couple from their Senior Ball forward. They enjoyed celebrating their graduating from high school together.

As much as Sarah was involved in music and sports, it was evident her main energy was to learn all she could for getting into the college of her choice. She graduated in the top 10 of her class with a GPA over 4.0.

After Sarah's graduation, Rube and I took her with us to Israel for a graduation trip for her, but to fulfill a long-standing desire we both had to visit the land. We were on a tour for ten days, but the remainder of the time we stayed in a small flat with our co-travelers and fellow Elders of Beth Yeshua, Al and Patty Kushner.

We experienced more of the culture by having to cook for

Sarah and Michael at their FHS Senior Ball.

At the Senior Awards Ceremony at FHS, Sarah (center in white top) and her close friend Mary Pham (to Sarah's left) were in the top ten students. Presenting was Vice Principal Mary Ames.

Michael and Sarah at the Baccalaureate for Florin High School's graduating class of 1996. Her dad Rabbi Rube helped officiate the ceremony.

In Israel with Patty and Al Kushner, Rube and Sarah. I'm taking the picture.

ourselves and adapting to local living conditions. We shared a flat in Jerusalem that only had a tiny enclosed porch as a kitchen. It was all pretty makeshift. A special part of the trip was reconnecting with our longtime friends, Connie and Eitan Shishkoff.

Sarah and Michael's story continued when she began college at UCD the same semester Josh entered his senior year, Fall of 1996. She traveled from Davis to Sacramento on Saturdays for our congregation's Shabbat services and also to see Michael. Often Michael traveled to Davis to see her.

On one of these occasions, Michael was driving back from Davis late one evening when he fell asleep at the wheel. He was driving a 1983 Mazda RX-7 that actually went under the back wheels of an 18-wheeler that was ahead of him on the freeway. The front end of his car was stuck there, amazingly not injuring Michael, but he and the car were being wagged back and forth until another car passing them signaled the truck driver to stop.

It was in the winter of 1998 that Michael met with Rube and me to ask for Sarah's hand. We wanted to be sure that Sarah's beau was supportive of the future she hoped for. Michael assured us of several things: he would make sure she got through Vet School, he would help raise their children to know they were Jews and they both would serve

God through Jesus the Messiah. The wedding was set for that next September.

That Spring of 1999, Rube and I were still living in Galt and acquired another Palomino mare, Shoshone, who was enfoal. We knew she was expecting when we bought her and were informed her delivery date was in late April or early May. During the wait, Sarah and Mike both kept spending nights with us keeping vigil for the foaling.

On *Cinco de Mayo*, a Wednesday, Shoshone's filly—we dubbed Golda Mare—came just after midnight. That night Rube was fighting a cold and both Sarah and Michael had returned to school and work, respectively. I was left to greet this spindly-legged newcomer by myself.

Having set my alarm for every hour, I discovered the foal had indeed come and was somehow outside the stall, out of reach of her mama. I tried picking her up by her body, but it was very difficult as she was heavy and springing up like a deer. Somehow I was able to hold her body upright while guiding her back around into the stall, much to my relief and Shoshone's.

Wouldn't you know she would foal when no one was around! We learned later that mares don't like to know they are being watched for this event. She was probably waiting for all of us to go away.

Ryan and Sarah Annemarie both had the opportunity to ride

Sarah, Rube and I in Israel Summer 1996 visiting Connie (far left) and Eitan (far right).

Shoshone and her foal Goldy were inseparable.

Sarah on Shoshone with Sarah Annemarie and Rube on Marilla with Ryan.

horses once Shoshone had foaled, which happened in May of 1999. Sarah and her dad loved to take them out.

On January 18, 2000, Rube and I had our 25th anniversary wedding ceremony under a chupa to renew our vows. All the children were there with us to celebrate. Life-long friend Rabbi Russ Resnik came from New Mexico to officiate. It was very special to us, especially since we had never had a formal wedding ceremony. We had declared ourselves married around Thanksgiving of 1973 and had legally married over a year later, February 16, 1975, at a small ceremony at Shalom Ministries in Santa Fe.

Sarah and Michael were married just before her senior year at UCD. Like

Josh and Rosie, their ceremony was planned for the second day of the Jewish New Year, which corresponded to September 12, 1999 that year.

Prior to the service, there was the traditional signing of the *ketubah*, the marriage contract between the bride and groom. In some traditions, it includes what the husband is giving to the bride, such as camels. Theirs included no camels.

Even though Rube was of-

Celebrating 25 years of marriage. Couples in back and front: Michael and Sarah Whitley, G'pa Jeff and G'ma Marjorie Boehm, Rube and me, Aaron – holding Ryan – and Monicqua Busch with little Sarah Annemarie, Joshua and Rosemary Rubinstein.

L to R: The Groom's parents Kimberly and Don Whitley with Ringbearer nephew Eddie Locks, Mike's mother Phyllis Whitley, Best Man Paul Duval, Groomsmen Kambiz Ahmadi and Joshua Rubinstein, Groom Michael, Rabbi and Father-of-the Bride Richard Rubinstein, Groomsman Jacob Guillon, Bride Sarah with her Maid-of-Honor Mary Pham, (back row) Groomsman Greg Glacken, Bridesmaids Kelly Glacken and Rachel Schley, Mother-of-the-Bride with Bridesmaid Rosemary Rubinstein and Matron-of-Honor Monicqua Busch, (front) Flower Girls Sarah Busch and Whitley Locks, Ringbearer Ryan Busch.

ficiating the ceremony, he and I both walked Sarah down the aisle.

The couple also chose to marry on the Capitol grounds as did her brother Joshua. It was a beautiful wedding that Rabbi Rube officiated. Joshua played an Itzhak Perlman violin piece for the processional, as he had for his own wedding.

The couple took up residence in the Sacramento area and Sarah commuted the 40-minute drive to Davis her last undergraduate year. During this time, Mike and Sarah took on the youth ministry at Beth Yeshua. In addition, Sarah sang on the worship team while Michael ran the sound system. They stepped in to fill the gap left by Josh and Rosie, who left for an 18-month ministry tour that turned into three years. In May of 2000 Sarah completed her BS in Animal Science at UCD.

Sarah chose to work in the veterinary field for a year before applying to UCD Veterinary School. 2001 became a momentous year. Sarah was working at a local veterinary clinic as a technician that spring when she got the news she was accepted into vet school. A couple of months later she and Mike discovered they were expecting their first baby.

Sarah asked for and got a delayed acceptance for vet school giving her a year to have the baby and get settled prior to beginning grad school. They couldn't

Rube and Shari escorting Sarah down the aisle.

Sarah's side of the family attending: L-R Uncle Jay and Aunt Anita Norris from Midland, TX, Uncle John and Aunt Johanna Thorpe, Uncle Brad and Aunt Katthleen Charon with their children Shy and Lucas from Utah, the Bride and Groom, her parents Rube and Shari Rubinstein, sister Monicqua and husband Aaron Busch with children Sarah Annemarie and Ryan, Rosemary and brother Joshua Rubinstein.

Michael's side of the family attending: L-R His parents Don and Kimberly Whitley, the Bride and Groom, Michael's mother Phyllis Whitley, Don's sister Laura and her husband Eddie Locks (not pictured) with their three children, back Courtney, front Whitley and Eddie.

Sarah's undergrad degree, BS in Animal Science, UCD. Flanked by Mom and Dad.

Corey Davis as a baby with Mom Sarah and Dad Michael.

have known, but it was good that she didn't try to handle vet school at that time because she was violently ill during the entire pregnancy. She would learn in her subsequent pregnancies, that being nauseated and throwing up was the norm for her entire nine-month experiences.

Michael continued working at Valley Motors Parts Department in Sacramento, where he was employed right after graduating from high school. He would later move to Maita Chevrolet where he continued learning about car parts and got his training in estimating damage to vehicles in their body shop. This field became his career during most of which time he owned his own business.

Corey Davis—sharing grandfather Rube's middle name—was

Family picture celebrating Sarah's DVM degree: Corey, Sarah, Michael Whitley; Rosemary holding Eliana with Josh Rubinstein behind; Jacob Rubinstein; Rube and me; Ryan, Sarah, Monicqua and Aaron Busch.

born February 27, 2002. Eight days later was our first family *brit milah*. It was a wondrous celebration, although little Corey might have described this event very differently if he could.

Mike and Sarah continued in their ministry at Beth Yeshua until Sarah finally began UCD Veterinary School in the fall of 2002 rendering her unavailable most Saturdays. The weekends were the times vet students were given access to labs. Corey was just over six months old.

Baby Raina Lee with Daddy Mike.

The next four years were very challenging for this little family. Michael did much of the hands-on childcare while still working in car damage estimations. They had some family help with watching the baby. For a short time Rube watched baby Corey, as I was still teaching full time. Even Rube's mom, grandma Marjorie—at age 80—took care of Corey for a while just before he was a year old.

Poppa Rube with grandson Corey and daughter Sarah on the 7th night of Hannukah 2008.

The family bought a starter house in Elk Grove, CA. Sarah commuted the 30 miles which could take anywhere from 40 minutes to an hour depending on traffic on the "causeway"—a long bridge crossing over agricultural, mostly rice fields that ran between Sacramento and Davis. Sarah's graduation was a very welcome event on every level. She completed her studies and graduated in May of 2006.

Sarah received several offers for jobs, and decided she wanted to work in an emergency hospi-

Rube and me with grandsons Corey Whitley and Eitan Rubinstein and granddaughter Raina Whitley. Eitan and Raina were both born in 2008, in January and April respectively. It was a very busy baby year for our family. In our Elk Grove, CA home.

tal. She loves doing surgery which is more in demand in an emergency hospital than in a regular practice. She accepted the position at Atlantic Street Veterinary Hospital where they live in Roseville, and continues in that job today. Recently she also began her own business of helping people say goodbye to their terminally ill animals in their own homes – Faithful Friend.

Once out of vet school, Mike and Sarah planned to continue having children. After Sarah's "usual" nine months of nausea, they welcomed baby Raina Lee to the family on April 29, 2008. Raina's features and coloring are much like Corey's: dark hair and eyes and a Mediterranean complexion.

We spent many holidays with our children and their growing families. Sarah and Michael hosted many of our gatherings. Sarah always had a special bond with her father, Rube.

After 15 years in Galt, Rube and I relocated ten miles north to Elk Grove which was much closer to all of our children and grandchildren. The added advantage was that the cousins got to spend a lot of time together and with us.

Another great baby surprise came for Sarah and Michael just a couple of years later, but only after the drama in the family took a devastating turn.

All Our Ships at Sea

As our children found their own places in the world, Rube and I took some trips on our own. The most fun for me was when we were able to visit my family at our reunions usually held in Ruidosa, NM. One of our last such reunions was in the summer of 2003. It has become rare for all seven siblings to get together, but that year it happened. This picture is permanently taped to my computer.

By 2005 Rube and I felt that our lifestyle in Galt was getting too demanding for us. We sold that property and bought a home ten miles north in Elk Grove. We not only sold our three horses to make the move, but we sold or gave away all vestiges of our previous hippie lifestyle. We no longer had a need for all his blacksmithing tools so gave them to a woman who was teaching that craft. We still owned a large stockpile of high-powered tools that went as well.

This move brought us closer to Rube's mother, Marjorie, who had recently relocated from Santa Rosa to Elk Grove. We were there for the process of her failing health. We took her in with us after she had hip replacement surgery. She recovered, but this began a series of health events that seemed to leave her a little weaker each time.

As it became more apparent that she was unable to live alone, we worked with Rube's brother Eric to sell her home and get her moved into assisted living. Since Eric was living in the San Francisco Bay area, and Rube's sister Jo was consumed by her own life trials, it was left to me and Rube to stay in Marjorie's life, which we did.

We had only been in the Elk Grove house a couple of years when I fully retired from teaching in 2007. I more fully immersed myself in the workings of

Beth Yeshua. I still co-lead the children's ministry with my good friend Carolyn Reese and work with a small team of "community coordinators" to organize all the festivals and other events of our synagogue. In addition to Carolyn, there was one of my oldest friends since coming to California, Evelyn "Evi" (Hall) Hardy, and lifetime buddy, Madelyn Childs.

Julia Schley continues as my longest standing California friend and ally. As a co-founder of Beth Yeshua, she is always reaching out, watching over Beth Yeshua. Our mutual friend, prayer warrior, and part of the original group meeting before Beth Yeshua was born, Carol Lerner, completed our merry band. She led the Women's Ministry, passing it to Evi when Noel and Carol moved to North Carolina several years ago. Carolyn and I are presently serving as the Financial Officer, so from time to time I step in to train Trustees who are empowered by the Elders to oversee all the financial matters of the congregation.

It seems that my having left full-time teaching was timely. Both Rube and I were struggling with Diabetes. Even though we neither were taking insulin, maintaining the optimum level of exercise and eating was a major challenge. We were doing so much in the congregation and in the family itself that we really

Rube and I are pictured at our Beth Yeshua Seder for 2009. By the next Seder Rube was very unwell.

Rube and I with his mother Marjorie when we took her to Kauai.

didn't pay enough attention to our own health conditions. We expended a lot of energy putting on the various Jewish festivals for our congregation and the community.

chapter

8

*Tsunami
Phase*

Sickness Enters

In the summer of 2009, Rube began to feel very sick. He had been dealing with Type II Diabetes for some years, as well as suffering from Psoriasis, Psoriatic Arthritis, high blood pressure and difficulty losing unwanted weight. By Thanksgiving he was quite ill. By that time he was on oxygen, dragging a little tank with him by day and using a larger unit at night at home.

At the same time, Josh and Rosie received unsettling news on the health of their yet unborn third child. It was discovered by ultrasound that their little guy had a severely twisted, underdeveloped heart. His tiny heart was about the size of a dime when they were able to diagnose this condition. It was recommended that the baby be born at the University of San Francisco so they were able to do surgery immediately after the birth. Essentially the little one would have been a "blue baby."

Josh and Rosie were fortunate to secure a room and shared bath at the Ronald McDonald house in San Francisco for them and their other two children so they could stay close to the hospital. Rube and I found a campground in Pacifica just south of the city where we could park our fifth-wheel trailer. We hoped to be close enough to help with childcare for when both Josh and Rosie needed to be at the hospital. This was no small feat due to Rube's declining health.

We had many pleasant trips taking our fifth wheel to Olema on the coast north of San Francisco. It became our home away from home. Rube would study for his ministry while I wrote. It was our home during the time Josh and Rosie dealt with Lev's health condition so we could be near them.

Lev Benjamin was born on December 22, 2009. The baby had to stay in the hospital for about a month. Surgery was arduous but successful. During that time, Rosemary pretty much lived at the hospital so she could nurse Lev. The medical personnel helped her find rooms where she slept and she alternated between there and the McDonald house. Rube and I drove over to relieve them when needed.

I will never forget the hospitality and love of the Ronald McDonald house. Their volunteer

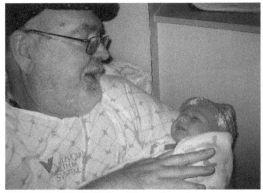

Zeyde Rube with newborn Lev. Rube was already on oxygen all the time.

groups brought in evening meals many nights. There were playrooms for the kids and since they were there over Christmas, donors supplied an amazing array of toys for all the kids living there at the time. Both Eliana and Eitan received tricycles as well as other toys and treats.

The large kitchen of the house was set up so that every family staying here was assigned a place to keep their own food. Even though the Ruby's had to share a bathroom with another family, it was HEAVEN to have a free place to be during their ordeal. We will always be grateful. Friends, family and congregants were able to come to visit the family there, which was so comforting.

During this time, Rube and I traveled back to Sacramento for the Saturday service most of the time. It was difficult since he was suffering so much. Sometimes he just had the Elders conduct the services because it was so hard on him to go back and forth.

When Josh's family was able to take Lev home, we drove our trailer back to storage and went home. As we began to put our energies into figuring out Rube's health, we were getting mixed messages from Rube's doctors. They seemed to be weighing all of his various conditions, but were not able to determine what was the major cause.

There was still the expectation of new life in the midst of the challenges all around. Our daughter Sarah was expecting the birth of the twins. She had her usual nausea-to-the-point-of-vomiting pregnancy. This was very stressful as she tried to

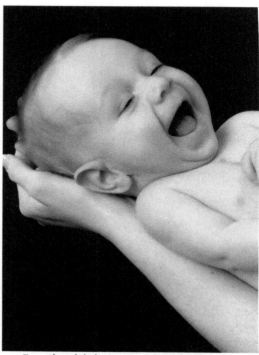

Even though baby Lev experienced a great deal of trauma in his young life, he was always a cheerful baby. Note the scar on his chest from his open heart surgery. Later as a 4-year-old he was proud of this scar and would flip up his shirt and show it to whoever cared to see it.

Spring birthdays 2010 gave us the opportunity to get a girls' three generation picture at my house in Elk Grove, CA. L-R: me, Rosemary Rubinstein, Grandma Marjorie Boehm, a pregnant Sarah Whitley, and Monicqua Busch.

continue working and little Raina was only one year old and Corey five when she started this pregnancy.

The Greatest Battle

Still in the midst of family trauma, we turned our attention more fully to what was going on with Rube's health. Rube and I were in and out of the hospital, usually by way of the emergency room. It wasn't until May 10th of 2010 that we finally had a diagnosis.

We had come in, once again, through the ER. While there, one of the doctors examining Rube noticed a lump on the side of his neck. He asked me what we had been told about it. I replied that they said it was a hematoma—blood under the skin. The D.O. shook his head and said "Lymphoma." Did he just say cancer?!

Rube was admitted and tests were conducted. Doctors and nurses were in and out that day, but all were very upbeat. An oncologist stopped by and was equally optimistic explaining that Lymphoma is very treatable. On that note, I went home for the evening. An official diagnosis was expected the next morning.

I arrived back at the hospital around 9 AM. Rube was alone in his hospital room reading something on his cell phone. The mood was palpably somber in contrast to the previous day's flow of optimism. I asked if the doctor had been in. He said they were and he received a diagnosis. He said it wasn't Lymphoma, but was a rare skin cancer, Merkel Cell Carcinoma. He was reading about it. It was always terminal. From onset life expectancy was nine months to a year with chemo. It was determined that this cancer had begun as early as November of the previous year—six months prior.

That began the most painful ordeal of our lives. Rube, fortunately, said he never really experienced physical pain. The doctors don't know why, but I know it was God's mercy! Mental anguish and physical discomfort were huge, however. Even though Rube decided to go for chemo—mostly so he could meet his yet unborn twin granddaughters from daughter Sarah—unless God intervened, we knew he had just a few months at best.

It was the summer of 2010. The congregation was 20 years old and there was its life to be considered as well. Not wanting to give up if God had plans to sovereignly heal Rube, I organized special rabbis to come in for the summer to preach for him. The two Elders expressed mixed opinions about inviting outside speakers, mostly because at least one of them felt he could handle the pulpit during Rube's absence. For a variety of reasons—not the least of which was my need to not see Rube "replaced" as Beth Yeshua's Rabbi—I pushed forward and secured a host of speakers from within the UMJC to come fill the gap.

By the end of summer, it was evident that Rube was getting worse. The chemo had indeed held off the disease for a while, and Rube did get to meet his newest granddaughters Hannah Marie and Olivia Grace, born July 24.

It had been eight months of struggling with cancer. He was very weak but still managed to have a twinkle in his eye holding Olivia and Hannah. This was October of 2010 on the occasion of Jacob's birthday.

Nothing was quite as uplifting for Rube and me than to have actual visits from the children and grandchildren.

During this time, from his sick bed at home, Rube began meeting with the Elders and with Josh. Rube and I both had felt for many years that God was grooming Josh to take over the congregation. I don't know if Rube ever verbalized it to Josh, but they were meeting weekly for many years while Josh was functioning as an assistant to his dad.

The twins with Mom Sarah and Dad Michael when they were brought to see their "Poppa" Rube. Olivia on the left – according to Mama, usually in purple or any color but pink – and Hannah on the right – usually dressed in pink or red. Notice Rube's reflection in the mirror in his sickbed.

One afternoon, when Rube was back in the hospital again, he called a meeting of the Elders and Josh. Josh felt he was to challenge the Elders about the future of Beth Yeshua. When Josh left the hospital room that night, I met with him in the hall. I asked him if he had prayed about whether he was to take over the congregation. Just asking such a question was a bit of a slap to his face since I knew him to be a PRAYING man, but ask him I did. I was amazed to hear that he had not done so, but that he would.

When he prayed with Rosie about it, they both thought he was to take over. This had to be a move of God since both of them had many concerns about the direction they saw the con-

We kept Rube surrounded with pictures of his grand-kids. The photo on the far left shows a proud grandpa, or Poppa as he is known to the Whitleys, holding the two-month-old twins L to R: Olivia and Hannah.

One of the visits of the Busches and the Whitleys. Me with my two Sarahs: granddaughter Sarah Annemarie and daughter Sarah, holding Sarah's twins, Hannah and Olivia.

gregation going.

Rube was released from the hospital to go home again and Josh came over to talk to him. Up until this time I did not know that Josh felt God told him to lead the congregation and that he had already spoken to the Elders about it. He said they treated it as an off hand remark by him and dismissed it and him. He did not tell his dad about it until this night.

Rube didn't have much strength, but he was energized by what I have to characterize as holy anger. He called for the Elders to come to him. Rube, the two Elders and Josh met and Rube pretty much chided the Elders for dismissing Josh as the potential new leader. At that time one of the Elders decided it was time for him to resign and he did, by letter, after the meeting.

Even with Josh presenting himself, the consensus wisdom was that there should be a search committee for finding the new leader. Some of the leadership felt we should try to find an ordained rabbi. I looked at the existing U.S. congregations to see how many were led by rabbis who had completed rabbinical yeshiva training. Only about 25% of the existing Messianic synagogues had such leaders. And, to top it off, there were not any ordained candidates seeking congregations to our knowledge, or at least not any that seemed to be a good fit.

Noel was the only Elder left, so the weight of this decision was on him. He said frankly that he was not sure what God wanted but that he would continue to pray and seek Godly counsel. It being October and time again for the Jews for Jesus Ingathering, Noel and his wife Carol attended. Noel took this opportunity to meet with several trusted men of God. The result was that they told Noel they believed Josh was the one God chose to lead Beth Yeshua.

Zeyde Rube with me and our kids: Monicqua, Joshua, Jacob, and Sarah.

The grandchildren visited Rube a lot. Ryan holding Hannah, top is Eitan with Sarah Annemarie holding little Lev, to the right of them is Eliana and Corey holding little sister Olivia.

One of these Godly men, Bob Trank, was one who was with us at the inception of Beth Yeshua and was co-leading our group for a while. I do not know or remember whatever discussion he and Rube might have had, but Bob left our group, disagreeing with Rube's being the leader. It was huge for this man to believe in Josh. To me that made it an even greater sign that Josh was God's choice.

Noel trusted what God spoke through the counsel he received and talked to Josh, telling him that he fully supported him to be the new leader. Josh said he wanted to be sure the congregation wanted him also, so he proposed to serve with Noel on the Elder Board and lead, but not take over for six months, at which time there would be a congregational vote. That was the plan.

This conversation was just a couple of weeks before Rube's death. Everyone was trying to keep the congregation going in the looming imminent death of its founder, leader, and beloved Rabbi.

The entire family filled our bedroom for a special time with their grandpa Rube. Josh played his violin for his dad regularly at the bedside. All but Raina – who I believe might have been sick at the time – were piled on our bed to be near Rube's hospital bed.

Rube's mother Marjorie and his sister Johanna and brother Eric came to spend as much time as they could with Rube. One of Rube's oldest friends, Eitan Shishkoff, was visiting from Israel and was able to come by and spend time with Rube a week before he passed.

With His Father

It was almost a year that this cancer had ravaged Rube's body. What first showed up as a small lump on his neck and another in the groin area, was evidently only the tip of the iceberg. We later realized he had a football-size tumor in his belly. The chemo held most manifestations at bay, but once Rube stopped chemo, tumors began to sprout all over his body.

What had been a nickel-sized "orange peel" textured bump on his ankle, suddenly became the size and texture of a pomegranate. It was evidently filled with blood. The oncologist recommended that I take Rube to a cancer center where they could administer radiation treatment to reduce the size.

We had an appointment and a scheduled transport since he had been in a wheelchair for months. When we got to the center, there had been a mistake and his appointment was not for an hour. They gave us a room in which to wait. Once there, Rube began to grow faint and I feared he was about to pass out. I rushed to get help. One of the doctors stabilized Rube and then left some nurses tending to him

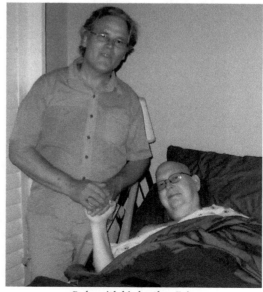

Rube with his brother Eric.

so she could talk privately with me in the hall.

She asked me what I knew of his condition. I blurted out that no one would tell me if my husband is dying. She said that she hated to be the one to tell me since we had only just met, but that he had less than a month to live. I can't explain, but I was both shocked and relieved at the same time. I needed to know. She immediately got an ambulance to take him to the hospital which was only one block away.

Once we were at the ER of the hospital, an admitting doctor met with Rube and me. It was then that the most amazing experience of my life happened. The doctor was explaining to me and to Rube at the same time that he had just a few weeks to live. Rube's expression was "beautific." It's the only way I can describe it. He looked absolutely radiant and was smiling out of a profoundly peaceful countenance. I broke down for the first time since his diagnosis and wept uncontrollably.

There were several in-and-out-of-the-hospital experiences while he grew sicker. But, once again, there was inexplicably no physical pain. At this point, we brought hospice in to help Rube be more comfortable. They showed us—the kids and I—how to administer anti-anxiety and pain meds when needed. The hospice workers were so helpful. For a week we all kept vigil watching him decline.

On one occasion, Rube stopped eating or drinking, and I was afraid he was dying, so I called in his mom and all of the kids. That night, all the adults stayed overnight with me and took turns sitting with him. He had been in a hospital bed beside our regular bed in our bedroom for months. Even though we knew it was close, he was still with us in the morning. All of the kids but Josh and Sarah went to work. Then Sarah had to go home to take care of her four children.

Typical Rube before his health declined. The way I like to remember him.

When it happened that morning, it was just Josh and I with Rube. I was keeping up an email blog to loved ones. For a couple of days, it actually looked like Rube's spirit might have already left him, but the machine—his body—was still working. I really felt it was time and so I asked Josh to sit with his dad while I went down the hall to my little office to update the blog.

I was there just a few minutes when Josh rushed in to get me. He looked stricken and said that his dad's breathing just changed.

We hurried back to the bedroom and each took one of his hands from either side of the bed. Rube suddenly just did not take the next breath.

Picking Up the Pieces

We had been planning for a memorial. Josh was working on a video in anticipation. We wanted to have a burial within a day per Jewish tradition, but it was Shabbat the next day so we waited until the following Monday. So many came from so far. We rented a very large church for the memorial. Earlier that morning, we held a private family burial in Sacramento's only Jewish cemetery.

One of Rube's oldest friends, Rabbi Russ, came from New Mexico and Rube's mentor Rabbi Michael from Florida to help officiate. Rube's uncle Harland and wife Donna drove down from Oregon. My sister Anita and her husband Jay came from Texas and were my strength during that time. Condolences literally came in from around the world.

Josh helped officiate the memorial, which I later realized interrupted his own grieving, but he would not have had it any other way. I spoke, telling some of Rube's story, but I was still in shock. It was such a comforting service. Our entire Messianic community and former colleagues in education were there to celebrate his life with us. We were blessed.

Once everyone went home, I

Cover of the program for Rube's memorial that our son Josh created.

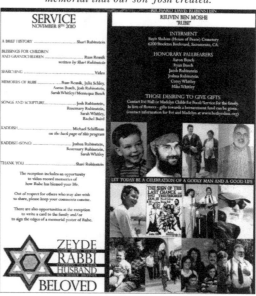

Contents of the program for the memorial.

stayed a few days with my daughter Sarah's family. It was hard to be home. Jay and Anita stayed a week with me. When I did go home, it was so hard to be in those rooms without Rube.

I wanted to stay in the Elk Grove area since I needed to continue taking care of Rube's mom. Rube and I had been doing it together. I saw her through her time in an assisted living facility until her death, October 7, 2014. The plan to move to Roseville began in earnest. I sold my Elk Grove home in late summer of 2016, while simultaneously purchasing another house in Roseville. Josh and Rosie's family had been dealing with a real estate agent to also buy in Roseville. We all made our moves on the same day – September 11, 2016 – almost six years after Rube's death.

Our daughter Sarah's family had moved to Roseville four years earlier, interestingly also on September 11 of that year. Monicqua's family had been in Roseville for over 20 years. We are all presently within four minutes of each other, except Jacob who lives 20 minutes away.

The family all spent a week in Kauai, HI in 2016. A treasured picture of everyone.
Family groupings, L–R: Monicqua, Ryan, Sarah and Aaron Busch.
I am in the center surrounded by Whitleys: Corey, Michael, Sarah, Olivia, Hannah and Raina.
Rubinstein family: Josh, Rosie, Micah, Lev, Eitan, and Eliana. To far right is Jacob Rubinstein.

9

chapter

*"Red Sky at
Night..."*

Surviving the Shaking

Rube and Noel were considering other men to bring into the Eldership and that was one of the first things that Josh and Noel did after Rube died. They wanted a broader foundation of leadership. They brought in four men: Bruce Granick, Steven Childs, Michael Levy, and Bob Hall. At the end of the six months "trial" period, Josh was voted in unanimously to be the congregational leader.

I am presently looking back at the nine years since Rabbi Rube died. During this time, there have been many changes in the congregation. Shocking and very sad, new Elder Bob Hall died of a heart attack while jogging that next summer, 2011.

Elder Noel and his wife Carol fulfilled a long-time retirement dream and moved to North Carolina to be close to one of their sons and the land from whence Noel had come. Our sound engineer and friend Ross Ramsay, along with his son, worship leader Sonny, and his wife Catherine, who was our toddler's ministry leader, moved their family to another area of North Carolina. One of the new elders stepped down to take care of personal issues, while another went on sabbatical. That left Josh and Steven Childs at the helm of Beth Yeshua.

In spite of all the movement at the top, there have been many good changes. Josh and Steven have built up a strong leadership team. They have helped Jews and Gentiles alike understand and appreciate their unique identities. They have led us to move out of a business district where we had converted space for a sanctuary and occupied for 13 of our 24 years. After an interim three-year stay at a business facility in midtown Sacramento, we recently took up shared residency in a facility with two congenial churches.

Our congregation is almost 30 years old. We weathered the national economic downturn of 2008. We have come back from the blow of losing our beloved founder and Rabbi in 2010. We are thriving. Rabbi Josh just stepped down from simultaneously serving a two-year post as the Vice President of the Union (UMJC). And did I mention that we also were blessed with another grandson, Josh and Rosie's Micah Gilad, was born September 26, 2014 – the tenth grandchild. We got our minion!

Hopefully minion plus one. Josh and Rosie, as well as Mike and Sarah, have always had hearts for adopting. When Sarah got pregnant with the twins, their energies necessarily were directed that way. Josh and Rosie recently began learning about becoming foster parents with the hopes of adopting a little girl. Before completing their training, they were given the opportunity to foster a baby with hopes of adopting.

At this writing little Ava Marie has been part of their—and our—family for sixteen of her eighteen months. As "big brother" five-year-old Micah prayed when he blew out his recent birthday candles, "I hope we get to keep baby Ava!" So say us all...

Wind in My Sails

I don't have to write what the ensuing years have been like. Anyone who has lost a loved one, specifically a spouse, can fill in the blanks. But I will say that I was fairly adrift for several years. The stages of loss are not exactly linear. They come and go and hit at odd times. When I see a sailboat, my heart and mind are drawn to memories of Rube and our life together. When I look into the eyes of my kids and my grandkids, I see Rube. When I take a trip to someplace we planned to go together, he is there.

My life is full in so many ways. I continue to work at various posts at the congregation that I spoke of earlier. I help with childcare of grandkids when needed. Since I live within several minutes of all eleven of my grandkids, I have many opportunities to interact with my family and be a presence in their lives, and they in mine. I am sad that little Micah and baby Ava never got to know their grandfather and that the younger grandkids probably can't remember Rube.

The calling I accepted in my youth is still central in my life – I still write. About five years ago, Josh got on board as chief encourager for my writing. He worked with me to help me publish my first book of perspective pieces in 2014 – *Shift: Tiny Tales to Lighten Your Load.* The second publication was in 2016 – *Phoenix: Rising Anew, Transformed by Fire.* I call these published volumes "My Littles." I expect that there will be many more "littles."

I have a teeming file drawer of my writing I have been adding to for over 40 years now, and am still composing more each week. I am working on ways to compile them that make sense to a reader, since essentially they are independent isolated pieces. Initially, Josh helps me get my pieces out as blogs on my website. I have several books outlined and most of their pieces written.

My personal pet, Annie the Vizsla, is the star of one upcoming book that should come out soon after I get this memoir published. It's entitled, *Annie: Canine Conundrums for the Human Heart.* I love the lessons we can learn from observing the animals we take as pets. My Annie is presently almost 14 years old, ancient for her breed. She's showing signs of demise. I hope to get her volume out before she passes.

I have several more books in the making at this writing. One new project I am co-writing with Dr. Sarah, my vet daughter. We both have a heart for children who lose their pets so we are creating a series of picture

A birthday celebration for me when I turned 70 in 2014.

books to help them learn to cope. Watch for the first one, *Maggie*.

That's full circle in so many ways. Sarah's father and I co-authored several children's books about the exploits of our Irish Setter some 40 years ago. *Rado the Red Dog, Returns to the Rubinsteins* is a Prodigal Son story.

We began the series and sent the originals to Jacob for Christmas. We later gave him copies, retrieving our originals. We had very little money for gifts, but we did have our imaginations.

Rado the Red Dog, Pursues Patience is one spotlighting a character trait we all need. Watch for these to be formally published. We wrote this the following Christmas, 1977.

Josh at about three years old with "his" dog, Colorado "Rado" who became the subject of some children's books we wrote. This picture was taken when we were camping out in California from our home in Santa Fe, NM.

As I interact with my youngest grandson, Micah, I am always intrigued by how he sees the world. I am working on a series about this red-headed kid. Watch for *Mickey G and The Train in the Wall.*

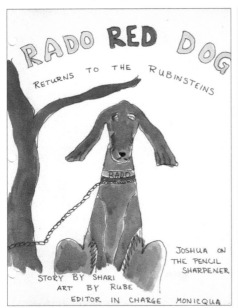

Original cover of our first Rado book written in 1976 featuring Rube's whimsical art and our collaborative writing.

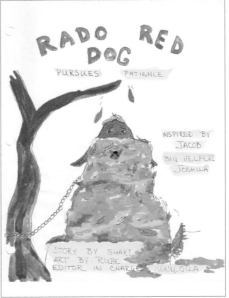

The original cover of the second in the series of the Rado books.

Children Thriving

This is the continuation of the stories of our children's paths since I interrupted it to tell of Rube's passing.

JOSHUA

Josh and Rosie's last two children never knew their Grandpa Rube. Micah Gilad came along almost five years after Lev was born, on September 26, 2014. Did I mention this one is a flaming red head? I remind Josh that he himself was "strawberry blonde" as a young kid. Given the dark brown of Josh's hair now, it is less believable to many. The beard he frequently grows has always been red.

Josh's family lived with me for a couple of years between their first and second homes when Lev was two. We all spent a summer in Israel and came home to this new living arrangement. I am sure it was stressful for them, but I loved being in the midst of them. The older children were in a charter school a few days a week with the remainder of the time in home school primarily with Rosie as their teacher. Fortunately my home included a great room which housed their classroom.

For a couple of years the family transitioned to a rental house just north of my Elk Grove home in the southern part of Sacramento. In September of 2016 their family purchased a home in Roseville, just to the east of Sacramento. I was in the process of selling my Elk Grove home at the same time. Our escrows went through at the same time and we both moved into our homes in 2016, as I wrote earlier.

Holiday picture at the end of 2021 of the Rubinsteins, L-R (top row): Eliana, Eitan and Lev, L-R (bottom row): Micah, Ava, Rosemary, and Josh.

Rosemary continues as a dietitian at a Davita Dialysis clinic in an adjacent city. She has been working at getting a health coaching business off the ground, *Real Food Rosie.* The whole family's attention has been redirected with their becoming foster parents to infant Ava Marie. As I mentioned earlier, they had hoped to foster and adopt a toddler girl and were in

Micah Gilad as a baby. That intent look is because his mind is whirling. Always thinking, that boy!

fostering classes when newborn Ava was brought to their attention.

Ava spent a month in the hospital and then had an emergency foster placement for a month before Josh's family took her in. She has been with them ever since and they are hoping to be able to legally adopt her. At this writing we are toward the end of the COVID 19 pandemic which caused the courts to close down except for emergency cases. Josh and Rosie are hoping to complete the process by the Fall of 2020.

Josh has always been very interested and gifted in electronics and also graphic design, computers, social media and other related software applications. He is an avid reader. After getting his degree from UCD in 1997, he worked at putting in home theaters before he began teaching high school. As I mentioned earlier in my narrative, Josh taught Government, Economics, Yearbook, and took over my Journalism Program at Florin High School. He went on to teach at Bradshaw Christian School before coming into ministry at Beth Yeshua in 2010.

He recently began teaching again. He heads up the journalism program which includes producing a magazine and school yearbook at a local high school while continuing as Rabbi of our synagogue. Because of the Corona Virus, all classes have been shut down for most of the second semester. Josh and his colleagues have been teaching using the internet. All are hopeful in-person classes might begin in the Fall.

SARAH

Sarah and Mike's twins' joyful births seemed overshadowed by their Grandpa's dying. Raina was barely two when they were born. Half way through this pregnancy, an ultrasound revealed two heartbeats. Carrying multiples, especially given how sick Sarah gets, was difficult on the whole family. She con-

The Whitleys in their 2021 Holiday Photo. L-R (back row): Raina, Mike, Sarah, Corey and Sarai. L-R (bottom row): Hannah and Olivia

tinued working at the emergency pet hospital, which was tough given her sickness.

Late in the pregnancy, Sarah had to go into the hospital as she was threatening to deliver too early. The medical team managed to keep the twins in long enough so that when they started to come in earnest only a few weeks early, there were fewer concerns as to their health.

This time when Sarah went to the hospital, the doctor assured her she was not ready to have these babies. Sarah insisted on staying in, and labor started in earnest in short order. They put her in an operating room as a precaution protocol for premature births. There were two complete pediatric teams to take care of the girls once they were delivered.

I was honored to be in the room when these two little ones came into this world, so I watched Sarah and Mike's reaction to having two little readheads with fair complexions and blue eyes. And they were identical. Hanah Marie came first followed within minutes by Olivia Grace. All four of their children look so similar, except for their coloring.

Sarah and Mike bought a new home in Roseville about nine years ago. Their house is the hub of a lot of parties. She does not work as many days at the hospital now, as she began her own business called Faithful Friend. She helps families in their homes when it is time to say goodbye to their terminal and/or elderly pets. Mike recently was offered an opportunity to go to work for one of his largest employers, who supplied his company with estimating jobs. He can accomplish his job by the use of technology from his home.

L-R: Babies Olivia and Hannah who are identical plus share a special bond. The picture was taken by my daughter Sarah's veterinarian colleague who also is a photographer, Dr. Nicole McArthur.

A picture of the Busch Family at the Whitley house for one of the Busch's birthdays. I suspect it is Sarah Annemarie's L-R: Aaron, Sarah Annemarie, Monicqua, Ryan.

MONICQUA

When Monicqua moved to California at age 20, she eventually got a job with the City of Rancho Mirage in the Palms

Rube and the kids dressed for Monicqua's wedding in 1983: Rube, Joshua at 8, Jacob at 13, Sarah at 5.

Aaron and Monicqua's wedding party. Third from left is 11-year old daughter Sarah and second from right 15-year-old son Joshua.

Rube and I, Sarah and Joshua as part of Monicqua and Aaron's wedding party.

New mommy Monicqua and proud Papa Aaron holding baby Sarah Annemarie.

Springs area. She met and married a man named Dan, who played music for the congregation she was attending. This marriage lasted a few years.

Monicqua was still working for the City of Rancho Mirage and became friends with some of the City Planners, of which Aaron Busch was one. They developed a friendship that eventually led to their being married on March 4, 1990. Both continued in their city work.

We all came down south for their wedding which was right after we had moved from Santa Fe to Galt. Sarah was about 11 and Josh 15. Sarah was one of her maids of honor and Joshua walked her down the aisle.

Neek and Aaron seemed content to stay in southern California. When it came time for her to give birth to their first child—and our first grandchild—Sarah

Annemarie, both my Sarah and I came straight from our stint at Jews for Jesus' Camp Gilgal—where I had been a counselor and she a camper—to attend the birth. We stayed with them for two weeks, waiting, watching, but that new little one did not come.

Finally, when it was the day before I was to report back to teach at Florin High School in Elk Grove for the fall semester, on August 23, 1993, little Sarah successfully came into the world. She has her daddy's blue eyes, but the blonde hair her mom had as a young girl. Auntie Sarah and I stayed one more day then returned back north to Galt.

Before the birth of their son Ryan—on March 17, 1997—Aaron, Monicqua and Sarah moved north to Roseville, which is a community just west of Sacramento.

Aaron worked as a City Planner for Roseville and worked his way up to being over building permits before moving on in his profession. Monicqua was working for Roseville Electric. A later picture of Ryan would reveal that he favors his dad and Monicqua's dad, Bob.

Aaron was hired by Yuba City to be in charge of City Development, where he stayed for nine years before being recruited by the City Manager of Rancho Cordova to join him as an Assistant City Manager. That manager lasted in the political appointment for a year, leaving

Four generations of Kluting women: left baby Annemarie Busch, mom Monicqua Busch, me and my mother, Jean Kluting Berryman at about age 65.

I am holding year-old granddaughter Sarah Annemarie at an Undulations Band coffee-shop event. Uncle Josh played violin with the band.

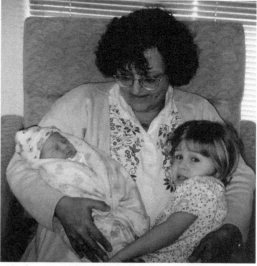

Newborn Ryan Matthew, Grandma Shari and new big sister Sarah Annemarie.

Grandma Shari and Grandpa Rube holding a young Ryan, lending credibility to the accusation that we routinely gave our grandkids sugar.

Jacob with his dad about 25 years ago. They had a strong bond.

Jacob and his siblings celebrating his 50th in Sarah's kitchen October 5, 2019: L-R Joshua, Monicqua, Jacob and Sarah.

his protégé Aaron to fend for himself.

As congenial as Aaron always makes himself, he realized this environment was not conducive to the upper mobility promised him by the outgoing City Manager. He was offered the Assistant City Manager job in Vacaville and was in that position for three years before recently being promoted to City Manager, just in time to deal with the impact of the Corona Pandemic.

Monicqua fulfilled a dream and completed an AA degree from our local junior college. She took classes for a long time, but disciplined herself to finish up the degree while also continuing to work. Monicqua later left clerical city work and began a job with Social Security. She continued in this work for several years before taking a medical retirement.

JACOB

Rube's son Jacob has become an expert on movies in general, but specifically those of superheroes. At this writing, he has produced a comic book introducing a new superhero of his making. She is somewhat like Super Woman, but is specifically dedicated to protecting the U. S. president, who is also a woman. The hero's greatest nemesis is her own twin sister. Jacob has had some book signings and has hopes that his comic book will be picked up for a movie.

For many years he has rented a condominium from his Aunt Patsy and Uncle Michael. Since Patsy's diagnosis of Multiple Sclerosis some years back, Michael hired Jacob to help take care of his aunt.

Jacob has always kept to himself, but he joins the rest of the family for all family events. Last October we celebrated his 50th birthday together.

Me with our four children in Hawaii in 2016: Joshua, Monicqua, Sarah, Jacob.

The Next Generation - From Oldest to Youngest

SARAH ANNEMARIE BUSCH
Friend of All Creatures

Monicqua and Aaron's daughter Sarah, age 26, graduated from UC Davis in Animal Science June of 2018. She was successful in landing a job in a large veterinary practice and hospital while she continues to take extra classes toward her goal of getting into Vet School.

She would be embarrassed that I believe she is beautiful in a Disney Princess sort of way. At one time she operated a small business of dressing up like Cinderella or other princesses and putting on little girls' birthday parties. She was very believable. She has recently moved into her own apartment in Roseville.

RYAN MATTHEW BUSCH
Compassionate Protector

Aaron and Monicqua's son Ryan, now 23 years old, continues living at home and attends Sierra Community College after

*Sarah at about 17 years old.
INSET PICTURE: A younger Sarah Annemarie.*

Ryan was in his element when the family went to Hawaii in 2016. INSET PICTURE: As a young child Ryan's determination was evident.

Corey really wanted there to be a picture of his beloved Sarai and him in this book. This was at her parents' home in southern California this past Thanksgiving.

The picture I love of Corey is with his dad on a Kauai beach in 2016. INSET PICTURE: A young Corey eagerly taking on the world.

having completed a year at Sacramento State University. He is returning to Sac State in the Fall of 2020.

Ever the industrious one, he holds down a job at a popular, upscale local Chinese eatery while he takes classes. He is the entrepreneur of the family and I fully expect he will launch some kind of unusual business that will do very well. Another garage prodigy!

COREY DAVIS WHITLEY
Steady and True

Mike and Sarah's son Corey turned 18 recently and just had a "virtual" graduation from high school last week, thanks again to the "no public gatherings" ruling for the COVID 19 Pandemic. His mother Sarah noted that his class is also the one born the year of 9-11.

Corey confided in me recently that he has decided he wants to teach history. I reminded him that both his grandfather, Rabbi Rube, and his Uncle Josh are history teachers. It is Corey who has been my lawn care person for several years. I get my yard done while getting to spend time with this special young man. In return he gets regular donations to his car account. He became a driver this year.

At this writing he is "betrothed" to a young woman he met at Jews for Jesus' Camp Gilgal when they were nine and ten years old. Their relationship began in earnest last summer at camp. She lives in southern California, while he lives in the northern part. She is hoping to move up to attend college with him.

ELIANA ROSE RUBINSTEIN
Rocks Our World

Josh and Rosie's first born, Eliana, is very musical and talented. She just turned 14 and had a virtual graduation from middle school. She will join her father next fall as a freshman in the high school where he teaches.

She has had several years of formal ballet. She takes voice and piano lessons and has been regularly singing on Beth Yeshua's worship team. She had a very successful run as Mrs. Darling in last year's school drama, "Peter Pan." She recently won the female vocal lead in this year's production in her school. Again, this performance was canceled due to the Corona virus.

She did us all proud becoming a bat mitzvah when she turned 12. She was invited to chant the blessings for the haftorah reading at the 2019 UMJC international conference and rocked it! This is the teenage Eliana about to embark on high school.

EITAN DAVID RUBINSTEIN
Scholar and Faithful Big Brother

The Ruby's second born and

Eliana Rose, several of us claim her as our "mini me." INSET PICTURE: A very dramatic picture of a younger Eliana.

Eitan David, Josh's mini me. INSET PICTURE: My favorite picture of a younger Eitan before the need for eyeglasses.

oldest son, Eitan, became 12 this past January. This is his first year in middle school as a 6th grader. This one is a wordsmith. He hears and sees nuances in words. I like to think he got it from me, but I know his parents and other grandparents are also very handy with words.

I noticed recently that he also has an "accounting" brain like my dad, Grandpa Monroe. My daddy worked as an accountant, and I love accounting as well. On top of that, this young man loves baseball and plays drums like a pro.

As of this writing, Eitan just celebrated his bar mitzvah. He has a deep love for their foster baby Ava. You can tell it is mutual.

RAINA LEE WHITLEY
Bright and True

Just three months behind Eitan is Sarah and Mike's oldest daughter, Raina. She just completed the same middle school as a 6th grader. This is another talented one who excels at drama. She has been in several productions and I expect she will continue to perform as well as serve on the production crew.

She has one of the sharpest minds I have seen in a long time, and that is saying something since I taught high schoolers for 40 years. She excels at organization. It is she I hired to help me organize the photos for this memoir. She was amazing.

She is the one I had thought might follow her mom into the veterinary field, but recently she shared with me that she might want to be a teacher. Regardless, whatever she sets her mind to, she will do and with a flair! If we do have Italian blood, she got it all. What a Mediterranean beauty!

Raina Lee is the perfect blend of her mother and father. INSET PICTURE: A younger Raina, bright with promise.

LEV BENJAMIN RUBINSTEIN

Knight of the Round Table

Lev is Hebrew for heart. If I ever need a lawyer, I hope Josh and Rosie's middle son Lev has my back. He is also another musical giant at the grand age of ten. He is like his dad, Grandpa Rube and my Dad, Grandad Monroe, in that he seems to be able to pick up any instrument and play it, and play it well!

He has been taking drum lessons since he was five and is a very intuitive drummer. He and Eitan alternate being the drummer for our congregation's worship team. He excels at playing piano and is able to improvise at will. On top of that, he has perfect pitch and a great singing voice. If he weren't so good at math, like his Grandpa Martin and Grandpa Rube, I would say he is headed for musical theater.

If that were not enough, he is getting very good at baseball. Whatever he does will be with heart, no pun intended.

Lev just before he turned 12. I call him "middle man" as he is the middle brother. He likes all things to be tidy and in their right place. INSET PICTURE: Lev Benjamin in an early picture showing how much he resembles Zeyde Rube about the same age.

HANNAH MARIE WHITLEY

The Queen of All She Sees

The older of Sarah and Mike's twins, Hannah is now nine and in 4th grade. I don't know how red hair can have gold streaks, but hers (and her sister's) does. Golden orange is a new hue. Gorgeous.

I don't think the twins realize

Hannah Marie in her fourth grade year. INSET PICTURE: Several years ago Hannah already had a glint in her eye.

how identical they are, but I'm not the only family member who sometimes confuses them. In fact, as I try to sort out who is good at what, I may get it wrong. I know they will correct me! If their mom had not designated colors for them as infants, we would have even more trouble determining who is who.

Hannah sets her mind on how things should be and can rarely be moved from that path. The positive flip side is that she is not easily deterred from following through with her goals. She has always seemed to be the more adventurous of the two, at least as far as ideas are concerned. Hannah does have a very tender heart and often just runs up to me and plants a kiss on my cheek and tells me how much she loves me. She is a gifted artist and loves to create stories.

OLIVIA GRACE WHITLEY
Full of Love

It is twin sister Olivia who has always seemed fearless to try physical feats. Both twins have played soccer for several years. Hannah plays a forward, while Olivia protects the goal. Their personalities are perfectly served in these roles.

It is Olivia who often gives in to both her sisters' suggestions. I have often wondered if she dislikes conflict. She seems to be the peacemaker of the family. Actually that was a role I played in my own family growing up.

All three of Sarah's girls are artists—as was she—but Olivia seems to be drawing all the time. She envisions that she will have a career with her art. Whatever her future holds, her compassion for others will surely be part of it. Need a back massage? Olivia will sense it and deliver.

Olivia Grace is her mother's mini me, which also makes her my mother, Grannie Jean's, mini me. INSET PICTURE: Olivia exhibits her tender side in all her pictures. Grace personified.

MICAH GILAD RUBINSTEIN
Protector of the Weak

Micah Gilad is Josh and Rosie's youngest son. At the big age of five, he is our red-headed wonder. He was the youngest for only four years, having happily yielded to their foster baby Ava this last year. He is a born big brother. He loves superheroes, especially Spider Man.

I watch him two half days a week after he gets out of the transitional kindergarten class. He calls his time with me "Bubbie Day." As soon as he walks in the door, he asks for an English muffin with peanut butter and honey, and he gets it. I wonder if he'll remember doing that.

He's a bright penny. I cannot fool this child! He lets me get away with nothing. He likes all things to be done in order, much like his big brother Lev.

Micah is red headed, and Zeyde had dark hair, even though he began with blonde hair. I think there is a striking resemblance between the two, even down to the freckles.

AVA MARIE RUBINSTEIN
Smart as a Whip and In Control

I have taken care of Ava two days a week since she came into Josh and Rosemary's family as a foster baby at two months old

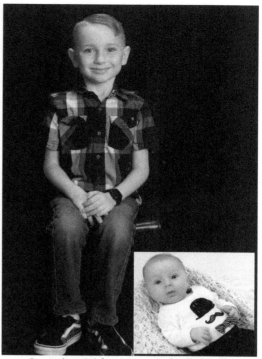

Our unique Mickey "G" - Micah Gilad at the end of 2021. INSET PICTURE: A bright-eyed Micah, ready to take on the world.

Grandpa Rube at about seven with an expression I see on Micah's face every day. This is the only grandson he never got to see. And, of course, he never met the last grandchild, Ava.

*Ava Marie at the end of 2021
showing off her vibrant personality.
INSET PICTURE: An early picture of Ava
about the time she came to the Rubinsteins.*

and she is 18 months now. Even though she had a rough beginning, it seems like we have always had her in the family.

She wears cute rubber-framed glasses. Evidently there is a gene in her birth family for lazy eye. The ophthalmologist says that correcting her vision now may keep her from developing this condition. She sure does look cute in her little spectacles, but she is very quick to pull them off and mostly chew on them since she is teething.

She's as smart as she is cute. She's proficient at sign language cues, but hasn't mastered many words. When she wants a cracker, however, she is especially clear, but she says "crack crack." Even without a large verbal vocabulary, she understands everything!

Can you tell I am a grandma...

My Supportive Siblings

Even though this narrative is not specifically about my six siblings, I want to give a shout out to them. We share a great love for each other. We do our best to get together at least once a year, which is not easy given Dwayne, Carol and Anita live in separate Texas towns, Linda Kay and Michael live in different New Mexico cities, Elaine lives in Colorado and I live in California. My brothers and sisters have always been there for me, and I have tried to be there for them.

My oldest sibling, Dwayne Truman Mings, was born to my father and his first wife, Cora Lee (Holloman) Mings. Dwayne's mother died when he was an infant. My father and mother married when Dwayne was three years old. All six subsequent children were from the same mother, Jean (Kluting) Mings.

I recently asked Dwayne how he felt about his childhood. I was concerned because I knew that he lived with his maternal grandparents much of his life. Dwayne said he had no complaints. He said he was a problem child with anybody he lived with. He added, "Most places I was accepted, but not loved." While still in Peacock living with his grandparents, he went to work on a ranch at the age of 17. He left there to go live with Daddy's sister Florence Allen in San Antonio, TX to finish his schooling.

Dwayne found the schools there were not geared to kids getting graduation credit for agricultural courses, of which he had many from Peacock High School. In order for him to graduate on time, he had to return to Peacock. The Principal told him it might be hard as he would have to go into second semester plane geometry and Dwayne had never had the first semester. Usually Dwayne was a straight A student. He did pass geometry with a 74%, and all other classes with A's so graduated on time. He was still living with his grandad Charlie Holloman who started charging him $60-a-month rent-and-board as soon as he graduated.

His grandad wanted to send him to Texas A & M, but Dwayne did not feel confident he could handle college level and didn't want to waste his granddad's money. Instead, Dwayne went to live in Aspermont, TX to work in the oilfield. About that time the oilfield there began to peter out.

Dwayne decided he was going to join the Marines. He got a couple of his buddies to go with him to Abilene to the Marine Recruiting Center. They snatched him right up and put him on a bus to report for duty. They tested him and put him in charge of a detail saying he had a "senior in college mentality."

During his time in the Corps, he would take leaves and go back and work for his uncle Bill Craft at his cotton gin. It was on one of those leaves Irvine introduced him to Patricia Mitchell who was in 11th grade at Lovington High School in NM. Dwayne said he was dragging his heels about getting engaged to Patri-

All my sibs at a family reunion in 2003 in Ruidosa, NM.
L–R, back: Anita and Jay Norris, Dwayne and Pat Mings, me, Carol Lester.
Front: Rhetha and Michael Mings, Elaine Mings, Rube, Linda Ragland.

cia. Our dad told him that if he didn't, he was a d##m fool. Dwayne said this was one time he accepted his dad's advice. He married Patricia in 1959, about a year after completing the Marine Corps.

Most of his career he worked for the Federal Government on the Border Patrol. He served most of the time guarding the New Mexico/Mexico border, but also spent several years serving in the Bahamas with the Patrol. He now lives in Texas. Dwayne was widowed some years ago.

Dwayne and Pat have four children: Cynthia, Charles, Wade, and Floyd. Cynthia works in a pharmacy and married an Air Force man. They now live in Utah. Charles' main line of work was as a lineman for the telephone company. He and his family live in Texas. Wade went right out of high school into the Army. He was based in Germany. He retired from the Reserves as a Master Sargeant and lives with his family in Texas. Floyd has had health issues and lives in Texas with his family.

The oldest girl in our family, Ramona Carol (Mings) Lester, has lived primarily in the three-state area of New Mexico, Texas and Colorado all her adult life. After graduating from high school in 1958, Carol met Kenneth Stinson while she was living in Kermit, TX helping her lifelong friend, Betty Bostick's, grandmother in an oilfield café. Betty's grandmother was the manager and cook. Carol and Kenneth got married in 1959. They have two children, Kenneth (Buddy) and John. They divorced when the boys were young.

In 1972, Carol gave birth to Cameron Peckham. When Cameron was two years old, they moved to Eunice, NM where Carol met and married Travis Lester in 1975. Carol always worked as an accountant/office manager. Travis died in 1996 from complications of Diabetes and cancer. She continued living in New Mexico until she moved to Texas in 2015 where she still resides. Carol said for me to tell you that she is the Big Sister and whatever she says goes!

Carol's older son Kenneth "Buddy" started in the oil business working in a refinery and worked while getting his teaching credential at Eastern NM University. After getting certified he taught elementary school in Lovington, NM. His family moved to the Dallas area where he got another teaching job. Now he works for a French-owned oil company as an environmental specialist. John is educated as an oil drilling specialist and has been a consultant to the oil industry for most of his adulthood. His family lives in Florida. Daughter Cameron Squires is a lawyer working for an international accounting firm. She lives in Texas.

The second oldest girl is Peggy Elaine. Elaine is the artist and historian of the family. I don't want anyone to think she is the only artist, as several others also create art, but she is the one who has been able to sell her work. I personally own over a dozen of Elaine's paintings and drawings. My home is her gallery.

Her earliest jobs were in accounting and doing audits. She married when she was 22 in 1965 and had her daughter Aimee' Atwood three years later. During this marriage her husband was in the Army stationed in Germany during the

Vietnam War. They were married for thirteen years during which time they traveled a lot for her husband who was playing music in a band after getting out of the Army.

After the divorce, Elaine started college at the age of 36 studying fine arts and archaeology. During the summers she worked for a museum at archaeological digs and excavation sites in the Four-Corners area of SW Colorado. After four years, lacking 12 college credits, she decided to stay in Colorado, because she felt it would be better for her daughter. She later petitioned the University of Colorado, having taken many extra classes off campus, to be able to get her degree at the age of 45.

She did some substitute teaching and working at an archaeology lab identifying and cataloguing artifacts that had come from earlier excavations. She picked up working more intensely on her art at that time. Her love of archaeology has never left her. She also has various stories she has been "mentally writing," and has wordprocessed some of them.

She is a great history buff in general. In 1997 when she was staying at our mom's, she organized, identified and created a family tree chart based on the photos of Grannie Mattie Kluting. Elaine has always been a detail-oriented person about where people came from and how they ended up where they are.

She designed and contracted the workers to build her house in Colorado. She wanted a vintage-looking house with modern technology. She also created and put in the landscaping for her "cottage" garden. Passersby called her the Flower Lady because her yard was so colorful and lush. Elaine told me she took an empty lot and made a good painting out of it.

Elaine still resides in SW Colorado and her RN daughter Aimee' (Atwood) Gunter and family reside in northern New Mexico. Elaine always tells Carol that she is the second in command and always wanted to override whatever Carol said. Classic.

The sister just two years younger than me is Anita Dolores. When our parents divorced, Anita was the oldest child at home being 16. She had a serious boyfriend, Ronnie Mahan, who had just moved with his parents to west Texas. Anita followed him and stayed with our mom's Uncle Austin Guess until she married Ronnie in 1963.

She worked as a waitress briefly then went to Business School. She went to work as a secretary for a trust officer. They had two children, Ron and Kimberly, moved to the country, had horses, and a beautiful garden. Having the horses was the fulfillment of a childhood dream for Anita. Ronnie and Anita were divorced after 22 years of marriage.

The rest of her career was working as a secretary for various businesses, including lawyers, bankers and interior designers. While working at a bank as secretary for the vice president, she later realized he was to become her future husband.

She married her banker boss, Jay Norris, with whom she has been married for 33 years. They have had no children together, but he brought a son, Alan

Norris, to the marriage, who was the same general age as her children, late teens. Anita reports they all got along very well.

Anita's talents are singing and writing poetry and songs. She has received one award for her poetry, but she has not pursued publishing. She has often made gifts of her writing. She especially likes to sing in church and at special occasion events. As young girls, we sisters often sang together. This will date you if you know this reference, but we considered ourselves to be like the Lennon Sisters who sang on the Lawrence Welk Show. Anita draws her singing inspiration from Mahalia Jackson's rendition of "In the Garden."

She always aspired to be a singer and actress. She got to fulfill her acting dream in a small way by being at the right place (Mexico) at the right time and being cast in a bit part in a movie starring Johnny Depp, Antonio Banderas, William Defoe and Selma Hayek.

Anita and Jay reside in west Texas, close to all three children. Son Ron Mahan, a landscape artist and vintage car enthusiast, and his wife Terry, a retired Postal Carrier and ruthless board game player, spend a lot of time with the family. Daughter Kim (Mahan) Green is an intelligent, self-taught medical person, while also advocating for animal rights. She is a fitness guru and has her own personal gym. Both Ron and Kim raised their children in Texas. Alan Norris is a RN and has primarily worked in a hospital in west Texas.

The baby girl is Linda Kay. This is exactly the way we thought of her. She was the cutest of us all. She did not get to enjoy the limelight long as our little brother was born when she was only a year old. Linda is another creative Mings. She is like our mom, and many of us, who love to garden. No matter where Linda lives, you will always find lush plantings. I guess you could say that about all my sibs and me. Linda is also a painter, singer and writer, although she has not pursued a professional life in any of these endeavors.

She was married at a young age to Kenny Fish. They had three children: Debbie Gae, Lisa Gayle and Ken Don. The family lived in Colorado some of the time but returned to the little town of Eunice just outside our hometown of Hobbs, NM. She learned drywall finishing and worked with Kenny in the construction field. He was also mechanical and was a professional drag racer. He taught Linda to work on cars. She and Kenny were divorced after 15 years of marriage in 1980.

Her children were 13, 12 and 8 when she met and married Steve Ragland who helped her continue raising the kids. Steve worked in the oil business as a hot oil truck driver. He became the manager of the company he worked for. They were married about 15 years when Linda lost Steve to cancer in 1994. Linda began taking college classes after Steve's death in her lifelong pursuit of being an artist. She got her AA in Art around 2002.

Some years later Linda and Bill Marr met and married. Bill also worked in the oil fields primarily as a pumper, but also a driller and a well tester. He also worked as an optimizer where he optimized production and fixed problems. They are both retired and still maintain the family home in Eunice, but she and

Bill spend most of their time in their second residence in Ft. Sumner. Their home sits on about 38 acres with a view of the lake. This is where they follow their passion for fishing, hunting deer and elk in season, and gardening. They just finished a pre-existing little house on the property for Linda to have a studio for her other loves of painting, jewelry making and other crafts.

Linda's oldest, Debbie, a gifted writer and painter herself, followed in her mother's footsteps and got her Associates Degree in Art. She had almost completed her AA in Fire Science when her health began to deteriorate. She went to be with the Lord one course short of getting her second degree. Debbie's children's families still live in New Mexico.

Lisa – another family history buff – and her family spent some time in California before returning to settling in New Mexico and Texas. Ken Don had his own landscaping business for a long time. He sold this and took a job overseeing the school buses, even driving for special events for Eunice where his children were attending school and their mother is a teacher.

The youngest child in our family is Michael Monroe Mings (3M). Michael is the only sibling who has primarily lived in our hometown of Hobbs, NM his entire adult life. Mike is the mechanical one of the bunch. His first "project" was when at the age of seven or eight he found our dad's pocket watch in a drawer and decided to fix it. He was not successful, but that was when we all saw his potential. His life's work was always about fixing things mechanical.

He married his sweetheart in 1969 at the age of 20. Mike had met Rhetha Jo McDaniel when she worked at the Reel Theater in the box office on the main street of our hometown of Hobbs, NM. He and his friends would be "dragging" Main and saw her in the little glass booth every night. Mike said she chased him until he gave up. Must have been a good match as they recently celebrated 50 years of marriage.

They had only been married a couple of months when the Vietnam Draft happened. When he first went into the Army he was offered a chance to go to a military academy, but it would have been another two-year commitment. Then the Army told him his scores were high enough to go to Officer's Candidate School, but it would have been a three-year stint. Staying longer was not appealing to this newlywed. After serving two years with the Army, including the typical combat commitment of one year in Vietnam, he completed his service and went home to Rhetha.

When he first came home, a friend's dad who owned the Toyota business in Hobbs hired Mike to sell cars, but ended up putting him in charge of the shop. He worked for a variety of businesses primarily working in car repair shops. Before he started his business of repairing HVAC systems – Joe Cool Air Conditioning – he worked for another air conditioning company and even owned an interim AC company.

His wife has always worked in Accounts Payable, primarily at a car-truck-tractor-trailer business in Hobbs. Rhetha continues this job, but somehow finds time to make a baby quilt from scratch every weekend, as well as writing out cards for all the life events of all of her extended, extensive family. She donates her quilts to needy babies.

Mike and Rhetha still live in Hobbs, NM where Michael is very active in Veterans affairs. He plants and maintains a magnificent garden – a family tradition – and spends countless hours in his "retirement" tending it and also working on rebuilding a vintage car.

Michael and Rhetha have two daughters, Katie Jean (Mings, Smith) Crowley, a teacher, and Molly Marie (Mings) Lasater, a photographer, real estate agent, former elementary teacher and current homeschool mom. The girls and their families reside in SE New Mexico and west Texas.

Coming from a big family gave me many playmates, a luxury that my children did not have. I tried to get back "home" once a year all of my adult life. On those occasions I got the opportunity to reconnect with my siblings, but the cousins also got some time together. My oldest, Monicqua, loved her time with my sibs' children. There are many family stories of the trouble she and Carol's boys, Buddy and Johnny, got into every time they were together.

— ❧ ❧ —

Epilogue

Sometimes I think that the impetus for writing about my life has been that I have not seen anyone with my history share their story. From a Southern Baptist to a hippie, from high school dropout to high school teacher, from seeker of spirits to Spirit filled Believer, and ultimately to worshipper of the Messiah of the world.

When I am listening to the news or watching historical documentaries, I can't believe what the media says about hippies. All they see is sex, drugs and rock 'n' roll. I hope my portrayal gets more to the core of a group of counter-culture folks who were sincerely seeking to find balance in a world they saw as chaotic. Let the story speak for itself.

Portrait of Richard as a baby.

Early picture of Rube's Uncle Don,
Uncle Harland and mother Marjorie.

Appendix A

Richard "Rube" Davis Rubinstein

August 2, 1945 — November 4, 2010

What I know of Rube's family life comes from stories I was told by Rube, his friends or my mother-in-law, Marge and some from my father-in-law Herb.

Rube's mother's family were all Nebraska farmers. His mother Marjorie "Marge" Moore had two brothers: Don and Harland. They lived through the Great Depression, but just barely.

Marge's father Ralph was known for wearing out Bibles from constant reading. The last one he owned became an heirloom to Rube. One of the ways this family survived the Depression was that Ralph took to robbing little country stores around the state. It did not come out for some time, but he was caught and served time for it. He was said to have never hurt anyone in the course of the robberies.

Marge's mom, Mildred, was a strong woman. She kept the family going in the

Rube's maternal grandfather,
Ralph Moore.

Rube's maternal grandmother,
Mildred Moore.

face of all the humiliation and the loss of the main breadwinner while Ralph served time. The children were all known for having a very strong work ethic. It was no easy feat to attend college, but all of them did. Don got a PhD in Nuclear Physics and worked in that field before somewhat retiring into farming and educational administration. Harland became an engineer.

The family never owned a car during their early years. I am not quite remembering the exact story of which brother, Don or Harland, rode horseback to school with Marjorie, but that horse was their only

*Rube's mother Marjorie
as a young woman.*

*Marjorie was no stranger to riding horses
as it was the way she got to school.*

*The young couple, Marjorie Ruth (Moore)
and Herbert Bernard Rubinstein.*

*Father Herbert Bernard Rubinstein
as a young man.*

Rube's paternal grandfather
Morris Rubinstein M.D.

Rube's paternal grandmother
Beatrice (Goldstein) Rubinstein R.N.

mode of transportation. Their farm was far enough out of town that they had to rely on the kindness of family or neighbors when they needed to buy supplies.

Marge came off the farm to live in town with another family so she could go to high school. She and her brother Don both attended college in California. Marge was a pre-med student at UC Berkeley when she met and married Rube's father, another pre-med student, Herbert Bernard Rubinstein. They both dropped out of school to get married.

Marge was a counter-culture person herself. She always bucked the system and fought for the little guy. Her personal philosophy manifested in her belief system, which was primarily communist. When she married Herbert, she evidently assumed he was a left-wing Jew and shared her political bent. He actually did not.

Herb came from a fairly conservative home in everything, including politics. Herbert's father, Morris (Moshe) Rubinstein was a medical doctor with the VA who had been raised in the Bronx, NY in a Jewish home.

Rube with grandpa
Louis Rubinstein in 1945.

Rube with his grandmother.

Herb's mother Beatrice (Goldstein) Rubinstein was also Jewish and raised in Brooklyn, NY. She became a Nurse.

Morris' father, Louis, immigrated from the area referred to as the Pale of Settlement by Poland in about 1880. It was probably during times of the horrible pogroms in that area. He was a locksmith and worked on clocks.

Rube's great grandfather Louis' grave had been unmarked until Rube and I found it and planned to put up a stone. Louis' son Morris had died during the year after Louis' death so was not available to erect the stone at the customary yartzheit (one year anniversary of the death).

We were interrupted from placing Louis' headstone by Rube's illness. When we set Rube's own headstone, we also set up the one for Louis in the cemetery where he was buried by Tracy, CA.

So there were many cultural and political differences between Herb and Marjorie. Their marriage was described as rocky but they appeared to always dote on Rube, who

Rube, the future Harley rider.

An early Christmas at the Rubinsteins: Herbert, "Dick" and Marjorie. They celebrated Christmas and Chanukah.

Four generations of Rubinstein men: Rube is the baby, held by his father Herbert, Herb's father Morris, and Morris' father Louis. Dr. Morris is in military uniform as he was an M.D. for the Veteran's.

was called Dick all of his young life. Both parents were keen on getting him out in the fresh air.

Even though Rube's father came from orthodox Jewish parents, he became part of Reform Judaism. With mother Marjorie being Gentile, Herb and Marge celebrated both cultures in their home.

Rube with his beloved Spaniel Dixie.

Rube as a young musician at the piano.

Rube the early "baseballer." Our son Josh's son, Micah, present age five, calls himself a "baseballer."
He plays T-ball. Lots of similarities in Micah and G'pa Rube!

Rube and sister Johanna about the time their parents divorced. Rube – sporting his first camera – was already very much into photography as was his father and his father's brother Walt.

Rube was always a dog lover. His first dog was a cocker spaniel named Dixie. They were very attached. Both Rube and I had spaniels as children and later raised Springer Spaniels on our land outside Santa Fe, NM.

Rube always thought of himself as an athlete. His favorite sport was baseball. Here he is at ten years old playing catch. The caption indicates it might have been Marge playing ball with him.

Rube was also brought up with an appreciation of music, taking both piano and clarinet lessons. He later taught himself guitar, accordian and harmonicas, to name a few.

Marjorie and Hebert's marriage lasted less than 15 years and produced then 12-year old Rube and his sister Johanna who was four.

— ❧ ❧ —

Later when Rube's parents divorced, Marjorie returned to school and became an English and Home Economics teacher. She

Rube's Dad Herb's only sibling, Walter Rubinstein, who also loved photography.

Herbert and second family, Christmas 1979. Seated: Herb and wife June. Standing: son Kevin and daughter Kathleen.

primarily taught in adult education programs. Herbert remarried and lived in East Lansing, MI with wife June and their two children, Kevin and Kathleen. Herb became part of the Episcopalian Church during this marriage. June was raised in England and had been Anglican.

Herb went on after the divorce from Marjorie to becoming a hospital admin-

istrator, after getting a Masters from Yale, but always meant to be a medical doctor as was his father. To his credit, when he was 60 years old he returned to school and became a nurse. His second wife was already a nurse. Sadly, he only lived a few more years after that. He died of complications after having surgery to restore circulation to his legs.

Early picture of Kathleen and husband Brad Charon, who had been widowed. His children, Lucas and Shy, became Kathleen's children.

— ❧ ❧ —

Early on Rube was a Boy Scout. He even earned Life Scout status when he walked back for help when a fellow scout was injured while on a scouting hike.

As soon as he was old enough to go around town – which would have been Oakland and San Francisco – he rented Toros and sailed about the San Francisco Bay. He always loved the sea.

Rube went on to help build a 46-foot Wharram catamaran. We lived on that boat when we first got together. Throughout our

Rube as a Boy Scout.

Kevin Rubinstein's three children when they were younger: Megan Elizabeth, Kevin William II "KJ" and Kaitlyn Marie at a beach. Their mother is Brenda (Liechty) Rubinstein. She and Kevin divorced.

marriage, Rube took every opportunity to sail. We owned a 24-ft sailboat chris-tened the "Osprey" that we kept at the Delta by Lodi, CA at the time of his death. The most authentic picture I have of Rube is from when we visited San Francisco to see the "big boats."

Rube's early years were actually quite typical, except for how his family connected with their synagogue. His Hebrew "religious" training was as a result of a Jewish parent co-op. These primarily mixed-marriage couples held their own meetings, separate from the synagogue. When they felt the need for a rabbi, they called on the local reform temple where Herb and Marjorie had been married. Rube was in training for his bar mitzvah at the time his parents split up.

He never had the ceremony, until much later as an adult, at which time he had be-gun to believe Yeshua (Jesus) to be the Jewish Messiah.

In school Rube was more of an introvert and what we might now label a nerd. He was

Rube always wanted to be sailing. This is the way I remember him. We were at San Francisco Wharf looking at the Big Boats.

Rube in a toga for Latin Club, far right.

Rube at about 12 in April 1957 when he would have been studying for his Bar Mitzvah ceremony.

in Chess Club and also Latin Club.

When Marge remarried, it was to a widowed, radical left-wing person of her own political ilk. Godfrey Emerson Boehm, known as Jeff, was a reporter-editor of a union newspaper and was very active in all the causes that Marge supported such as: stopping troops going to Vietnam, boycotting grapes to support Cesar Chavez, picketing nuclear power plants. Jeff brought his son Eric, then about nine, into the family that included seven-year old Johanna and Rube at about fifteen.

Jeff's wife and younger son Karl had been killed in a tragic car accident a few years prior when the family had just set out on vacation. His wife was driving and Karl was behind her on the driver's side when she ran a stop light and was hit by a car. Jeff was badly injured and hospitalized for a year. Eric was physically fine, but lived with neighbors for that year. It was very emotionally terrifying for him.

Jeff and Marjorie were married until he died at the age of 93 in May of 2000. It was always assumed that his health and life expectancy was diminished for both his having been a Prisoner of War (POW) in WWII and also having been in that horrible car accident.

I found an obituary for Jeff on KeyWiki published after his death. It sums up his life very succinctly. It also illustrates the political tone of the household in which Rube grew up:

Probably the first Christmas together as a newly-formed family in 1961. Marjorie's parents were visiting. L to R: back row - Marjorie, her parents Mildred and Ralph Moore, Jeff Boehm. Seated in front: Eric Boehm and Johanna Rubinstein. 16-year-old Rube (known as Dick then) was taking the picture.

Marjorie and Jeff considered themselves to be soul mates.

***Godfrey Emerson Boehm** was a founding member of the Newspaper Guild and devoted a lifetime to journalism and labor organizing. He died of congestive heart failure on May 23rd 2000, at his home in Santa Rosa. He was 93.*

Boehm interrupted his work as a journalist to serve as a combat pilot during World War II. He spent 15 months in a German pris-

on camp after being shot down over Italy. After his return, he was blacklisted and forced to work as a janitor for several years. Ten years later, Boehm returned to journalism and co-founded the Union Gazette, where he worked until his retirement in 1983. In 1957, he received the International Labor Press Association award for excellence in journalism. Boehm was also awarded the Purple Heart and an Air Medal for his valor in service, but Boehm returned the Air Medal in 1986 to protest US foreign policy.

Boehm was survived by his wife, Marjorie (Moore) Boehm, his two sons, Eric Boehm and Richard Rubinstein, and his daughter, Johanna (Rubinstein) Thorpe.

Likewise, Marjorie was a national political figure, serving in many offices of the Women's International League for Peace and Freedom (WILPF) including being the U. S. Section President from 1977-1981. I found her obituary written by a WILPF friend and colleague, Ellen Schwartz. This article reflects the esteem with which my mother-in-law was held, as well as further setting the political tone in the house where Rube was raised:

Marjorie Boehm, *April 15, 1922 – October 7, 2014*

With great sorrow I share the news that Marjorie Boehm, former Women's International League for Peace and Freedom (WILPF) U.S. Section President, and one of my oldest friends, passed away on Tuesday, Oct. 7. Marjorie was active and committed to WILPF from the time she joined in 1963, until declining health made it impossible about 2 years ago.

She was elected to the WILPF National Board as Vice President in 1975, representing the Western Region, then served as U.S. Section President from 1977–1981. Marjorie represented WILPF as part of international delegations to Cuba and the USSR. Before and after that she was active in the leadership of the San Jose Branch, until moving to Santa Rosa in 1990 with her husband Jeff, esteemed California labor union newspaper editor.

In 2002, she moved to the Sacramento area to be closer to family and immediately became involved in the activities of the Sacramento branch.

In Rube's teen years, he bought into the family causes. He was once arrested for stopping the troop trains going to Vietnam. For this act of Civil Disobedience, he was put in jail. Rube fought their trying to cut his radically long hair, which earned him a

The three children at Jeff's memorial service: sister Johanna, brother Eric, and Rube.

stint in solitary.

One of the strongest convictions held by Rube's mother and stepfather, Jeff, was the plight of the migrant workers, especially the Mexicans working in California fields. During Rube's senior year in high school, he wrote a report entitled "California Migratory Workers" for which he received an A and special commendation of his Economics teacher, Mr. Winston, on July 27, 1962. His conclusion epitomizes his fervent sentiments:

If we close our eyes to these conditions they do not disappear. We must do something about them. I suggest a plan of action in which the migrant workers be given the same opportunity as other workers in the country. Among them: mimimum wage, federal camps, a health plan, federal education, regulated working conditions, in general the chance to become decent, first class citizens.

This report quotes heavily from *Strangers in our Fields*, written by Ernesto Galarza, Secretary of the National Agricultural Workers' Union (AFL–CIO). His book was published by the U.S. Section of the Joint United States-Mexico Trade Union Committee in Washington, D. C. Jeff Boehm was the Editor of the Union newspaper during all this time. Galarza also wrote *Barrio Boy* and was the champion of what he perceived to be the downtrodden workers the U. S. had imported from Mexico for cheap labor. Ernesto was a family friend and was engaged by Marge and Jeff to tutor Rube in writing.

Rube's father was at this time a remarried hospital administrator in Illinois.

Rube's senior picture for high school. He attended Oakland High in the San Francisco Bay area.

He tried to help keep Rube out of the war in Vietnam after learning he had received his notice to report. Herb appealed to the Draft Board to let Rube serve as a porter in a hospital where he was the Administrator for his "community service" as a Conscientious Objector. He was refused, and instead Rube was put to work at a local Goodwill where he remembers having to sort a lot of old shoes. Rube resisted the draft, ultimately by threatening to throw a chair out a window of his military interviewer. He was labeled "Undesirable" by the recruiter. He was the family hero.

Rube was compliant in his involvement in these causes, but he was fairly typical in wanting to have his autonomy. At his high school graduation party—thrown by his mother and including all her "radical" adult friends and colleagues—one of the guests asked Rube – who still used the nickname

Dick then – where he was going to attend college. Rube replied, "Ask my mom!"

He matriculated at UC Berkeley where he lived in co-op housing and bicycled everywhere. His stepfather refused to sign for him to get a driver's license, which was required for anyone under 21. Being very bright and well-read, he did very well, except for his Russian language classes. He failed this course two semesters running and was put on probation from Berkeley. This was ironic since his immigrant grandparents spoke Russian. During that time he attended a local college to get his grades up and was consequently readmitted.

While at Berkeley (1963-1965), Rube was in touch with more radicals than he had ever known, which was saying something. Rube characterized the political scene as getting very dangerous on campus as almost everyone was carrying a gun, Rube included. Rube made the decision to transfer as a junior to University of California Santa Cruz (UCSC) in his junior year. This university was just starting up, the year being around 1965. He was also changing his major from pre-med to history.

This UC only had two colleges at the time, one of which was Cowell – Social Sciences. At this time Rube's double major was U. S. Social History and Middle Eastern History. He loved the counter culture atmosphere of this campus. Teachers did not give grades, but rather wrote a paragraph about each student indicating whether they passed or failed. He said it felt like an extension of his beliefs being there.

He struck up friendships with some like-minded fellow students, several of whom were incoming freshmen, Russ Resnik and Eitan Shishkoff included. Several of them formed a band for which Rube played guitar and harmonica simultaneously—shades of Bob Dylan—while Eitan played drums, Jeffrey Becker keyboard, and I never knew if Billy Eschenbach played an instrument or was just their friend. They pretty much wrote their own stuff or played Bob Dylan's songs. They called their band Sunburst. The flyer advertising their last performance was called "The Sign of the Last Chance Dance."

Their dubious "claim to fame" was being asked to "open" for a performance of The Grateful Dead. Rube told of smoking dope with Jerry Garcia and hanging with his band. What Rube never told me—I learned about five years ago from Eitan—was that their little band did not realize they were to supply their own sound system. They did indeed play on that stage, but not many could hear them as I alluded to in the main body of this writing.

Rube's band's flyer - The Sign of the Last Chance Dance. Gwendolyn and Jeffrey Becker, Eitan and Connie Shishkoff, Mary and Rube with Billy.

During this time he also held down a job at a local lodge that was owned by lifelong family friends. He was a prep cook and did some cooking on the weekends. It was here he met his first wife, Mary Dolan. She was a waitress from Moss Landing. The story goes that one day they were in a laundromat together doing their laundry when they decided to be married. Rube declared them so. He had recently sent off for a $5 Universal Life license that entitled him to perform weddings.

Most of these few fellow students became lifelong friends. Eitan Shishkoff, Russell Resnik and Jeffrey Becker were in the group that founded their commune at Big Basin. It was also out of this environment that Rube's wife of some five years decided to move in with Jeffrey as they left the Big Basin property, leaving Rube behind, at which point I met him.

Prior to Big Basin, this group felt the need to leave California, and actually to leave society in general. Another of their friends, Andrea, was in possession of a property her parents bought high up on the Continental Divide in New Mexico. There was a tiny "stop" – no real town there – called Lindrith. Rube always characterized it this way, "There was a post office and a bar where a person could get a hamburger and a beer."

When Rube was in his senior year at UCSC, those around him were getting more agitated to be out of the predominant culture of America, which they perceived to be greedy, fortune oriented, anti-personal freedoms, and where big business was in control. The Man.

This piece of land was so remote, they were definitely secluded. They somehow believed they could do subsistence gardening, but when we lived there we found it was almost impossible to grow much on that rock. There was more than one reason they called it Stone Mountain.

So, a small group moved there. This was after Rube and Mary had Jacob

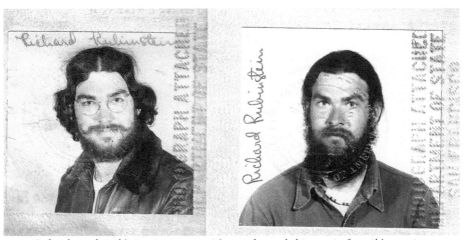

Rube always kept his passports current in case he needed to escape from this country. Note the changes in his face as he became more entrenched in his opposition to world events. The first was taken in 1968 – when he would have been married to Mary – and the second in 1974 after he and I were together. I also kept my passport current.

who was about one year old. The couple used an old treadle machine to make a teepee in which they lived. They romanticized Native Americans in their commune, so living in a tepee was a natural choice. The tiny fire in the center was the hub of their existence.

It was particularly rough living in it, however, as little Jacob was in a full body cast at the time—having only recently been discovered with a dislocated hip from birth. He could not walk but dragged himself around on the dirt "floor." When winter hit, it was intolerable as the temperature got down to 40 below. That was when Rube decided to take his family and return to UCSC to finish his last semester of college.

A friend named Adam had built the only actual house on the property some years prior. It was constructed against the side of the hill, which formed its back wall. The structure was tiny with a dirt floor, but it did have the whole front side of windows. A small loft served as the bedroom, the downstairs being the eating and sitting area. Square footage was probably about 200: 20 by 10 downstairs, smaller upstairs.

No electricity, no actual kitchen nor indoor plumbing. There was a 55-gallon drum for water and a hose from the garden well feeding into it. So, yes, there was actually running water as there was a spigot and there was a sink inside.

This is the house that Rube and I moved into when he brought me to this remnant of their commune a couple of years later. At that point, all but one of the others had moved on for various reasons.

The only other dwelling place was a hogan built by Eitan and Connie. It was dug out of the earth and was covered by the kiva roof typical of these Na-

The goat house at Stone Mountain.

tive American homes. The only other structure was the goat house, which also housed chickens. There are times when people shared this animal shelter.

In order to have water, the group dug a well, which they did by hand. At this time Rube and Mary were back in California, but when Rube got out of school at UCSC on a Friday, he drove nonstop more than 1000 miles to Stone Mountain, helped dig for a day, then turned around and drove back to school. It was on one of these trips that Rube fell asleep at the wheel and flipped his jeep. He amazingly came out pretty much unscathed.

Couples Eitan and Connie Shishkoff and Russ and Jane Resnik moved from Stone Mountain to a place called The Mesa where they established a home in an existing adobe structure. It was here that minister Don Compton from a Santa Fe based organization called Shalom Ministries, came to talk to this ragtag band about the Lord. In due time, they all came to believe that Jesus is Lord.

With that realization came change. They remained there for a short time, actually long enough to help Rube and I come to the Lord, after which they all relocated, Eitan's family to Santa Fe and Russ's to Albuquerque.

Don Compton held a vision of sharing Jesus with hippies who were predominantly Jews and bravely, faithfully set out to do so. He was instrumental in leading a great number of Jews to accept their Jewish Messiah. Rube and I credit him for our salvation as well, since he nurtured us after our declaration of faith. Don is a true, Godly man and continues ministering to those in prison in the Santa Fe area.

I will add, as somewhat of a disclaimer, that all I have learned about Rube's life before me was gleaned from snippets told by all the aforementioned persons. I do not claim that I have the timeline, nor even the impact of the events well represented. I add this appendix to give the reader a sense of who Rube and his friends were leading up to our life together.

A final word about Rube. No one is perfect. I have to say that he worked so hard at being a Godly man. Did he ever have flare ups? Yes. Did he lose his temper? Yes. Was he ever unkind? No! He always said that kindness trumps everything. "Always take the path of greatest kindness." I can honestly say that is how he related to me.

The Reader probably has a good idea of how headstrong I could be. When Rube and I argued, pretty much I was to blame. Let's say 99.7% of the time! One of my close friends, Carolyn Reese, corrected this statement and declared "99.9%." But this man that God gave me was ALWAYS FIRST to ask for forgiveness. He was always the one who restored me and he did so with kindness and meekness. He epitomized Gala-

Early picture of Rube, Mary and little Jacob.

tians 6:1. Somehow he always felt that if we had an argument, at its core he was to blame as the spiritual head of the family. He took full responsibility.

He was very genuine about this sentiment and acted on it, always right away. He was a proponent of "not letting the sun go down on his anger," so I can count maybe two times in our almost 40 years together that we went to bed without resolving an issue. That is his greatest legacy. I truly hope all of his kids and grandkids can live their lives that way.

Rube was inspired by the Holy Spirit to write many songs of his faith in Yeshua. He probably wrote at least 20 such songs. There is one that truly captures his heart, his angst, his path to redemption. I am including it here in his own handwriting, his edits and all. He usually got a song in its entirety and had to tweak it very little. We sang them together in churches and even on the radio. They all had a country/western sound. We sang them less as we came into Messianic Judaism. The song says it all.

Rube and I singing one of his songs from his personal songbook. We were so young!

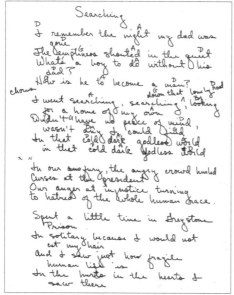

The song "Searching" by Richard "Rube" Rubinstein - in his own handwriting.

Appendix B

My Mother
Jean (Kluting, Mings) Berryman
August 18, 1920 - July 13, 2001

My mother's mother, Martha "Mattie" (Guess) Kluting, was reported to be of Irish and Chocktaw Native American heritage. She was a very strong woman, which was fortunate since she had to raise the children much on her own, due to the "spells" my father Chester Large Kluting would have. When he was af-

flicted, he would go off for weeks and even months with no word. Once he came back to himself, he returned to the family.

My grandfather Chester came from an immigrant, reportedly German father and a Cherokee woman, William Kluting and Rebecca Rosetta (Large) Kluting. It is a long family story. Grandad's middle name, Large, was the family's surname. His family was still on the reservation in Oklahoma. His mother was a teenager when she left to marry. My mother remembers when her aging, widowed Grandma "Rose" lived with her family during Mom's teen years. She

My maternal grandmother Mattie (Guess) Kluting as a middle-aged woman.

Granddaddy Chester as a baby with seven of his siblings and his parents L-R: William "Willie" April 1889, Bertha Emma Aug. 1887, William Wesley March 1864 holding my grandfather Chester Large Aug. 1899. Back center Maggie Sept. 1882, Nannie Feb. 1885, Front Rebecca Rosetta "Rose", Annabelle April 1891-2, Louise Jan. 1893. Front Center: Iva March 1897 (He is a boy. Dresses were worn for early years.) Picture taken 1899 when William was farming Chocktaw land in Oklahoma. Later there were three more children born: Rose, Hallie and her twin Buck.
Courtesy of "family historian" Elaine Mings.

taught Mother to quilt. I learned it was a Cherokee tradition.

I remember when Granddaddy suffered from TB. He visited us after he had been healed. He was never healed of the desire for strong drink. Grannie finally divorced him when Becky was still a girl. Grandaddy Kluting lived to the age of 74, as did Grannie. He did not remarry after the divorce.

In later years, Grannie married a man we were instructed to call Mr. Russell. Grannie Mattie was always such a cheerful person around her grandkids. She was a large woman and typically jovial. She indulged us with sweets and great baked treats when we visited her at the boarding home she owned and operated in Alamogordo, New Mexico, just outside White Sands Proving Grounds.

Grannie was very intelligent and possessed many talents. She was a writer, for one thing. I was actually given her Woodstock typewriter that one of my sisters had ended up with. My youngest sister Linda now has Grannie's industrial sewing machine. Grannie was probably best known for being a seamstress. In fact, she was able to earn enough to help the family through those hard years. I was told that she was often called upon to do alterations. Every time the styles would change – length of skirts, coats – she would be employed to shorten or lengthen clothing. She also was a quilter. I have one of her last unfinished fronts of a quilt. It is made up of some of the bottoms of coats she was left with after shortening clothes for people.

Grandad Kluting, son Lester on leave, and Grannie Kluting while they were still together.

She and Mr. Russell owned a boarding house for men in Alamogordo, NM. The meals around her table were always sumptuous and plentiful. We often visited her as a family and played on the grounds while she and Mother visited. The house was roomy with lots of nooks and crannies. Unfortunately, Mr. Russell would often try to get one of us girls alone in one of the many rooms. We told Mother and Grannie. They were not pleased. It was a problem all of that short marriage. Grannie divorced him.

While Grannie was still in Alamogordo she remarried a man we were instructed to

A later picture of Grandaddy Chester on one of his rare visits to our family in Hobbs, NM.

call Mr. Hollenbeck. He died while she was still living there. She then moved to Hobbs and met Mr. Jim Barnes at the rest home she was living in. He was blind. They got married and moved into a little house together.

Grannie had several health issues that were developing over the years, the worst being Diabetes. She lost a toe to the disease. When she died, she donated her body to the medical school at the University of New Mexico for study. It was evidently puzzling how she did so well with many illnesses each of which could have ended her life. She and Mr. Barnes were still together when she died at the age of 74.

I don't know if it is a testimony to how lax people used to be about public records, but I find it intriguing that my mother's birth certificate shows her name to be Gene, and the handwritten certificate reads Jene. It was supposedly Imogene or even Imajean, but they just put Gene. Even then the spelling Gene was a man's name. My mother has spelled her name "Jean" all my life, so at some point she just made that switch. I doubt she ever made it legal. Her wedding certificate says Imogene.

My mother was the oldest girl, with only one older sibling, Durward, in a family of nine living children. Iona died as a baby. With all but the youngest being born about two years apart, Grannie had children over a 21-year span: Durward, mother born in 1921, W.A., Kenneth, R.D., Lester, Terrell,

Mother as a young woman with a hair-style of the late 1930's. I just realized I have her teeth!

Mother played volleyball for Peacock High School. She is fourth from the left. Her cousin Idell is the third girl from the right. I believe the coach is the Principal.

Louanne and then Rebecca, born five years later in 1939.

Somehow my mother managed to play tennis in competition while in high school and her claim to fame was having won her county's tennis tournament. She also played volleyball in school. She worked as a switchboard operator in Peacock after graduating from high school. When she and Daddy lived in Washington state, she worked in a dress shop before getting on at the Kaiser boat works as "Jean, the Pipefitter's Assistant." Daddy told us that it was too distracting to the men building the ships for her to be down there with them. The bosses agreed and made her a payroll clerk.

Most of our early years she was a stay-at-home mom. During the Flying Saucer years, she helped in food preparation, pie making and waitressing. In later years she was back to being a switchboard operator, this time for the Leawood Motel in Hobbs, NM. In those days, all phone calls went through an operator. It was a popular spot for oilfield executives and workers.

Since Mom's whole family helped work the farm, it was up to my mother to do a lot of the inside chores such as cooking and cleaning while the boys were field hands. This was a very hard life even with that many ready workers for all the chores. My grandfather Chester proved to be little help as he had those long periods of absence during all their lives. Grannie was left to manage the farm and the family.

Every week Mother's brothers got some kitchen duty. On washday, water was heated on the wood-burning stove and pots of water were set to boiling. Not wanting to waste wood, the family took the opportunity to do a lot of baking. There was bread-making and, of course, the washday cob-

Uncle Durward, wife Edna and son Bob.

bler, which was usually peach since peaches are native to that part of Texas. Evidently Uncle R. D. made a great cobbler even to the day he died an old man.

I was around my mother's siblings when I was a young child. We rarely lived close geographically, but we found times to get together. They were always very entertaining. The oldest child was Durward who was quite the kidder. Every time he was around, I seemed to get into trouble. He was always "egging" me on to do something I shouldn't. These weren't truly bad things, but just contrary tricks. I remember most the story

Uncle W. A. on a rare visit to Mother's house in New Mexico.

of his having me put my bowl of oatmeal on my head as a little kid. Mom wasn't amused.

It was Durward who married Edna. They weren't able to have children. They adopted Bob who was the child of a relative. The family lived in Washington state and later Alaska. It was rare to get a visit from them due to the distance. We wrote letters to keep up.

Mother had two brothers who were given initials for names. It seemed to be a Texan thing. W.A. really did not have names for the initials. The story is that when he got to the Armed Forces, they insisted he have "real" names so he became William. Never mind that one of his younger brothers was already William.

W.A.'s wife Marjorie at a young age. She was a beauty.

My cousin Barbara and I were just a couple of months apart. She spent her later years in a home supportive of disabled persons. Here older brother Billy was visiting.

W. A. married a woman named Margie with whom he had five children. I was best acquainted with the oldest boy, Billy, and a daughter my age, Barbara. Barbara and I were only months apart, but she had been born with Down Syndrome. I was told much later that Margie was devastated by Barbara's condition which evidently was exacerbated by their comparing the two of us. My mother was so sad that Margie took it so hard. I think she even had "survivor guilt" and didn't let on how I was progressing so as to not distress Margie more.

W. A. and Margie's younger children were Dennis, Dean and Phyllis. We never lived close to them, but when I was 12 we visited them, traveling from New Mexico to Napa, California by car one summer. That trip was the first time I realized that someone could have feelings for a cousin! I was a bit smitten with cousin Billy. When we all got to go to the movies, he bought me bonbons, which I never knew existed. I always had a soft spot for Billy.

Kenneth was the mystery brother who was between W.A. and R.D. Kenneth was a long-haul truck driver and traveled all over the place. His first familly was when he was married to Thelma (Galloway) Kluting with whom he had two children, my cousins Marlene and Linda.

As a family we didn't have as much contact with his two subsequent families, although his daughter Charamin (Kluting) Gomez has been participating in family reunions in the last few years. I spoke with Aunt Becky about Kenneth recently. We both kind of suspect that he suffered with the "family" condition. I speak of his probably being bipolar like our granddaddy Chester. Everywhere that disease has hit in our family has left stranded, wounded folks.

The next brother, R. D. did have names for his initials – Robert Damon. R. D. was such a playful person. I can't think of a time when he was around that there wasn't a lot of good humor. He lived in southern Texas, a couple of hundred miles from where I grew up in Hobbs, NM. He is one of the uncles I saw the most. He and wife Martha were family favorites and usually the hosts for family gatherings.

Martha and R.D.'s childen are Robert, Steven, Cheryl and Mark. I had less connection with the boys as a kid, because I naturally wanted to play with their sister. Cheryl contracted Polio when she was about two. She and Mother's sister Louanne got it the same year. Cheryl's type was paralytic and she was left needing crutches to walk, but she survived. Louanne contracted bulbar and paralytic polio and did not survive.

Uncle Kenneth in his Navy uniform.

I think Cheryl was one of the strongest people – both physically and mentally – I have ever known. She not only survived her condition, but thrived for many years. My best memory is when their family came to visit us in Hobbs from their home in Aspermont, Texas. Mom put all us kids on pallets made up of blankets on the living room floor so the adults could have our room and beds. We tried to fall asleep knowing they were coming in late. Cheryl came in quietly, set down her crutches and sat on top of me. That is how I woke up. She was great fun.

As an adult Cheryl held down a job in the next town over from Aspermont, which meant she had to drive there. She bought a van and figured out how to rig up a system of pulleys, with a dog leash as her handle, for getting her wheel chair in and out of the van. She loved being independent.

Cheryl went on to have a surprisingly normal life, marrying and having a family. At some point she had a rod put in her spine, which broke when she was in her bathtub for protection against a tornado that struck near her home. She had many

A typical picture of Martha and R.D. at my mom's house in Hobbs.

Here are Martha and R.D.'s three boys: Steven, Mark and Robert.

Cousin Cheryl with her van and the pulley system she invented for not needing help to load her wheelchair in and out.

Cheryl and husband Shorty were a strong couple.

Uncle Lester, wife Doris Ann and their daughter Laura.

surgeries before she ended up in a wheelchair, having spent much of her earlier life getting around with crutches.

The next one of my mother's siblings after R.D. was Lester who seemed like a giant Teddy Bear. He was tall – about 6' 4". He and his first wife Jesse and daughter Pat rented a ranch house surrounded by the cotton fields they were paid to take care of. The property was in a remote area of eastern New Mexico. There was a carved wooden plaque over the entry gate that read "Rat Camp Ranch." It was here that I encountered the fateful Tarantula.

They had moved to a nice brick home in Roswell, NM, which is where they were when they divorced. I was 12 and was visiting them when they told their daughter Pat they were splitting up. This house had a large backyard with a barbecue grill and an expansive front lawn. Lester asked me to go sit in the shade of their big tree while they broke the news to Pat. We were all devastated.

Lester later married Doris Ann and they had Laura. Lester always worked as a long-haul truck driver. Lester died a few years ago in his 80's. The years of driving were blamed for shaking up his insides. Laura and her husband Wallace live next door to where Doris Ann remained as Lester's widow in Las Cruces, NM. Doris Ann also died recently.

The other William of the boys was the youngest son, William Terrell. The immediate family always called him by the second name. Mostly I remember that he met and married a Japanese woman when he was in the service overseas. Her name was Fumikio, but we called her Aunt Mickey. She was always amazed at what seemed to her an abundance of appliances Americans owned. The family story is that she pushed Uncle Terrell to get them for her when their budget was not sufficient. They produced a son, Jeff, but their marriage did not survive. Terrell remarried later to a woman named Bertha and had two children – Teresa and Bill. They did not stay together and we lost touch with him for a long time.

At a family reunion that Rube and our family attended, Terrell asked to be baptized. Rube did so in the river there at Ruidoso, NM. Recently we have renewed contact with cousin Bill at a family reunion. Teresa died a few years ago.

The story of the Kluting girls is much shorter. My mother only had three sisters, one of whom died as a baby - Iona. As I mentioned when talking about cousin Cheryl, mother's little sister Louanne died as a teenager from Polio.

Since Louanne's case of Polio was both paralytic and bulbar, it affected her lungs. She couldn't breathe. She was in an iron lung for two weeks in Carrie Tingley Hospital in the town that was then named Hot Springs, NM – the town's name having since changed to Truth or Consequences to win a prize from the game show of the same name.

People didn't know what to do for Polio victims then. The medical professionals thought they had some kind of flu until they started becoming paralyzed and couldn't breathe unassisted. Louanne only lasted two weeks.

Aunt Rebecca "Becky" is the baby and, as of this writing, the only surviving sibling. Since she is just one year older than my oldest sister Carol, she has always been like a sister to us. When Becky was young, she lived in Las Cruces, NM where she was a cheerleader in high school. One time we invited her whole squad to our house while they were there for a tournament that included our high school. They brought a lot of happy energy to our house. Becky has al-

Uncle Terrell was a very handsome man. This picture was at a family reunion in Ruidosa, NM.

Aunt Louanne about the time she died of Polio.

A younger picture of Louanne.

Mother and her youngest sister Becky who were twenty years apart. Mother was about 65 at this time.

Becky and her children: Candace "Candy," Becky, Craig, Tammy, Janeene.

Becky and two of her daughters, Tammy and Janeene, and I believe Tammy's granddaughter at the Kluting Family Reunion in Ruidoso, NM after Mother died. The dog is Pepe', that was Mother's dog at the time she died. He took right to Becky.

ways seemed like a celebrity to me, and is still an all-time favorite. I planned to name a daughter after her, but it never happened.

I always thought that Becky was so much older than I, but I realized she is only five years older. When she was just 16 she was already married and had her first child, Janeene, prior to turning 17. I kind of followed in her footsteps, not consciously, having married at barely 17 and having given birth to my first daughter, Monicqua, before I was 18.

Becky was in two marriages. Don Nelson was her first husband. Their Janeene was born in Roswell, NM before they moved to Artesia, NM where the remaining three children were born. Twenty-two months after Janeene was Tammy, then Craig three years later, and Candy eight years later. The family moved to Eunice, NM for Don's oil pipeline job when Craig was a junior in high school and Candy was in 2nd grade. The older girls were already married.

Don and Becky were married 26 years, divorcing in 1981 when Candace was 13. In August of 1982 Becky married Leroy Phillips who had also been married before and brought with him two boys, Craig 14 and Keith 13. They were raising three teenagers at the same time. Leroy owned an oilfield business in Eunice and sold it once all the kids were out of the house, the youngest three being in college.

They took the proceeds and bought a ranch in Oklahoma in 1987. Their house was on 160 acres. A few years later they bought another 240 acres to have more space to run cattle. They kept mixed breeds but were having trouble with successful birthing of their calves. Leroy heard about the Salers cattle from France. They were advertised as not only having good milk but also easy births. It was a big investment but they managed to buy 40 head.

Leroy and Becky were divorced on October 30, 1999 after a lengthy and emotional process. Becky now alternates living with two of her daughters: Candace in Las Cruces, NM and Janeene in Elephant Butte, NM. She is still my hero.

Mother died just before her 80th birthday from a stroke. This picture was taken at a family reunion in Ruidosa, NM where we celebrated her 75th birthday. She is flanked by two of the most gorgeous members of our family, on the right my sister Anita and on the left Anita's daughter Kim.

My mother's family had a big impact on my siblings and me as we grew up. To this day, all of them live the cowboy lifestyle. They have made it a point to keep horses, and some even still run cattle. Becky has shared how important it is to her and her kids that the grandkids all know that way of life. They live by example. There was something about them that made us feel loved and secure. I miss them. I miss my mom.

Mother at 75, five years before she died.

— ❦ ❧ —

Appendix C

My Daddy
Houston Monroe Mings

February 3, 1914 – April 14, 2000

Monroe, as he was called, came from a hard-working, tough mother, Beatrice "Bea" (Williams) Mings, who raised her three children by herself after her estranged husband, my grandfather Vance Mings, committed suicide when my father was just five years old. This would have been about 1910.

Daddy at two months old.

At the time he died, Vance had come to get the children to take them for a visit since he and Beatrice were separated. He was driving a horse-drawn buggy with Bea's brother who was always called Sambo. Vance picked up the kids – Cecil, Florence and Monroe (my dad) – with infant Jiggs staying behind with his mother. They were driving to Sambo's house, where the visit was to take place, but Vance asked Sambo to stop at a pharmacy on the way. Sambo didn't pay attention to what Vance bought.

When they got to Sambo's house, Sambo observed Vance drinking from a small bottle after he got out of the buggy. Sambo realized it was a poison due to the labeling on the bottle. It was strychnine. Vance immediately got sick and Sambo got him into the house. The kids were not only watching as their father convulsed and died in front of them, they also immediately became ill. Vance had put the poison on apple slices and given them to the three children. Florence didn't especially like apples, which saved her. Cecil evidently ate the most and was quite sick. My daddy Monroe ate less but was also sick. All the children survived.

I know my grandmother – Mama Ross, as she preferred to be called after marrying a man about 20 years her senior, W. O. Ross – had to have some help in supporting her

Vance Mings as a young working cowboy. He apparently has an injury to his left hand.

family. In those days women had to have a husband to provide for them. Sadly this alliance proved difficult for her children.

W.O. had several grown children of his own at the time of the marriage: "Uncle" Tobe is the only one I remember. He rode with us on that family trip from New Mexico to Oregon when I was 12 years old. I always assumed his name was Tobias, but don't recall anyone saying.

W.O. and my grandmother had two children together: Pete and Peggy. Pete was a very studious looking man. I remember he had what we then called "Sugar Diabetes." There was almost nothing to be done for this condition at the time. I remember when Pete and his wife Bell and sons Michael and Ronnie came to visit us. They were amazed at my mother's pies she made weekly. They never had eaten pie since the family stayed away from sugar for Uncle Pete's sake.

Dad's youngest brother, Calton Vance "Jiggs," is not at this visit. We almost never saw him because during WWII he went AWOL from the Navy and stayed in California. Just before V-E Day in 1945, Jiggs had been on leave from the damaged cruiser Chester while it was docked for repairs at Mare Island in San Francisco. After Jiggs gave himself up, years later, he told reporters that he was in a "dazed" condition when the ship returned from the Pacific war zone. He explained he was attempting to find solace in drink. During leave he got

*Mama Ross in middle age.
She was a tall woman.*

*Daddy's sibs and spouses: L–R (top) Mother and Daddy, Half brother Pete and Bell Ross.
(front) Harry and Florence Allen – Dad's sister, brother Cecil and Leona Mings.
The time was evidently about 1946 since that little girl pushing her "baby" up the stairs is me.
I don't know where Aunt Peggy is, but she was probably away at school.*

drunk and did not make it back to the ship before it left to go back to the war. In wartime that is desertion that carries the Death Penalty.

This began Uncle Jiggs' double life, as the media called it. For almost 14 years he had an alias and primarily worked as a ranch hand. During this time he fathered three children with Wilma but didn't marry her because he didn't want to do so with an alias. When he turned himself in, he received a Court Martial and had to serve six months at hard labor. He and Wilma were subsequently married. The children were 11-year old Carl, 8-year-old Joseph and 2-year-old Angie.

Daddy, Mother, Elaine, Carol and me with our cousin Rodney Allen on one of our vacations to see Daddy's sister Florence, who lived in San Antonio, TX. The Alamo was amazing to visit. My younger siblings were probably back at Florence's house.

Daddy's sister Florence "Flo" seemed to be the wealthy family member, due to her husband's work in selling insurance. Flo and Harry had only one child, Rodney. They lived in San Antonio for as long as I can remember. They hosted us in their home many times in my childhood. I know we were there for at least one Thanksgiving. Flo's table was loaded for the occasion, but given the fact that there were eight or nine of us, it was probably just the right amount of food. Flo was very generous to us.

Aunt Peggy was my dad's last surviving sibling. She was strong physically and mentally to the end, having died a few months ago at age 94. I remember being told that it was she who came to help Mother after I was born when we were living in Tacoma, Washington. She is about the perkiest person I have ever known. If she can't cheer you up, you're already dead!

She became a nurse and married Robert McCorkle who became a D. O. They worked together in his practice. They had a daughter named Judy and a son named John. They lost Judy to cancer in early adulthood. John lived close to his mom in east Texas and was there when she died.

I remember vividly when their family would come to visit us. I suppose being in the medical field made them very fastidi-

Aunt Peggy in her 60's. Her beauty was from a joy she had inside that she said the Lord gave her.

ous about germs. We considered ourselves clean people, but their understanding of cleanliness was at another level!

My father's telling of his childhood was so sad. Farmers in those days generally had a tough lot, but my dad believed his stepfather had a mean streak in him when it came to the children from Mama Ross's first marriage.

Daddy says that he never had a birthday cake as a child. Seems odd, even unlikely, but there it is. He also tells of a Christmas time when Mama Ross and W.O. went off on a vacation for two weeks and left the kids at home to fend for themselves. Cecil would have been about 12, Daddy 10 and Florence 8 so Jiggs would have been about 5. The way Daddy told it, they didn't even have enough food. I can only hope his memory was skewed, because my grandparents did not seem to be that kind of people.

This is a picture of him and his fifth and final wife, Daphne, at the celebration when Daddy turned 80.

My memories of Daddy are of a handsome, fun-loving, but strict father. He loved to get down on all fours and chase us kids

Daddy a few years before he died. He died at the age of 86 from metasticized prostate cancer. He was visiting my sister Anita and her husband Jay in Midland, TX.

Daddy as a young man.

Daphne Mings, Monicqua Busch and baby Sarah Annemarie, Daddy, me and my son-in-law Aaron Busch.

around the house, usually barking like a dog. I never wanted to cross him because when he got angry, he could yank out his belt to whip our bottoms quicker than any gunslinger could get out his gun. It felt just about that fatal as well. He must have been so frustrated as his predominantly female household started growing up and getting interested in boys. He did his best to instill in us his moral compass that he derived from his reading of the Bible and being part of the Baptist faith.

Daddy always loved basketball and golf. When we lived across the street from Hobbs High School and had access to their ample grounds, he would often cross the street to practice his golf swing. I joined him on many occasions and benefitted from his tutelage on the proper grip, swing and hitting of the ball.

The forever image of my father for me is his leaning his foot on a running board of a delivery truck with a toothpick dangling from his mouth and that ever-present glint in his eye. When he wrapped his arms around you, you knew you were loved. I miss that certainty.

Appendix D

Mother and Daddy

Daddy met my mother in their hometown of Peacock, Texas, when she was still in high school. As it was a small town – it is said it swelled to 100 when all came in from the farms and ranches – they could not have avoided an acquaintance. My mother remembered that Daddy was invited to speak at the high school about students preparing to become part of the workforce. He was about six years older than my mom. She said that was when she became enamored with him.

Even though she graduated from high school at 16, she was probably still 16 when she and Monroe began corresponding. She had the offer to go away to college with a scholarship, but I was told it felt too "big world" for my mom.

It was about 1938, when Monroe went out to California to work to help his family. I have read the letters he wrote Mother, which were fairly gushy. Her letters to him were just as personal.

When he returned, one day he went to her house and said, "Let's get married." She had just done a mayonnaise treatment on her hair – evidently it was common practice to nourish hair this way – so she tried to wash the goo out so they could get married. I don't even know how they could acquire a license that fast, but marry they did on August 25, 1938, in a relative's front room.

Daddy was actually a widower at the time. He had married his childhood sweetheart, Cora Lee Holloman, who died when their son Dwayne Truman (born May 24, 1935) was a year old. Mother knew she was also taking on a three-year-old son. By the time their children started coming, they had moved to Stanford, Texas, where Ramona Carol was born on August 18, 1940 and Peggy Elaine on February 10, 1942.

Before I was born on March 25, 1944, Daddy and Mother moved to Tacoma, Washington, to work in the shipyards during World War II. Mother took the train from Texas to Tacoma with their three kids: Dwayne, Carol, and Elaine. As I alluded to in the main body of this story, Dwayne tells the story of how sick Elaine became on the train ride which made it a very tedious trip for the family.

Daddy started working for Kaiser Shipyards and Mother joined him after I was born that spring. Prior to this she worked in a dress shop. Aunt Peggy came to help take care of the kids. The family lived all scrunched up in a little apartment over a bakery. To this day I LOVE the smell of bread and other goodies baking!

Mother wasn't the much-advertised wartime "Rosie the Riveter," however, she was "Jean the Pipe Fitter's Assistant." That was her job until they put her in Payroll. Daddy said her good looks caused too much of a commotion on the shipyard floor so they moved her upstairs to the offices.

When I was just over a year old and the war was over, the family set out to return to Texas. As they came to Hobbs, New Mexico, they stopped to visit friends and relatives, and never left. The last three children were born there: Anita Delores on September 26, 1946; Linda Kay on May 14, 1948 and Michael Monroe on August 24, 1949.

Daddy's first job in Hobbs was at Good Eats Bakery, working for Mr. Randolph. At first he was a baker but was promoted to being a delivery man.

Daddy also drove a wholesale delivery truck supplying local establishments with candy and cigarettes. We had a free-standing garage where he stored these products. They were definitely under lock and key or we kids would have munched out on the candy.

The first part of a letter Mother wrote to Daddy when he was working picking fruit in California. Note that she went to "the candy making" with someone else.

Daddy realized a long-time dream when he took out a lease on The Flying Saucer when I was a pre-teen. Having this burger joint was a lot of hard work, but Daddy seemed to love it.

His last formal job was with Ponca Wholesale where he again drove a delivery panel truck. He worked his way up to being the accountant for the business. His career ended when he was caught embezzling funds, which I explained in the main text of this memoir. As I said, Ponca chose to fire him, and not press charges.

This came in 1962 when I had been married for a year and had given birth to my first child, Monicqua. I was living in Colorado by this time so did not

The second page of the letter Mother wrote to Daddy. Sounds like he is jealous thinking she was seeing others. Postmarked February 26, 1937.

get in on the intimate details, but, suffice it to say, Mother and Daddy split up after that. They were just shy of 25 years of marriage. Mother was left raising the three youngest children alone, who were then Anita 16, Linda Kay 14 and Michael 13.

Mother subsequently married a man named George Berryman who was many years her junior. He was a "pusher" in the oil fields, which meant he got crews to work the rigs. About 20 years later he was killed on one of the lonely roads to the oilfields. It was when he was driving his pickup to work one early morning that he came over a rise and hit a horse in the road. By this time all of my siblings were grown. I was in my mid-thirties and was teaching at the State Pen in Santa Fe.

It was odd to get state-level news on the radio, but I remember hearing on

The first two pages of one of Daddy's letters to Mother before they were married. In this one we learn that he had an early dream of owning a little cafe.

my radio while driving to work at NM State Pen that an oil worker in Hobbs was killed by hitting a horse that flew into the cab of his pickup truck. I received a call at work telling me that it had been George. Mother never remarried. She lived alone with a series of toy poodles, the last one being Pepe'.

Right after my parents' breakup, Daddy married a woman named Lenore, which lasted a few months. Not too much later he met and married Lorene. This lasted seven years. They had differences of opinion on several things, but the heaviest – according to my dad – was concerning her teenage daughter. Lorene owned a delicatessen when she was widowed. When she and Daddy married, they ran it together. Dad said the girl had her hand in the till with her mom's approval.

Daddy was always the romantic. By this time he had relocated to Ruidoso,

The second page of the letter Daddy wrote to Mother. Daddy realized his dream to own a cafe much later when we got The Flying Saucer. Written March 23, 1938.

All of the siblings back home for George's funeral.
L-R front: Linda Kay and Anita. Back row: me, Michael, Dwayne, Carol and Elaine.

New Mexico, where he met and married Madge. He was working at the horse racing track as a guard at the horse owners' gate. It was a treat to visit him there as we got to be up close and personal with the horses. This marriage also lasted seven years.

His sixth and final marriage was in Kermit, Texas, to a woman named Daphne. They were married for 14 years at the time he died at age 86 from complications of untreated prostate cancer with which he had suffered for most of their marriage. Dad didn't like going to doctors.

My dad could never sit still. His money-making project in late life was collecting cans along the Texas highways. He drove his pickup out a few miles, picking up cans fore and aft. He raised enough money to leave $1000 to each of his seven children at his passing. That's a lot of cans!

Lessons Learned

My parents left an indelible mark on me. From Mom I learned to be systematic, thorough and intentional about whatever I am doing. I also learned to be kind, especially to strangers. She always welcomed everyone we brought home to her table. Mother was continually singing hymns or Country Western songs around the house as she went about her chores. "The Tennessee Waltz" was an all-time favorite of hers and mine.

From Dad I learned to be persistent, fun-loving, loyal and a truth teller. The deepest betrayal was to try to deceive my father. Both my parents taught me the value of setting a goal and accomplishing it through hard work. In fact, it was Dad and his mom, Mama Ross, who kept us hopping with chores our every waking moment. To this day I have a hard time "allowing" myself to be idle.

Daddy whistled or sang pretty much his every waking moment. Mostly Daddy's choice of music was old Baptist hymns or Country Western songs. He loved music. It was he who bought a violin and encouraged all of us to take lessons. Several of us did, but only Elaine became proficient.

I learned much later that Daddy could play any instrument he picked up. He evidently played violin, guitar and harmonica. I suspect that was in his earlier years, because I rarely saw him have the time to pick up an instrument. It had to be daunting to support a family of seven kids.

Through both my parents I developed a deep love of music. I am also always humming, whistling or singing songs to the extent that I have become annoying to many!

I don't know how they did it, but I always felt that I had individual significance to each of my parents even though I was the middle of seven. The traits they imparted guide my life. I hope I have passed them to my own children, and now my grandchildren.

About the Author

— ❧ ❧ —

Shari Rubinstein is a wordsmith. She is an avid reader with her studies focused in a variety of life's teachings.

Her educational preparation includes a BA and MA in English, as well as an MA in Special Education.

Shari is a retired English and Journalism teacher. She has written for more than half her life. Shari has previously published two collections of her perspective pieces: *Shift: Tiny Tales to Lighten Your Load* and *Phoenix: Rising Anew Transformed by Fire.*

Shari lives in the Sacramento, California, area surrounded by her children and grandchildren and a loving community of friends.

To enjoy more of Shari Rubinstein's writing please visit:

www.sharirubinstein.com

On her website you can enjoy her regular blog posts
(which often become her books!) ... and you can order
one of her books for your friends!

If you enjoyed this book you will love Shari's other works:
Shift and *Phoenix*. Each of these is a series of pieces that help
the reader navigate the pain and joy of life's seasons.

To learn more and read previews visit: sharirubinstein.com

CPSIA information can be obtained
at www.ICGtesting.com
Printed in the USA
LVHW070039180222
711373LV00009BA/145